Boy from the Valleys

MY UNEXPECTED JOURNEY

LUKE EVANS

EBURY
SPOTLIGHT

Ebury Spotlight, an imprint of Ebury Publishing
One Embassy Gardens, 8 Viaduct Gardens,
Nine Elms, London SW11 7BW

Ebury Spotlight is part of the Penguin Random House group of companies whose addresses can be found at global.penguinrandomhouse.com

Penguin
Random House
UK

Copyright © Luke Evans 2024

Luke Evans has asserted his right to be identified as the author of this Work in accordance with the Copyright, Designs and Patents Act 1988

No part of this book may be used or reproduced in any manner for the purpose of training artificial intelligence technologies or systems. In accordance with Article 4(3) of the DSM Directive 2019/790, Penguin Random House expressly reserves this work from the text and data mining exception.

This book is a work of non-fiction based on the life, experiences and recollections of the author. In some cases, names of people have been changed to protect the privacy of others.

Lyrics for *La Cava* written by John Claflin and Laurence O'Keefe

Photo credits:
Trae Patton/NBC / Contributor (page 6, bottom image)
PA Images / Alamy Stock Photo (page 7, top image)
Matt Frost/ITV/Shutterstock (page 7, bottom two images)

First published by Ebury Spotlight in 2024
www.penguin.co.uk

A CIP catalogue record for this book is available from the British Library

ISBN 9781529917857
Trade Paperback ISBN 9781529917864

Printed and bound in Great Britain by Clays Ltd, Elcograf S.p.A.

The authorised representative in the EEA is Penguin Random House Ireland, Morrison Chambers, 32 Nassau Street, Dublin D02 YH68

Penguin Random House is committed to a sustainable future for our business, our readers and our planet. This book is made from Forest Stewardship Council® certified paper.

MIX
Paper | Supporting
responsible forestry
FSC® C018179

To my mam and dad, my everything.

And to little Luke, I gotcha, kid.

PROLOGUE

November 2023, Duke of York's Theatre, London

I was back on the West End stage for the first time in nearly fifteen years, playing the late Queen Mother's butler in a comedy called *Backstairs Billy*. The company of actors was wonderful; the reviews were so fantastic there wasn't room on the front of the theatre for all the glowing quotes; and despite my worries about returning to theatre after so long working in movies, I was loving every second of it.

It was only a week into our three-month run, but I had already established a habit of turning up an hour and a half before the curtain rose to take a quiet moment for myself. I'm not superstitious, but I liked the ritual of going up to my dressing room, lighting a candle and putting on some music. It helped me prepare for what was basically a two-hour cardio workout: I was running around on stage in a tail suit and wig every night and by the end of the show the sweat would always be pouring off me.

Back in my musical theatre days, I'd always had to share a dressing room, so it was a treat to have a room to myself – and this one was far more luxurious than anything I'd had before, with a new carpet, freshly painted walls and a bed, because I can nap for Wales. As I relaxed into my chair, my eyes wandered around the room. All of a sudden I had a jolt of recognition; a long-ago memory flashed into my mind. My heart racing, I sat up and looked around the room – *really* looked at it this time. My eyes flew wide. It had been redecorated but still, I couldn't believe I hadn't noticed it before. This was the very same dressing room I'd been in for my penultimate musical theatre performance, in *Rent Remixed*, fourteen years earlier. Back then I'd been a struggling, skint actor on the verge of quitting the business, until one night, in this very room, I opened a letter from a stranger that would go on to change my life. That letter set off a crazy chain of events that sent me in a wildly different direction to where I'd been headed, and now here I was, with forty-five TV and movie projects under my belt and a career that satisfies me every day. And the incredible thing is that none of it had been expected or planned – none of it had even been on the cards – until the night I had read that letter, in this very spot, all those years ago.

ACT ONE

1

31 December 1975

A few hours before midnight on New Year's Eve, young David Evans pulls up outside a house in Trinant, a hilltop village in the valleys of South Wales. The pubs were packed with revellers as he sped past on his motorbike, but out here at the edge of the estate all is silent and still, the only light coming from the front window and the moonlight silvering the tops of the trees on the opposite valley.

The nineteen-year-old is dressed in shiny monkey boots and big flares, like his musical heroes, Bowie and Bolan, and is tall, slender and super-handsome. He's known as a cool guy round here: the quiet, good-looking one who lives with the elderly couple down the valley.

David's here to see his on/off girlfriend Yvonne Lewis, who's babysitting for a local family. The pair started dating a few months ago after their eyes met across the car park of the local youth club (and for David at least, it was love at first sight) until Yvonne's dad got wind of the courtship and summoned his sixteen-year-old daughter for a talk. She knew it was serious, as he usually left all the parenting to her mam.

'I've had some information,' he said, his face grave. 'You've been seen with a man.'

'What? Dave's hardly a *man*,' scoffed Yvonne.

'Well, we're having none of that. You're far too young for that nonsense.'

David had asked if he could meet Mr Lewis, hoping he might talk him round, but he'd refused and that was that. He shrugged off the heartbreak by taking up with Denise Hayes; still, he hasn't stopped thinking about Yvonne.

As David walks up to the front door, he's got butterflies, but it's not just at the thought of spending the evening with the pretty bottle blonde. He's got something he needs to tell her, something so huge and wonderful and utterly terrifying that he can't get his head around it himself. As an apprentice to a bricklayer, for the past few months David's been working on a building site with Alan, who's a Jehovah's Witness. David doesn't come from a religious family, but he's always had questions about what happens when you die. His father passed when he was young and as the family drove away from church after the funeral he remembers looking back to see if he could see his dad's spirit floating up to heaven. As a child he never got any answers, but when Alan began talking to him about the Bible it all started to make some kind of weird sense to him.

Alan explained that the world has been under Satan's influence for thousands of years, but that his rule is now coming to an end, and one day very soon God will step in and put everything right. On this day, known as Armageddon, God will destroy all the wicked people, resurrect the dead and transform the earth back into a paradise where the righteous can live in harmony, free from violence, disease and death. And according to the Jehovah's Witnesses, Armageddon will happen on 31 December 1975. In other words – tonight.

'Make sure you spend the evening with the ones you love,' Alan had warned him, which is the reason David's here: to be with Yvonne.

He knocks, and moments later the front door opens.

'Hiya, Dave.' She smiles shyly; in photos from this time, Yvonne has a look of a young Princess Diana. 'Come on in. The kids are asleep.'

They sit on the sofa together and watch the New Year's TV specials, and soon David forgets all about Denise Hayes; he has no doubt that it's Yvonne he wants to be with, regardless of what her father might say.

And, as the clock approaches midnight, he knows it's time to share the momentous news.

'You'll never guess what's happening tonight,' he says.

'It's becoming 1976?'

'Yes, but ...' David takes a breath. 'I think the world may be ending.'

Yvonne frowns, then snorts with laughter. 'Yeah, right ...'

'It's true! I've been speaking to the Jehovah's Witnesses and they've worked out 1975 is a marked date.'

On the television, Big Ben begins its countdown.

'It's been prophesied in the Bible,' David goes on, his voice urgent. 'Armageddon could happen tonight.'

Yvonne just stares at him. *Well, I didn't see that one coming*, she thinks.

As Big Ben bongs its final bong she holds her breath, with no idea what to expect. After a few moments, when nothing happens, she breaks into a grin.

'Still here then,' she says, giving David a jokey shove.

But he is looking deadly serious. 'Honestly, Yvonne, there's so much going on that we don't know about.'

He tells her about his conversations with Alan, and his tone is so earnest and sincere that she finds herself hanging on his every word. Yvonne is fascinated that this quiet, reserved young man has been so affected by what he's heard, and by the time he's finished talking she's decided that she wants to find out more about these Jehovah's Witnesses for herself.

From then on, the young couple start going to meetings at the local Kingdom Hall together, studying the Bible and learning new moral standards. They are welcomed by a community of kind, smiling, smartly dressed people that they quickly realise they want to be part of. David and Yvonne commit themselves to the religion – and to each other. Within a year, my parents are married at the local registry office.

. . .

I was born on Easter Sunday, although there was still snow on the ground in the Valleys. While the rest of the country was busy hunting chocolate eggs, my parents were stuck in a small room at Pontypool Hospital waiting for my arrival. Not that they would have been bothered about missing out on the Easter festivities; as Jehovah's Witnesses, they are forbidden from celebrating worldly occasions such as Christmas or Easter, or even birthdays.

Mam had been woken by the contractions at 5am and soon after she was in Dad's transit minibus on the way to hospital. She describes the birth as horrendous. She was tiny and only nineteen – barely out of childhood herself – and I was a big baby: a hefty 8lb 5oz. As the contractions intensified, the midwife offered gas and air, but it just made her feel sick. My dad stayed with her throughout the labour, praying more than he'd ever prayed before. He was worried about the blood; not because he was squeamish, but because transfusions are forbidden by their religion, and he was terrified what would happen if things went wrong.

By late afternoon, Mam was exhausted. While Dad offered up more prayers, she was taken away for an episiotomy, a cut in her vaginal wall to help the baby out, which even in her weakened state struck her as a terrible idea. I still refused to budge, so out came the ventouse suction cup, and eventually at 5.55pm, after what my famously hard-working mother describes as the hardest day's work of her life, I made my entrance, Down Stage Centre (literally!) crying.*

The hospital room exploded in relief and joy. As Dad whirled the small Irish midwife around the bed, I was cleaned up and presented to Mam. Near delirious with exhaustion, her first thought was: *Why does this tiny baby have Dave's face?* But she was instantly in love. She put a

---

* This was to set the tone for the rest of my childhood. My mother will romanticise this – 'oh, he was a *lovely* child' – but if you ask my aunties and cousins they'd say I never stopped crying, though it wasn't that I was an unhappy kid – far from it.

little cap on my misshapen head, which had been sucked into a lopsided pixie hat by the ventouse, and stared in wonder at her new son.

My little dumpling.

They already knew my name. Luke George Evans. George after my paternal grandfather, and Luke because it was 'a lovely biblical name', according to Mam, suggested by one of the elders in the congregation. And I'm sure that's true, but remember, this was 1979. *Star Wars* had come out two years before and *The Empire Strikes Back* was looming on the horizon: the fledgling movie franchise was already a worldwide phenomenon. Even in Crumlin, the mining town where my parents lived, you couldn't walk down the street at that time without hearing the name 'Luke Skywalker', and I can't help but wonder if their choice of name had also been somehow subliminally influenced by this.

Mam's not having any of it, though, and it's true my parents were unlikely to have seen *Star Wars*. The Bible condemns all aspects of the supernatural, although sci-fi wasn't strictly against the rules. As a result, I wasn't allowed to watch those Saturday morning cartoons like *Dungeons & Dragons* or *He-Man & the Masters of the Universe*. He-Man's famous cry of 'I have the power!' would have been particularly problematic: it's not He-Man who has the power, it's Jehovah.

While Mam and I stayed in hospital, Dad went back to work. He came to visit us the next day with a gift, a copy of the single 'Bright Eyes' by Art Garfunkel, which had just become number one, though I think this was less a comment on his new-born son, and more to do with his love of music. He had every record you could imagine, from Petula Clark to The Beatles and The Drifters, Acker Bilk to Elvis, and growing up I would spend hours with headphones on listening to his record player. There was always music in the house, and Dad would usually sing along – though the correct lyrics were always optional and rarely adhered to. Why deny yourself the chance of singing a song because you don't know the correct lyrics? I remember him changing the words to the Madness song 'Our House'. He would sing: 'Our house, in the middle of School Street, our house ...'

Three days after I was born, we all went back to the house on Kennard Terrace that my parents had bought two years earlier for £4,000 (that house in the middle of School Street was still a few years in our future) and so my life began.

2

Until I was sixteen my world was contained within a few square miles of the Welsh Valleys. The collieries were closing when I was a kid, but the mines had been the backbone of the community and had left their mark as starkly as a smudge of coal on the skin. Driving to the market in Abertillery you'd still see the huge colliery winding wheels, monuments to an abandoned world beneath, while many houses in the village had a shiny brass miner's oil lamp by the fireplace: beautiful pieces of engineering but no longer of any practical use except as decoration (and perhaps a gauge of how thorough the woman of the house was with her polishing). And everyone was related to someone who had worked down the mines, but was now employed in a quite often soulless job at the new factories that were mopping up the local workforce. The Valleys have changed a lot these days, with massive industrial complexes and plush housing estates, but back then it was mostly mining villages made up of narrow terraced streets. If you spotted a semi-detached, you knew you were in a posh area. And between these pockets of grey and grit it was all green: fields, forest, grass and the endless rolling hills dotted with sheep.

My parents grew up a five-minute drive from each other: Dad in Crumlin, at the foot of the mountain, and Mam in Trinant at the top, where most of her family live to this day. It's not just their birthplace they have in common: they're both one of six children and both have twin sisters. But while my mam's upbringing was typically working class – six children crammed into a terraced house, three or four single beds to a bedroom, all noise and chaos – Dad had a less conventional start in life. His mother was in her late forties by the time he and his twin sister Diane came along, by which time her eldest, Bryan, was twenty-four and already married. You can imagine in these circumstances that if you got landed with two newborns, rather than the one you'd been expecting, you might feel that it was all a bit much. Given the option, in fact, it might seem wiser to … *outsource* part of the job. And that's exactly what my grandmother did. She kept my dad's sister and gave David to her childless sister-in-law to raise.

Alice – or Lala as she was known – was in her late sixties by the time her new son arrived. Her husband, Arthur, died while my dad was still young, but there was another man in the house who could take over paternal duties: Tom, the lodger. He was a small man, possibly even smaller than Lala, with brushed-over thinning hair and two missing fingers thanks to a gunpowder accident as a kid. An engineer, he had moved to Crumlin in the 1950s to work on upgrading the cast-iron viaduct – the tallest in the UK – that carried coal across the valley to Newport and had rented a room from Lala and Arthur. After a few years the work on the viaduct was complete, but Tom never left. He continued to rent Lala's spare room, helping out with maintenance and jobs around the house, and after Arthur's death the pair of them lived happily together – platonically, by all accounts, although I do hope there was some affection – until the end of their days. I remember Mam telling me that when Lala went to visit Arthur at the chapel of rest, she walked up to the open casket and stroked his face, the first and last time Mam witnessed any physical contact between them.

My dad's 'real' family lived just across the valley, but we didn't see as much of them. Auntie Lala and Uncle Tom were as much my grandparents as my mam's parents, and we visited them often. Lala died at the age of 90, when I was seven, but I can still see her as clearly as if she was here now: sitting in her armchair by the kitchen fire, her arms reaching out for the enormous hug she'd always give me when I came round, enveloping me in the scent of floral talc. I often worried I might disappear inside those hugs. Lala seemed like a giant of a woman to me: tall, with big hands – though her wedding ring always had a bit of blue J Cloth tied around it so it didn't slip off her finger. She was a snuff addict, horrible brown stuff that was like the cocaine of old ladies back in the day, and though I never saw her take it – she was far too ladylike for that – she always had a telltale runny nose and powdery brown residue round her nostrils to prove it, though like many old ladies at that time she always had a big old hanky at the ready.

. . .

While Lala seemed very grand to me, with her singsong voice and old-fashioned manners, my mam's side of the family, the Lewises, were soundly working class. I've inherited traits from both my parents, but I'm very much a Lewis at heart: bolshy, opinionated and with a knack for telling a funny story – just like my grandmother, Enid.

Nana Lewis wasn't someone who needed to be liked, but we all adored her anyway because she was such an institution. She loved being naughty and could make you laugh until you wet yourself. I remember sitting with her at a family wedding reception, watching the newlyweds' first dance.

'This is nice, isn't it, Nan?' I said.

'Ooh yes, it's lovely. Lovely.'

I nodded to the bride, who was whirling around in a froth of chiffon. 'Bethan looks gorgeous, doesn't she?'

Nana's nostrils flared. She took a sip from her vodka and orange, her one alcoholic drink of the year, and paused for a beat.

'She looks like a pig in a wig.'

This kind of stuff was always coming from Nana. She loved to be controversial and I loved her for that.

Nana's favourite things were gossip, Mars bars, Trebor Extra Strong Mints and Regal King Size cigarettes. I always remember her smoking

– there was none of the worry about second-hand smoke around kids in those days – and as the tip of her cigarette burned down, she'd slip off the back of her leather mule slipper and flick the ash into the heel. A short woman, Nana favoured functional clothing: a plain overalls and simple dresses. What was the point in getting dressed up? It wasn't as if she had anyone to impress. It was the uniform of a woman who'd spent her life raising her kids, her kids' kids, and her kids' kids' kids. There were always children in my grandparents' house: you'd go round to visit and it was like a nursery. They'd be jumping all over Nana and Gransha, yelling and demanding things. Not that my grandparents seemed to mind; the children were about all they talked about. I think it's a Valleys thing: babies are everything.

If it wasn't screaming kids, you'd have to compete for my grandmother's attention with *Play Your Cards Right* or *Coronation Street*. It didn't matter if we hadn't seen them for weeks; the television never went off and the volume never went down. Nana would always sit side-on to the TV, one eye on you and the other on *Strike It Lucky*, and you could be in the middle of telling her the most amazing story but if something caught her attention on-screen you'd have to wait to finish it. 'I don't like him,' she'd suddenly announce, her lip curling at Michael Barrymore or whoever, and you'd know you'd lost her for a minute or two.

If the house was very much Nana's domain, the back garden and countryside beyond belonged to my grandfather, Gary. Gransha was a true countryman. For years, I thought the design of toby jugs was based on him: he had the same white mutton chop whiskers and wide smile. A big, burly man, he was funny and entertaining, with never a cross word for any of us kids. He was a tinker in his younger years, that's for sure, but I've always admired him as a man who knows how to survive.

Around Trinant, he was known as 'Gary the Gardener'. Their entire garden was given over to vegetables, with immaculate rows of marrows, beans, cucumbers and peas, and he also had an allotment where he grew more produce and kept chickens. They must have been almost entirely self-sufficient. Then all those beautiful organic vegetables would boil away for hours on Nana's stove until they were barely holding their shape and you could drop a knife through them.

From a young age, Gransha would take me and my cousins on epic walks for miles across the countryside, crazy distances for kids of our age. He was like the David Attenborough of Trinant, with an encyclopaedic knowledge of local plants, and would pick berries and nuts for us to try as we walked. We'd watch as he took a bite from a random leaf he'd plucked off a tree, smacking his lips with relish as if it was ribeye steak, then he'd pass it around us kids to have a taste and the bitterness would pucker our mouths and make us squirm.

One summer's day, when I was in my early teens, we were walking up the Sugar Loaf mountain alongside a stream. The sun was beating down and we were desperate for a drink. As we trudged upwards, Gransha spotted a freshly discarded old Coke can in the shallows. He swilled it out, then filled it from the stream and took a long drink.

'Lovely!'

I watched, equal parts horrified and fascinated.

Gransha saw me staring and held out the can.

'Go on, then …'

I hesitated, but I was so thirsty. Besides, Gransha was drinking it, so it must be okay.

Well, I've never been so sick in my life. I spent the whole night on the loo. And the next day, shaky and pale, after vomiting and shitting all night, I thought I'd phone Gransha, because I knew he must have been suffering like I was. Nope! He was absolutely fine. And I just thought: *What is this man made of?*

If we passed a pub (and more often than not we did; in fact I often wondered if the pub was the point, rather than the walk) we'd stop for Gransha to have a pint while I shared a packet of Golden Wonder with my cousin Dean. He's my mum's twin sister Elaine's son and there are only seven months between us, so we're more like brothers than cousins. I could listen to Dean's stories for hours, especially if he'd just had a birthday or was looking forward to Christmas. It was a glimpse into a very different life to the one I lived as a Jehovah's Witness. I remember him once telling me about the Easter egg he had at home. 'Can I see it?' I asked, goggle-eyed. 'Can I *try* a bit?'

Our walks with Gransha would usually end up at the same place: the skips round the back of the factories. The man was a magpie, always on the lookout for something that might be useful or worth a bit of money: an old microwave, copper cabling, a broken bike that he fixed up and which lasted for years. He apparently once found a Rolex in one of those skips, though I never saw it. He had several sheds and they were all packed to the rafters with stuff other people had thrown out. They were like walking into a Guillermo del Toro set, filled with headless dolls, rusty drill bits, old horseshoes and an anvil. One of the factories, Venturepak, was especially exciting at Christmas, when we'd find bagfuls of chocolates in broken packaging. Another time we unearthed an old pram, then piled all our treasures into it and pushed it down the lanes, through a leafy tunnel of arched trees, all the way back to Trinant.

Gransha was a big drinker, although that's a description that would fit almost every man in the Valleys at the time. It was just the way things were. After work you'd drop off a portion of your earnings to the wife, then head to the pub to spend the rest on pints of very cheap beer, sing songs with the lads and then stagger home at the end of the night. On Saturdays you'd watch the rugby at 2pm – more cheap beer – then go home, eat your tea and fall asleep in front of the TV. Things are slowly changing, though there's still the same institutionalised culture of drinking to this day. At eighty-seven Gransha can no longer handle his drink, so for his birthday I bought him a six-pack of Guinness 0.0% and didn't tell him it was alcohol free. He was as happy as Larry enjoying the placebo effect.

Gransha used to work down the mines, but later became a drayman for Bass Brewery, travelling the Valleys and delivering kegs to pubs; probably not the best job for a man who loved a pint or six. Nana must have had it tough: stuck at home looking after six kids – all of whom she gave birth to in that house – while her husband blew his wages down the pub, leaving her barely £20 to last the week. My mam remembers sitting on the floor with her siblings, counting out used bottle tops, which they would then exchange for money. When she was growing up you ate fast, or else one of the other five kids would snaffle the food off your plate.

With all that in mind, it's perhaps understandable that Nana never seemed to like Gransha very much. I'm sure she did, but she was always having a go at him.

'Here he comes, stinking of booze, the drunk sod,' she'd mutter, the moment he stepped foot in the kitchen, although he was never drunk around us kids – at least, I wasn't aware of it if he was. As far as I was concerned, Gransha was just always smiling. 'Get out! The kids are in here', she'd yell. 'Go on, stay out there!'

We used to find it funny that she was always giving him a hard time, but you have a different take on things as an adult. Once her kids were old enough to support her, I think all Nana's anger and bitterness towards Gransha must have come out. There was never any question of them splitting up, though; it was just how things were. They didn't even argue. My grandfather would just go, 'Oh, wrap up, Enid', in his good-natured rumble, and head back to the garden shed and all his trinkets.

Nana died of Alzheimer's three years ago, and I miss her to this day. As for Gransha, he's still going strong, if a little forgetful, and a horror to take shopping as you'll occasionally find something in his pocket that wasn't there when he left the house that morning. He looks exactly the same, though the sideburns are getting a little threadbare, and he still lives in the same house, looked after by my favourite auntie, Helen. She has always lived there, caring for our ageing grandparents; I don't think I'd still have a gransha at the age of forty-five if it wasn't for her. And to this day, that house is still busy with grandkids, great-grandkids and great-great-grandkids.

3

I stared down at my plate. A slice of lamb (no gristle or fat – Mam knew better than that), a single potato, three peas and two coin-shaped slices of carrot, in a pool of congealing gravy. The other dishes on the table had long since been cleared, probably washed and put away as well. My dad had left the room an hour ago, out of patience with me and my tears.

'Roy can hear you', he'd said gravely, nodding at the wall we shared with our neighbour, a lifelong bachelor who kept greyhounds that barked the whole time in the garden. Dad was brought up to be respectable in public. It wouldn't have bothered me, though; I'd inherited my mam's fire. I couldn't give two hoots if Roy could hear me.

'Come on now, Luke, please.' Mam's voice, though tender, was edging towards desperation. 'You need to eat something. Just one carrot. It's good for you.'

'I can't, Mam.'

This wasn't an exaggeration: I literally couldn't. The smell, the texture - it would make me retch.

She cut the coin of carrot into quarters and speared one of these tiny pips onto the fork.

'How about this one little bit?'

'I can't, it makes me feel sick!'

Mam sighed, then after a moment pushed back her chair and left the room. I have no idea how she stayed so calm in the face of my hysterics. She was dealing with a child who refused to eat as soon as he could say the word 'no'. Mealtimes, courtesy of me, were hell. To this day, I'm phobic about the sound of people chewing thanks to the hours spent in silence, listening to my parents eat, while I sat rigidly in front of my plate. It's to Mam's credit that I can only remember her snapping on one occasion, when after an hour of her begging and me refusing to even try a morsel of her homemade lasagne, a square of which she had specially made with extra tiny bits so as not to offend me, she grabbed a handful and smeared it in my face. I can still remember sitting there in shock. *You've gone too far this time, Luke.*

Today, though, Mam wasn't giving up. A moment later she was back at the table with a tube of mints. She unwrapped a Polo and held it out to me.

'Just one bit of carrot. Please, Luke.'

I wiped away my tears. There was a deal to be had here, which could work in my favour! My eyes fixed on the mint, I forced down a quarter of the carrot slice, trying not to retch, chewed it as little as possible and then grabbed the sweet.

Mam let out her breath; the tension in the room eased a little. After a moment, she unwrapped another Polo.

'How about a pea, love?'

I was seven at the time, but this could have been a scene from any moment during my childhood. A lot of kids are picky, but I was on another level. It's easier to say what I would eat: chips, ham, white bread with crusts cut off, maybe a bit of fruit. That was about it. I had to take a packed lunch to school – obviously – and it would always be the same thing: jam sandwiches, a bag of crisps (preferably crushed to crumbs before eating), a Twix or Club – or whatever the Kwik Save 'No Frills' equivalent was. We were on a tight budget when I was growing up.

I know Mam was in despair over my refusal to eat. I was a skinny kid and once had whooping cough for weeks, which in her mind was directly linked to the lack of nutrition. What made my issues even weirder was that I come from a family where plates were not only cleared, they were licked clean. I remember going for tea at my Auntie

Elaine's house, staring in horror at the shepherd's pie on my plate, and my cousin Dean muttering, 'What's wrong with you?'

It was a question my whole family asked.

'That child's not right, Yvonne. You need to sort it out.'

I remember my nan getting involved on one occasion.

'Come on love, just one little mouthful for your nana. Just a spoonful.'

'No. I don't like it.'

'If you don't eat your vegetables, you won't grow up to be a rugby player.'

'I don't want to be a rugby player. I want to be a ballet dancer!'

I was no Billy Elliot; I'd never even seen ballet. It was just the most opposite thing to a rugby player I could come up with.

'Oh, we've got trouble here,' muttered Nana, dropping fag ash into her slipper.

My war on food continued until I was fourteen, when a chance encounter with some pickled beetroot showed me the light. It's got quite a sweet taste and made me think that perhaps not all vegetables were equally horrible. From there, it was onto salad cream – which I realised I could smother on tomato, lettuce and cucumber to force them down – and I was away.

Nowadays I'll eat anything and will go out of my way to try new things, but the trauma I put my family through for all those years stayed with them for a good decade afterwards. My nan would visit me in London and when we went out for dinner I'd catch her watching me, mesmerised at the sight of me willingly putting food into my mouth.

'Look at him eat, Yvonne,' she'd murmur, shaking her head. 'Will you look at that? You'd never believe it was the same kid.'

· · ·

The one food I never had any problem with was sugar, and by happy coincidence my uncle Tom owned a sweet shop. It sold all the essentials, like toilet paper, sliced bread and milk, but it was the penny sweets that I cared about, laid out in trays next to the till so that 'Tom the Shop', as he was known in the village, could keep an eye on the kids' hands. Not that I would ever dream of nicking any; Jehovah saw to that. During my childhood, He (or She/They/Whatever) kept me out of the trouble that other kids regularly got into.

My favourites were the jelly cola bottles, although they were nothing like the ones we have today. They were small, flat and very hard, and you'd have to really chew on them. It's no exaggeration to say that as an adult I've searched dozens of sweet shops, both actual and virtual, but have never found the cola bottles of Tom's shop. Haribo have had to be a last resort.

Blessed with a sweet tooth that wasn't even satisfied by Frosties (I'd sprinkle *extra* sugar on the top) and with a near-constant supply of sweets, it probably won't be a surprise to hear that when I was seven I had to have most of my milk teeth taken out under general anaesthetic. I was left with just my top incisors, which is probably why they're so long now. Apparently teeth keep growing until they touch something, and for a long time there was nothing in my lower jaw to stop them, a quirk of dentistry which many years later would prove fortuitous when I was cast as the daddy of all vampires in *Dracula Untold*, although the studio didn't even realise I had my own set of fangs until the first camera test.

Some children might have been traumatised at becoming virtually toothless overnight. Not me; I felt special. Nobody else I knew had so few teeth. Not only that: as a reward for being such a good little patient my parents bought me a tape recorder. It had a speaker, a handle on top – your basic eighties kit – but oh, how I loved that machine. I took it with me everywhere; not to listen to music, but to record interviews. I would ask people about what they were up to that day, question them about their lives or just tape them singing a song. Family, friends, random visitors to our house: nobody was safe from Luke and his tape recorder.

If I didn't have anyone to grill, then I'd record myself reading a book. Not a chapter; the entire thing. An hour of me reading *Goldilocks and the Three Bears*, doing all the different voices and describing every picture. I know this because Mam still has all the tapes.

My interviewing technique was inspired by the presenters on *TV-am*, ITV's breakfast show at the time. I loved telly, and in those days of terrestrial broadcasting, the TV schedule provided the framework for my days. After school it was Phillip Schofield and Gordon the Gopher, *Newsround* with John Craven, *Blue Peter* and then tea (in the Valleys tea is dinner and dinner is lunch). The weekend belonged to Cilla Black: *Blind Date* on Saturday night and *Surprise, Surprise* on Sunday evening, which always made me and Mam cry. The highlight of my week was *Crimewatch* on Thursdays. We attended a Jehovah's Witness meeting that night and as soon as it finished I would rush my parents out of the Kingdom Hall, a quick stop at the chippie, then back home for *Crimewatch* to start at 9pm. More often than not I ended up going to bed in terror. The presenter once mentioned that a murder suspect had been wearing a pair of leather shoes from Ravel. A cold stone of fear formed in my stomach. *I* owned a pair of Ravel leather shoes! I was frantic with worry: what if I was accused of murder? Should I phone in and tell them they weren't mine?

It's probably obvious that I had a very vivid imagination. I was never interested in shop-bought toys, like Lego or *Star Wars* figures. When I was twelve I begged my parents for a Sega Mega Drive because all the other kids had one and within a month I was done with it, although I kept it in my bedroom to impress friends. I would much rather build a den, create a shop or make a cake, though I wasn't content just to stir the mixture or lick the bowl like most kids. Baking with Mam was an opportunity to star in my own cooking show.

I was mesmerised by cooking demonstrations on television – they still fascinate me to this day – and would do my best to recreate what I'd seen. I'd empty the kitchen cupboards of bowls and cutlery and would get Mam to weigh out all the ingredients into separate containers prior to showtime.

'Oh Luke, this is just so much washing-up ...'

'Please, Mam? Just the flour and sugar and the butter and milk? And can you pre-crack the eggs?'

In those days the most famous TV chef was Keith Floyd, who always cooked with a bottle of wine on the go, so I'd get a wine glass and fill it with white pop (lemonade), then we'd put on aprons and we were ready to go.

'Good afternoon, and welcome to the cooking show!' I beamed into the imaginary camera, which was the kitchen wall of our narrow terraced home. 'Here with me is my assistant, Doreen.'

Mam was always Doreen; the name tickled me. Every time I said it I'd laugh. I was an unusual kid; my humour was quite specific.

'Hello, I'm Doreen, and—'

'Thank you, Doreen, that's enough.' (This was *my* show.) 'Today we're going to be making a Victoria sponge ...'

I'd go through the process of making the cake, describing each stage to camera, and taking a swig of 'wine' every now and then, just like Keith Floyd, though I'd lose interest by the time it went into the oven. The process of making it was the fun part.

Another favourite game was shopkeepers. I was obsessed with the idea of standing behind a counter. I was always very clear: *I* am allowed behind the counter, but *you* are not. As Dad always had building materials in the garage, I would prop up some scaffolding planks on breeze blocks to make shelves and a counter, create a curtain so I could open and close the shop, then arrange my stock: tins, mud pies, potatoes, whatever I could find. I would then force my mother to come shopping.

I use the word 'force' advisedly here: I never really gave anyone a choice about whether they got involved in my games. If it wasn't Mam, it was usually my cousin.

Poor Dean. His dad was a real man's man, so at his house he played rugby or built go-karts, but when he came to us I would make him pick wildflowers, crush the petals to make some rancid perfume and then go round the neighbourhood trying to sell it to the old ladies in the street. Dean, bless him, always went along with it, but I'm sure he must have thought: *What the hell is Luke doing?*

I was clearly very persuasive, because nobody ever said no. I loved putting on shows: I would take Dean out into the side passage and make him learn a speech or song then march him back into the room to perform it. I would stand there, eyeballing him, and if he didn't get it right I'd be furious and make him do it again – four or five times if need be – until he got it right. I would perform Bible stories and sketches from *French and Saunders* ('Star Pets' and 'Whatever Happened to Baby Dawn' being my favourites) and everyone would get roped into it.

Yet at the time, the idea of performing for a living – as an actual job – never crossed my mind. You didn't have far-fetched ideas like that where I grew up. Besides, as a Jehovah's Witness you weren't encouraged to have career ambitions. You would need to have a job as an adult, obviously, but that was only to support your main work, which was spreading the word of Jehovah. From when I was little, though, everybody in the family could tell that I wasn't going to be content with life in the Valleys. There was something different about me and the way I saw the world. My mind was always sparking with plans, coming up with ways to make our lives better and enhance our existence. And I was very aware of it too. From a young age, I knew there was another life waiting for me beyond the Valleys.

4

Mam pushed open the front gate, which was hanging off by a hinge. The garden before us was a mess – an old sofa sprouting weeds and springs, a pile of half-burned plastic toys, grass up to our knees – though we'd seen worse. The other day we'd had to edge around a large, angry-looking pony to get to a front door.

It was 9am on Saturday morning, and while most children my age were at home on the sofa watching *Going Live!*, I was dressed in a suit and tie, knocking doors in a village up the valley with my parents and other Jehovah's Witnesses to spread the word. I had been doing this every single week since I was born – an hour and a half on Saturday mornings, again on Sundays and throughout the school holidays – but it never became any less of an ordeal. A few months ago we'd been in New Tredegar and a bunch of teenagers on bikes had followed us down the street, shouting 'Fuck off, you Jovie bastards!' Sometimes, when people started throwing things or set dogs on us, we would get in the car and leave, but this time we'd ignored the shouts and carried on.

As Mam and I picked our way up the path my feet made a pleasing tapping noise. I'd persuaded my parents to fix metal caps to the heels and toes of my shoes, as I loved the sound they made and would occasionally bust out some amateur tap moves on the pavement. For a while this made these weekend outings slightly more bearable, because the only time I wore these shoes was to knock on doors – though if there was a way to convince my parents that I was too ill to join them then I would always try it.

Like me, Mam was smartly dressed. As a Jehovah's Witness you always had to look respectable, because you were representing the religion. We always smelled nice; we smiled a lot and had neat hair. There was a lot of deprivation in the Valleys and when people saw us at their front door, looking so clean and fresh and happy and hopeful, it must have been a powerful draw. *Look what's happened to us since joining the religion*, our immaculate appearance seemed to say. *Join us, and you could be like this too!*

Mam was armed with a leather briefcase, inside which were copies of the Jehovah's Witness magazines, a Bible and a stack of report sheets, which would be filled out with notes such as: *Number 48: do not call again* or *Number 16: come back same time next week*. She was a Pioneer, which is what the religion calls those who knock on doors regularly. Mam used to spend upwards of sixty hours a month doing the rounds of the villages of South Wales in a bid to save souls.

Mam knocked at the door; a few moments later a woman opened it.
'Yeah?'

She was in her nightie, hair all over the place, a cigarette clamped between her lips. You could tell she was ready to say no even before she knew what we were there for – and really, who could blame her? Even at the age of nine, I was well aware that nobody wanted to hear about the Bible on a Saturday morning. It's the first day people have off from work and we're forcing them to come to the door and stand in the cold, letting all the heat out, to talk about something they most likely don't give a shit about.

'How are you this morning?' asked Mam. 'Do you have a hope for the future?'

The woman scowled. 'You what?'

It was then that I noticed the boy. He was standing in the corridor behind his mam wearing Spiderman pyjamas and, to my horror, I recognised him instantly. He was in my school, and he was looking at me with such utter disgust that I wanted to disappear inside my oversized suit, bought so that it would last me a bit longer. I must have looked so different from him: the big shoulder pads, the stupid tap shoes. I *was* so different from him. Everything we stood for, how we lived and spoke and dressed: we stuck out like sore thumbs. And I just thought: *This is not going to help me at school next week*. The kids at school already thought we were freaks, and now we were coming to their houses on a Saturday morning! That's how we were treated, and that's how we felt. Like freaks, oddities, weirdos.

The door had been slammed in our faces before Mam had even had a chance to finish her spiel. She smiled down at me, undaunted as ever, and we made our way back down the path, with me clip-clopping like a bloody shire horse, my cheeks burning with shame.

I hated knocking on doors. I hated forcing our ideas on people who had no interest in them, hated trudging around the rainy, grey streets when I could have been at home playing or watching TV. But I knew that there was no point complaining. It was our moral obligation as Jehovah's Witnesses to give as many people as possible the chance to come to the truth before Armageddon. We didn't knock on doors because we wanted to; we did it because we had to.

The Jehovah's Witness movement began in America in the 1870s, though it wasn't until the early 1900s, when the organisation's then president, Judge Rutherford, hit on the idea of driving with a gramophone on his car to spread the word, that the religion really started to grow.

Judge Rutherford thought there was a different way to understand the Bible. For instance, unlike traditional Christian doctrine, Jehovah's Witnesses don't believe in the Trinity: the Father, Son and Holy Ghost as one. To them, Jehovah alone is God, while Jesus is one of his angels, sent to earth as a sacrifice for the sins of man, and the Holy Spirit is the power Jesus used to perform miracles. Witnesses believe solely in what it says in the Bible, considering it both historically and scientifically accurate, and they follow the rules that were set out for the Israelites by Jehovah, which is the ancient name for God. They refer to the religion's set of beliefs as 'the Truth', which speaks volumes straight off. As far as Witnesses are concerned, these are not stories – this is *fact*.

It was Judge Rutherford who came up with the concept of Armageddon as God's war on the wicked, the central event that underpins the whole religion. Armageddon has been just around the corner for all my life and for seventy years before that, though after the disappointment of New Year's Eve 1975 they're now deliberately vague about the exact date. The last book of the Bible, Revelations, talks about the 'Signs of the Times': the rise in earthquakes, pestilences, wars and famine that show the end of the world is coming, and by those criteria you can certainly understand why Witnesses believe Armageddon will be happening any day now.

Though it's been portrayed in movies as this monstrous, terrifying thing, the prospect of Armageddon didn't scare me as a child. As far as I was concerned, it would just be God stepping in and stopping all the bad stuff that was going on in the world. Besides, I knew that my parents and I were going to be saved and would then live in paradise on earth, free from violence, pain, war and crime – which is a lovely idea, regardless of your beliefs. It was everyone else who was going to die in the storm of hail, earthquakes, floods, fire and sulphur at Armageddon (and I assumed that the rest of our family would hop over to our side of the fence when the big day came). That was about as far as I wanted to engage with the concept. I didn't need specifics, though I did have questions about the fact that the dead were going to be resurrected at Armageddon. Did this mean Hitler would get another chance? And what if you'd been cremated, would you just be … put back together? The answers were always annoyingly vague.

My parents were brilliant at door-to-door work; they still are. They can talk to anyone. I remember taking them to the premiere of *The Hobbit*, and in the car home Mam told me that she'd had a lovely chat with a man who had Welsh heritage.

'He was so nice,' she said. 'He told me this fascinating story about his childhood.'

'What was his name?'

'Oh, I can't remember. He had a funny beard.'

Well, that could have described hundreds of people in *The Hobbit*.

'He was short,' Mam went on. 'And had a funny accent. Australian, maybe …?'

I stared at her. 'Peter Jackson?!'

'That's it! Who's that then?'

'He's the director of *The Lord of the Rings* and *The Hobbit*.'

I couldn't believe it. Peter Jackson is a very lovely man, but quiet and reserved. I spent a year in his company, working with him and having dinners with his family, and barely knew anything about the man, yet my parents had drawn out these deeply personal stories in a matter of moments in the chaos of a movie premiere party.

My parents' conversational skills were a mixed blessing, though, as it meant that people often ended up inviting us into the house. I'd end up sitting in a stranger's living room clutching a cup of tea I didn't want, shooting looks of silent desperation at Mam, which she of course ignored. If someone wanted to hear about the Bible, it was our duty to tell them.

The door work wasn't always about converting people, though. It was about being kind. A good Witness is someone who leaves a positive impression. People often wanted my parents to come back because they hadn't spoken to anyone else all week, and we were nice and kind and would listen to them. In a way, it was like social work. Mam helped one young woman get to safety after she tearfully admitted her husband was beating her. Other times she bought food for people whose kitchen cupboards were empty. I'm sure this was part of the reason why a lot of new people came to the congregation when I was young. They were often fragile or vulnerable, and needed support and love as much as the religion itself.

When I was four, we moved from Crumlin to the nearby village of Aberbargoed to be closer to the Kingdom Hall, which is the Jehovah's

Witnesses' church and meeting house, and from then on our life was entirely within the religion. Being a Witness coloured every aspect of my life, although it just felt normal to me. My days were bookended by prayer. We would read a passage of scriptures at breakfast and say a blessing before dinner. On Tuesday evenings we'd go to one of the congregation's houses for an hour of Bible study. On Thursday evenings and Sunday mornings there would be a two-hour meeting at the Kingdom Hall. Saturday mornings, of course, were spent knocking on doors.

We were discouraged from mixing with 'worldly' people, which is the name for anyone outside the religion, so all my friends were living the same life as I was. There was a boy called Gavin on the street behind and we'd sometimes ride our bikes together, but he was really my only non-Witness friend. We would have 'get-togethers' with other families in the congregation: Saturday afternoons in the park with a Frisbee and picnic, beach trips in the summer, cheese and wine nights for my parents. It was a community of kind, like-minded people who were there for each other through life's hardships. You stick to the rules, you've got friends for life. And if you don't? Well, that's a story for later.

It's not that I thought we were better than everyone else, but I was aware that being Jehovah's Witnesses meant we'd survive at Armageddon while other people would not. We were reminded how lucky we were to have the religion: *Look at those poor people! They smoke, they drink too much, they swear. They have no hope for the future* … It's the reason Jehovah's Witnesses aren't allowed friends outside the religion: to protect the flock. Otherwise, you might discover that there's more to life than you're being told. Worldly people might get a bit drunk and say the odd 'shit' and 'bugger', but they also have successful careers, a nice car and several holidays a year. And if your eyes have been opened, and you've found out how great a 'worldly' life can be, then Bible meetings and caravan holidays might just start to lose their appeal.

5

'Good morning, class. Please open your books and write today's date at the top of the page.'

I did as I was told. *Monday, 15 April 1987.*

I frowned, staring at what I'd just written. The teacher had moved on, but I wasn't listening. There was something about that date …

'Oooh!' I was so excited that it came out as a shriek. 'It's my birthday today!'

The classroom fell silent. At the back, somebody sniggered. I turned around to see a sea of faces staring back at me, their expression one big *What the hell?*

You can understand why. *This kid doesn't know it's his own birthday? What about when he woke up and opened his presents? Hasn't he been planning a party? Didn't anyone wish him 'Happy birthday' this morning?*

But no, none of those things had happened. I'm not sure my parents would have even remembered it was my birthday, and if they had, they had been told by the religion that celebrating was forbidden, so they'd have kept quiet about it. To this day I'm still not sure when my parents' birthdays are. One's in August and the other November, I think. When I left home and celebrated my first birthday – my eighteenth – I tried to enjoy it, but I felt guilty, and that guilt stayed with me for a long time thanks to this early conditioning.

Perhaps if I'd been around other people celebrating their birthdays it might have been different, but I wasn't. It would be like if you'd never tasted ice cream before, or better still cola bottle sweets: you wouldn't know what you were missing. We didn't go to my cousins' parties and when there were birthdays at school they knew not to involve the Jehovah's Witness kids. We would sit there quietly at the back of the class or in the corner while everyone else sang the song and ate the cake. Other children were always horrified at the thought of not getting birthday presents, but my parents were very generous and if I wanted something I usually got it, so I never felt left out. Plus, I got presents all year round, rather than on just one day, so in my mind it was even better.*

Christmas, however, was less easy to ignore, because for a few weeks every December the world was transformed into a tinsel-trimmed, fairy-lit, mince-pie-eating wonderland. When we were knocking doors at Christmas I'd always look at everyone's trees and choose the best one on the street. We might not have celebrated it ourselves, but the fact that everyone else did brought considerable benefits for me.

Most importantly, Christmas meant a holiday from school. It meant snowy days flying down hills on carrier bags and cosy fires at home. And the telly! All the best films and TV specials would be on: *The Snowman, Raiders of the Lost Ark, Mary Poppins*. I would record them all on VHS tapes to watch throughout the year. In the weeks running up to Christmas I'd beg my parents to visit our families so I could see their trees with all the lights and baubles. It was magical how their houses were transformed, though I'd listen to the adults telling the kids that Father Christmas was on his way and I'd think: *Do they honestly think a fat, bearded man is going to come down their chimney in the middle of the night?* I'd been told straight off that Father Christmas didn't exist and it seemed ridiculous to me that anyone would actually believe it. They all had gas fires, so he couldn't have made it down the chimney anyway (ironically, we had real fires in our house, so there was more chance of him visiting the little Jehovah's Witness family in School Street). Still, I did

---

* Nowadays I have epic birthdays. I make the biggest fuss over them and I love it.

love seeing the piles of presents under the tree and when visiting one of my aunties' houses, or even better Nana and Gransha's, would always subtly check if there was something there for me.

'Mam, I know you're going to give him a present,' my mam would tell my grandmother. 'We'll come up a week before, so he doesn't get it on Christmas Day.'

Nan would roll her eyes. 'Whatever you want, Yvonne love.'

My grandparents accepted their daughter's decision to join the religion, but I don't think they ever understood it. To our family, Jehovah's Witnesses were just a bunch of 'Bible bashers'.

The only events we were allowed to celebrate in the religion were wedding anniversaries and the Memorial of Jesus' Death. This was the most sacred occasion of our year and was marked with an evening service at the Kingdom Hall on the night of the Last Supper, when Jesus was taken away to be killed.* The memorial usually took place around Easter, but was based on the date of Nisan 14, from the ancient Jewish lunar calendar that was used during Jesus' life. The service always fell on a full moon, and afterwards, as we left the Kingdom Hall, Mam would bend down to me, point up at the sky and whisper, 'Look, there's a full moon again!' She'd always try to make things exciting for me. And I'd be amazed that yet again this had happened on such a special, solemn day, blissfully unaware that it was anything but a coincidence.

During the memorial, unleavened bread and wine were passed around the congregation, but the only people allowed to taste them were the anointed. I should explain here that the concept of death is different to Jehovah's Witnesses: they believe that we don't actually die, but go into a sort of sleep, waiting to be resurrected after Armageddon. Some Witnesses, however, believe they are among the anointed, the

---

* Jehovah's Witnesses believe that Jesus died on a stake with his hands tied above his head, rather than on a cross. I'm not sure why; perhaps because crucifixes are so synonymous with traditional Christianity.

144,000 people mentioned in the Bible who have been chosen to go to heaven to rule alongside Jesus when they die. We knew a few of these and they were hugely respected and somewhat revered within the community, perhaps because we knew we'd never see them again after Armageddon because they'd be in heaven. I have no idea how they knew they were anointed – I don't think there were any tests per se – but you couldn't question it: if they told the elders they were one of the anointed, everyone had to believe them.

You can probably see a theme developing here: don't question what you're told. Do as the Bible says. Stick to the rules. And I guess this is fine, as long as it's not doing anyone any harm, but for me it's another matter entirely when it comes to the Jehovah's Witnesses' prohibition of blood transfusions.

In the Bible, blood is portrayed as a sacred gift given to us by God. It's not ours, so to pass it around is to break the sanctity of the gift. This was obviously written long before the invention of lifesaving modern blood transfusions, but because it's in the Bible, the Witnesses are sticking to their guns. If you voluntarily accept a blood transfusion – even if it's to save your life – you will be shunned by the community.

I can't even begin to get my head around the ridiculousness of this. There was a young woman who died after she started haemorrhaging while giving birth and refused a transfusion. 'It's okay, I'll be resurrected and will see you in paradise,' she promised her husband and newborn baby. It's the most extraordinary belief.

Unfortunately for my parents, I was first in line for accidents when I was growing up. One time I was messing around in the car park at the Kingdom Hall with my friends when I slipped and fell on my bottom, right onto a shard of broken glass. I could feel that I'd ripped my trousers, so I sheepishly went off to tell Mam.

She was talking to someone in the foyer.

'Mam?'

'Just a second, Luke, I'm busy.'

I stood there waiting. Weirdly, I don't remember much pain. Eventually, she finished her conversation.

'What is it, love?'

'I'm sorry, Mam, I think I've torn my trousers.'

I turned round to show her and apparently the back of my trousers were completely soaked with blood, so much so that it was pooling onto the carpet of the Kingdom Hall.

They rushed me to the little hospital in Aberbargoed and while I was having stitches in my bum, my poor, traumatised mother was passed out cold on the bed beside me.

Another time, I was out on my blue and gold BMX with some other kids and we came across two boys having a fight up the lane. Stopping at a safe distance, we watched as one punched the other in the stomach and he buckled over in tears. As the victor stalked away – in our direction – the other kid managed to get to his feet, then grabbed an old metal dustbin lid that had been wedged in a hedge and threw it as hard as he could at his opponent. We watched as it flew over the other kid's head, then over our heads and then, as if in slow motion, the wind caught the lid and it came flying back, hitting me straight on the head. I fell off my bike; dazed, I gingerly touched my head. 'BLOOOOOOD!' I shrieked, sending the other kids screaming and scrambling to get away. I was hyperventilating with the shock, so it was really pumping out of me. I pushed my bike home in tears, so much blood pouring down my face that the world turned red. I will never forget my mother's look of horror when she opened the front door to me.

Thankfully, I always managed to hold on to just enough blood to avoid the issue of a transfusion, though I've been left with a ridge on my head and quite an impressive scar on my right bum cheek.

∴

Like most Jehovah's Witness families, we had a picture book at home called *My Book of Bible Stories*. I enjoyed reading about Adam and Eve, Noah's ark, and Moses leading the Israelites out of Egypt and would sometimes re-enact them with Dean as my reluctant co-star.

'You're going to be Joseph and I'll be Abraham. Do you know that story?'

Of course he didn't; he watched *ThunderCats* like most normal kids.

'Don't worry, it's going to be fantastic! You put this tablecloth on – no, not like that. Over your head, that's it … Right, stand over there and then I walk in …'

There was one story that always unsettled me, though: the tale of Lot's wife. Basically, God tells Lot that he has to leave the cities of Sodom and Gomorrah, along with his wife and daughters, because the other inhabitants are wicked and immoral. God destroys the cities and their people, and as the angels lead Lot's family away they are warned not to look back, but Lot's wife disobeys and is turned into a pillar of salt.

It was the picture that went with the story that scared me. Lot's wife is turning slowly to salt, looking back longingly at the home she's had to leave, while in the background people are running around in flames, sulphur and fire raining down on them. It's pretty terrifying for a children's book.

The story is actually intended to be about the perils of being materialistic. Don't hang on to worldly things like Lot's wife; the biggest television and nicest car isn't going to help you when Armageddon comes. What matters is your faith in God, because he will save you. Yet as I got older and learned more about that story, I discovered the reason the people of Sodom and Gomorrah were considered so abominable was because they were homosexuals.

The Bible doesn't mess about when it comes to homosexuality: 'detestable' is the word that's used. According to the scriptures, 'Men who lie with men' are right up there with thieves, adulterers and murderers and will die with the rest of Satan's wicked at Armageddon. It gradually dawned on me that those poor people at the back of the picture were dying a horrible death simply because they were gay. God clearly considered that be enough of a reason to burn them alive. And if you were a kid who was just starting to get a sense of who you were, and perhaps beginning to realise that you were different from other boys … Well, that picture was more than enough to make you keep quiet about it.

6

The first sense I had of being gay – or at least different – was at the age of eight, when our class got a substitute teacher for the summer term. He played rugby for Llanelli and had a sharp haircut and a two-seater sports car. He was handsome and sharply dressed; all the girls fancied him, and all the boys wanted to be him. I remember staring at him in class, muscles busting out of his shirt, and just thinking: *Wow*. Even then, I knew I was looking at him in a different way from the other boys.

Our house was opposite Aberbargoed Juniors and one morning I opened the front door to discover that he had parked his sports car right outside. Heart hammering in my chest, I went over to take a closer look. It was an open-top kit car and the first thing I saw was the word LUKE emblazoned across the shoulder harnesses. It was the brand name of the harnesses, but all I saw was my name. I'm sure my mouth must have dropped open.

A few days later, shortly after I'd arrived at school, he came over to speak to me.

'Luke, was that your mother I saw with you just now?'

'Yeah, that's my mam.'

I probably stammered it out because this handsome giant was talking to me.

'Ah, right.' He paused. 'And your dad is still, um …?'

I knew what he was getting at instantly. I suppose it was hardly surprising; my mother was very pretty and still in her twenties – they were probably about the same age, come to think of it – but I remember the shock of the realisation. *He fancies my mam!*

Three weeks later our usual teacher returned and I never saw him again, but the memory of the feelings he awakened stayed with me. I was still very young, so it clearly wasn't a sexual thing, yet I was acutely aware of an urge to be around this strong, masculine man. Looking back, I wonder if part of the attraction was the knowledge that a man like that would be physically powerful enough to stand up and protect me. My dad took very good care of us, but he was never the kind of man who would have a shouting match or swing a punch – and at this time in my life that was exactly what I needed.

I was bullied for being gay before I even understood what it meant. For a long time I assumed 'bender' was just another random insult, like 'wanker' (another word often thrown my way that I didn't understand) until it dawned on me that the floppy-wrist gesture that often accompanied these taunts was aimed at something very specific in me. Perhaps it was because I was a little more sensitive and delicate, more passive in dealing with aggression, or maybe it was just because I was more into art than rugby – who knows? The names kept coming: 'Jovey' (their shorthand for Jehovah's Witness), 'Shirt-lifter', 'Bible-basher', 'Bender', 'Gay boy'. I think the worst one was 'Jovey Bender', because it combined two aspects of my identity that could never be reconciled. It wasn't possible to be a 'Jovey' and a 'Bender' because being gay was strictly forbidden by the religion. And so began a tormented tug of war in my head that would go on throughout all my years at school. It's a terribly dark place to be as a child, knowing you're somehow 'wrong', but with no idea why that is or how you can fix it.

I hated school. Children can be horribly intolerant; evil little bastards some of them. Anything slightly different about you and you're immediately a target – and I was different in almost every way possible. I wasn't good at sport. I wasn't the least bit competitive, perhaps because I had no siblings to compete against. Instead of playing football at break, I preferred to hang out and chat with my best friends, Emma and Debbie.

The other boys wore Adidas tracksuits and trainers, but I had never had any branded stuff – it seemed a waste of money to be paying double for a logo – so instead of a Nike rucksack mine had a picture of Garfield the cat, though I got the piss taken out of me so badly I had to stop using it after its first outing. And, of course, I was a Jehovah's Witness, which was the cherry on top of the icing on the weirdness cake. I also happened to be the most visible of the Witness kids in my year, as all the others were girls (apart from one boy who had nine siblings and was as badly bullied as I was). Because the religion is a patriarchy, as a boy I was the one who would have to stand up in class when we got a new teacher and spell out exactly how different we were.

'Hi, me and these other guys here are Jehovah's Witnesses, so that means we abstain from RE lessons and assemblies, we don't sing Christmas carols or hymns, we don't celebrate Easter, birthdays, Christmas, Harvest Festival ...'

Looking back, I didn't stand a chance.

The bullying was mainly verbal in junior school, though nonetheless painful for it. The other kids made a deliberate point of excluding me. It wasn't just that I was the last to be picked for sports teams – although I was, along with the boy who always had snot hanging from his nose – but they made it clear they didn't even want to be near me. I remember a maths class where the only free seat was next to me and this boy wouldn't sit down. To be treated like that as a child and made to feel there's something intrinsically wrong with you ... it's just so painful, and it stays with you. Even now, if you asked me what I looked like as a child, I would automatically reel off the things I was bullied about: big ears, skinny legs, hair that would never go spiky or lie in curtains like the other boys'. I felt inadequate physically, and that feeling grew with me into adulthood. You might imagine that becoming famous would have helped, and I do have brief moments when I think: *My God, people actually think I'm handsome?!* But it's all so separate from my daily reality, and that voice inside my head – the one telling me I should look younger, have better muscle formation or smoother skin – often drowns out any compliments I might be lucky enough to receive. Thankfully I'm in a place now where I can get these negative feelings under control and appreciate myself, but I've really had to work at it. As for many of us, it's an ongoing battle, but we have to love ourselves. As the great RuPaul said, 'If you don't love yourself, how in the hell you gonna love somebody else?' Amen!

It wasn't that I was a weak kid, but I was sensitive and not especially brave. I didn't know how to argue back or swing a punch (hard to believe if you watch half of my movies!) and I didn't have any well-rehearsed retorts because I was an only child: there was no big brother to practise on at home. I couldn't even fight back with a few swear words, the easiest and most accessible of weapons, because swearing was forbidden by the religion. All in all, I was the perfect victim for any of the louder, brasher kids to attack.

One late autumn morning, I went into the garden before school to feed our rabbit and noticed that the water in the top of a flower pot had frozen into a disc, trapping a scattering of fallen leaves inside. I carefully lifted it out, thrilled by this miniature stained-glass window. I was sure the other kids in my class would be just as fascinated as I was, so I thought I'd take it into school to show my teacher.

As I hurried across the playground, a boy ran up to me.

'What's that?'

'I found it in a flower pot. It's ice, you see, and these leaves have got—'

With one swipe he knocked it out of my hands. It smashed on the concrete. I looked at him with total incomprehension as he ran off laughing with his mates. Why would you want to destroy something so beautiful? Looking back, I assume that this kid probably hadn't been brought up with the same sense of wonder and appreciation for nature that I had, but back then all I knew was whenever I tried to be myself I was ridiculed for it.

If the teachers noticed what was going on, they never addressed it. Nobody ever asked me if I was okay. As a young person you would usually have someone older who you could ask for advice, but I didn't have anyone to talk to. If my mother had realised how prolific the bullying was I know she would have stepped in, but I couldn't tell my parents because their first question would be to ask what I was being bullied about, and I was too ashamed of the names I was being called to tell them. After all, the Bible states that homosexuals will die at Armageddon along with the murderers, thieves and adulterers. So I stayed quiet, kept my head down, stuck with the other Witness kids and threw myself into my studies and you wouldn't have had a clue from reading the glowing comments in my school reports from this time that I was anything other than blissfully happy at school.

...

As an adult I became an ambassador for The Prince's Trust and saw first-hand the terrible damage years of consistent bullying can do. It can totally fuck you up. You think you're a failure because of what you've been told for all those years. Your confidence is crushed and your ambition dies. People turn to drugs or alcohol as a way to deal with the pain, sometimes even consider taking their own lives.

In a way I was one of the lucky ones. The bullying didn't destroy my drive or ruin my future. Maybe it was because I had a lot of love at home, but even in junior school I knew it wasn't me that was the problem, it was the bullies. As an only child I was around adults a lot more than kids of my own age, so perhaps I just grew up faster and developed a more mature perspective – an old head on young shoulders. But throughout my childhood, whenever bad stuff happened, there was a refrain going through my head: *This is only temporary*. Even at a young age I had this clear-eyed view. Once school was over, I knew my life would begin.

7

Mam was everything to me. She was the one who stood at the gate to wave me off to junior school in the morning and would be there to welcome me at the end of the day. I would come back to have lunch and watch *Neighbours* with her whenever I could, and would even sneak home to use the bathroom between lessons, running there and back before the teachers knew I'd gone. I don't think I once used the toilets at Aberbargoed Juniors the entire time I was there.

When we lived in Crumlin, my first home in a different valley, Mam worked in a sewing factory making leather gloves, but she gave up work after we moved to Aberbargoed and I started school. It was Dad who was the breadwinner, working on a building site all day and coming home late and weary in the evening, which is perhaps why we didn't have a deep connection until I was in my late teens. We're very close now, but back then I don't think he understood me or really knew how to deal with children in general. It can't have helped that he'd been raised away from his siblings by a seventy-year-old woman who wouldn't have been regularly mixing with young families and who clearly had very different ideas about how children should be raised. Seen but not heard, perhaps?

My closeness to Mam was intensified by the fact that I didn't have any brothers or sisters. Her own childhood had been a struggle, with so many kids in the house and little money to go round, and Dad had effectively been raised as an only child, so my parents made the conscious decision to pour all their love, energy and hard-earned cash into making our lives better. They wanted to give me the opportunities they hadn't had, especially when it came to schooling. Neither of my parents received a decent education. My mother is impressively practical – she can cook, clean, make clothes and curtains, even reupholster furniture – but when I was growing up she struggled to read, and the only thing she was confident writing was her name. If she was in school today she would quickly be diagnosed as dyslexic and given the appropriate support, but back then the teachers just labelled her ignorant and naughty and treated her as such.

Thanks to technology such as predictive texting, Mam finds things much easier these days. It's admirable how well she's coped over the years, as nobody ever suggested she might be dyslexic and so she never sought help, but throughout my childhood I was very much conscious of her limited ability to read and write. It created a curious dynamic in our relationship: as much as I felt loved and cared for by her, I was also aware of a strong need to protect her. This was most apparent at our Bible study meetings on Tuesday nights, where the congregation would take turns to read from the scriptures. I would sit next to her, my heart rate shooting up as I waited for someone to say: 'Yvonne, would you like to read this next passage?' I would sense her instantly tense up; her terror at getting it wrong in front of all those people was palpable. It was always a huge relief when she had finished, and she usually made very few mistakes, as she was so familiar with the Bible. Though if she picked up a copy of *HELLO!* magazine she wouldn't have had a clue, because she'd have been unfamiliar with the words and structure.

By the age of seven my literacy skills had overtaken hers, and from then on I would take care of any writing that needed doing at home, such as filling out deposit slips for banking cheques and putting together estimates for Dad's building jobs, as his schooling had been just as bad. While it was undeniably handy to be able to write my own school sick notes, it wasn't easy to accept that I was better at reading and writing than my parents. I knew I could run rings around them if I wanted to, though I never did. I hope that doesn't sound arrogant: it was simply down to the fact that I was able to read better, so could access more information. Plus, I was a very curious kid. My parents were content with the scope of their lives, but I was insatiably inquisitive about the world outside the Jehovah's Witness bubble. This was obviously long before the internet and there were rarely any newspapers or magazines in our house, and almost all the books were religious, except for a sprinkling of encyclopaedias, so it was up to me to find ways to feed my hunger for knowledge.

Keeping pets was one such resource for me. We had animals throughout my childhood; as an only child, they provided entertainment and companionship, and I loved the sense of responsibility they gave me. I was never content with just caring for them, though – I had to know every tiny detail about them. For a time I had an aviary of birds and Mam still has the notebooks I filled with records on their diets, breeding and habits.

Gransha had helped me build that aviary around a honeysuckle bush in our garden. It took us all day to finish – fixing the frame, covering it in chicken wire and connecting it to our shed via a hole where the birds could nest – and when it was finally ready, my parents stood watching as we released my five new zebra finches into their new home. The scent of honeysuckle was heavy in the air as we watched them flitting around; it was a beautiful moment. One of them landed on the fence, gripping the wire close to where we were standing, but our delight turned to shock and confusion in an instant when the little bird suddenly flew out. It was so tiny it had slipped straight through one of the holes in the chicken wire! A moment later another of the birds flew away and then a third tried to follow, but cut its neck on the wire and was left dangling on the fence. Frozen in horror, I could only watch as the final pair made their escape. They perched on the washing line and as they sat there, smugly ruffling their feathers, I still remember our panicked conversation: *What are we going to do? How are we going to get them back in?* Moments later they took flight, heading off over the rooftops, and that was the last we saw of any of them. The prison break had been a complete success.

I was mortified. The aviary lay empty for several weeks until we bought some new birds (and some smaller-holed chicken wire). Yet despite the unpromising start, my aviary turned out to be a real success. I later kept canaries, and in the summer would sit watching them for hours while they splashed under the shower I'd rigged up over the honeysuckle bush and sang late into the evening.

Primarily, we were a cat family, and over the years we had a cast of characters to rival Andrew Lloyd Webber's musical. Our first was Pussy, a huge, ugly old thing who was scratchy and standoffish, but would occasionally deign to play. Then there was Fluffy, who came to us as a rescue. When we first got him, his fur was matted to the skin, and I remember Mam sitting there, patiently loosening the mats with talcum powder, crying her eyes out over this poor, neglected boy. Fluffy had a beautiful coat with distinctive ginger markings and, according to my cat book, was a dead ringer for a rare breed called a Turkish Van swimming cat. Well, that was it. As far as I was concerned, Fluffy was a pedigree.

'Oh yes, he *is* handsome, isn't he?' I would say. 'He's a very rare Turkish cat who likes to swim. I know! Quite unique, really ...'

Fluffy probably wasn't a Turkish swimming cat. I was desperate to put him in the bath to test it out, but Mam wouldn't let me. Still, this was typical of me as a child. It wouldn't have been enough for me knowing that we had a pretty cat; I'd want to think he was *special*.

There was a family who lived at the top of our street who were known for screaming matches in the garden and their large number of cats. They didn't care for them, so they often found their way to our house, where they were sure of a warm welcome. I had been feeding one of these cats for about a year, a ratty, smelly boy. One day he turned up with another cat, a beautiful little grey one, barely into adulthood, who seemed pitifully hungry. In my imagination they were brother and sister, and it was almost as if he had brought her to us to look after. I named her Laura and began feeding her every day, gratified to watch her putting on weight. Quite a lot of weight, actually ...

One particularly chilly winter night I sneaked Laura into my bedroom, as I couldn't stand the thought of her being outside in the cold. When I woke up the next morning – a Saturday – I reached a hand out from inside the cocoon of my covers to turn on my little black-and-white telly so I could watch *Going Live!* before the door-to-door work, and heard a faint squeaking coming from under my bed. Curious, I hung down over the bed to look, but it was too dark to see anything, so I grabbed the TV, put it on the floor and turned up the brightness so the screen shone under the bed like a torch. There was Laura, curled up in a nest she'd made with my flannelette blanket, with her five new kittens. She hadn't gotten fat: she'd gotten pregnant! Well, she couldn't go home after that. We had her spayed, gave her a collar and a new name – Polly (I didn't think Laura suited her now she was a mother) – and she went on to have a beautiful new life under witness protection. I was allowed to keep one of the kittens and named him Squeak, though when a Jehovah's Witness family with two daughters wanted a cat Mam offered him up. Well, I called those two girls every name under the sun. 'Those little bitches are *not* taking Squeak!' I should mention that I would never have dreamed of using this word in any other circumstance. Until this point, the worst I'd done was to call my mam and dad a witch and wizard – mild to most people, but dire insults in a Jehovah's Witness child's mind. I caused absolute ructions over that kitten; nevertheless, Squeak left.

Polly had a number of admirers, including a neighbour's enormous black cat called – what else? – Sooty. He started spending so much time at our house that the neighbour told us we might as well keep him. Sooty was an absolute delight, but a total juvenile delinquent.

He would sit for hours in front of my aviary and sometimes I'd hear the birds screaming and rush to the window to see Sooty clinging to the fence, his face smooshed up against the wire. 'Sooty!' I'd shriek. 'Don't you dare!'

I always knew Sooty wouldn't live long and one morning there was a knock at the door to tell us he'd been knocked over. Still in my pyjamas, I ran up our street to the main road, stopped the traffic and picked up what was left of poor little Sooty. I buried him at the top of the garden in a solemn ceremony, sobbing my heart out.

I was always hit hard by the death of our animals. Possibly the most traumatic was the loss of Tigger, another of our cats. We had been on one of our caravan holidays and when we returned the girl who'd been feeding him told us that she hadn't seen him for the past couple of days. We eventually found him stuck in the hedge that divided our garden from our next door neighbour's. The poor thing had been shot with a lead pellet and had to be put down.

There was only one suspect: our neighbour had a pellet gun and an aviary of budgies he was excessively worried about. I remember Mam, furious and heartbroken, yelling over the fence.

'I know you're in there. You come out and explain what's happened here. We know what you've done!'

Mam kept shouting, but he wouldn't come out. Such a terrible thing to do.

Anyway, I own his house now and any animal can come and go as they please.

8

I lived for the school holidays. The moment I set foot outside Aberbargoed Juniors I felt normal. I wasn't hiding who I was or keeping quiet out of fear of being bullied: I was equal to other kids and wasn't treated any differently by them. Outside school I was friends with two Jehovah's Witness brothers, Ben and Joel, real boys' boys who loved *Star Wars* and rough and tumble games, and the prospect of them finding out about the bullying was terrifying. I think I would have been too embarrassed to hang out with them if they had known about the names I was getting called in school.

Summer holidays usually meant caravanning in Wales, whether it was the Forest of Dean or the coast. Most often it was at Saundersfoot in Pembrokeshire with my cousin Dean and his family. Auntie Elaine and Uncle Gavin had a smart new caravan, whereas my parents – as ever overly worried about being flashy – had a horrible, second-hand Swift Sprite that looked as if it would blow over in a stiff breeze. It was tiny and very old (and smelled every year of it) and the walls were as thin as cardboard, so you could hear every cough and splutter from your neighbours. I was always mortified when we parked up alongside the other modern-looking caravans in the park.

I have such happy memories of those summers. Long, hot days riding our bikes, scrambling through the forest and then, as the sun went down, night-fishing on the pebbly beach with Dean and his siblings, Adam and Donaleigh. There was a big rock just near the water's edge that would fit all of us and we'd clamber up there and sit in a row with our fishing rods, the moonlight glittering on the water as we waited for a bite. We never caught anything, although one time as we waded back to the beach we found a large flatfish wedged under a rock, which we proudly took back for our parents to cook.

Nobody could make me laugh like 'our Dean'. He would make up silly names for the other people at the caravan park. At one site the manager looked exactly like Basil Fawlty, gangly and moustachioed, and we'd crack up every time he strode past. He had the ability to find something funny in everyone. We would crack up on the bus, at the supermarket – he always seemed to find the funniest-looking folk. Even when Dean wasn't trying to be funny he was entertaining. He once fell into the sea fully dressed and had to walk back to the caravan park in nothing but his Superman pants. He was furious, which made it all the funnier for the rest us.

The first time I remember going on a plane was when I was eleven. We had been invited to Benidorm by another Jehovah's Witness family who went there every year and had a daughter who was about my age.

We stayed in a little apartment in La Cala de Finestrat, which is just next to the main strip, and every morning Mam would make us ham, tomato and cheese baguette sandwiches and wrap them up to take with us to the beach (I'd remove the cheese and tomato). I thought it was magical: I loved the dazzling, intense heat, although none of us realised quite how strong the sun was in Spain. Mam usually just used baby lotion when she sat out in the garden at home. I ended up in hospital after getting so badly sunburned my legs swelled with huge blisters. Poor Mam was mortified; she still remembers the looks of disgust from the doctors and nurses. Still, it lives on in my mind as the most joyous holiday. Even while having to wear long socks on the beach to cover my blistered ankles, I felt like any other normal kid. Years later I spent a lot of time in Alicante, just down the coast, and remember this place so fondly.

. . .

You'll remember that my parents married very young and I arrived soon after, so they hadn't had much time on their own as a couple. Also, my dad was not much of a romantic. He worked hard and paid the bills, but there's so much more to a marriage than these practicalities. He never thought about the little gestures, such as buying flowers or taking Mam out for dinner; I don't remember them going on a date when I was young, not even once. It wasn't that he didn't love her – and I'm sure this wasn't at all uncommon among men at the time – but my mother struggled with his lack of thoughtfulness. Where Dad was reserved and calm, she was emotional and passionate. Mam needed to know she was loved and appreciated, but he just didn't seem to get it.

The only secular events Jehovah's Witnesses are permitted to celebrate are wedding anniversaries, yet Dad always forgot to buy a card. He'd say he'd been too busy, clearly having no idea why it was important to her – it was just a piece of paper, after all! But to Mam this was yet more proof of how little he valued romance and the outward expression of love. After all, he'd never seen any between Lala and Tom when he was growing up. To Mam, it felt like he couldn't be bothered to make that one small effort, even when he knew how much it would mean to her. Every year, like clockwork, it would upset her.

The dissatisfaction must have simmered on for some time, but like many married couples my parents just got on with it. Life was busy, and they had a small child who consumed most of their attention; besides, divorce was severely frowned upon in the Jehovah's Witness community. Perhaps they would have plodded along like this for many more years, but then one day, when I was eleven, my mam decided she'd had enough.

My parents' friends had thrown an anniversary party for them; once again, Dad hadn't bothered to buy her anything, not even a card. On the way home I could feel the bad energy in the car. They weren't talking, but it was obvious Mam was angry and upset. When we arrived back she calmly told me to go in the house, but as soon as I closed the front door the shouting started. Even from inside, I could hear every word. Mam was screaming and crying – she sounded completely broken – while Dad was quiet, unable to find the right words. Even when she told him she'd had enough, that she was done with it all, I still don't think he understood the seriousness of the situation. I did, though. I was absolutely petrified.

I don't know how long they were in the car for, but at some point I picked up the phone and called an older Jehovah's Witness couple I was very fond of, called Dave and Iris, to ask for help. Dave was a big barrel of a man who loved singing and had the loudest voice in the Kingdom Hall, while Iris had enormous backcombed hair, a mahogany tan and very long nails.

It was very late and they arrived in their dressing gowns – Iris with her usual giant hairdo – and managed to calm my parents down. Meanwhile, I was packed off to bed as if nothing had happened.

This was the beginning of a year-long period that nearly led to the break-up of my parents' marriage. I was painfully aware of what was going on, the shouting and loaded silences, but my parents never once spoke to me about what was happening. Neither did Dave and Iris. Nobody asked how it was affecting me. I suppose they were consumed by their own problems and probably thought I would be too young to understand. They were still only in their twenties, after all; I very much doubt I would have dealt with this any better at that age. Left to deal with the chaos and uncertainty by myself, I lived in a constant state of anxiety. Our little house was open plan – there were no doors to close for privacy – so I'd stand in my bedroom doorway in the darkness listening to them fight. My knees would literally tremble, imagining at any minute that Mam would come marching upstairs, pull me out of bed and take me away. But where? I had no idea where we would end up living if she left Dad, or how we would survive. If there had been an argument the night before, I was terrified I would find our suitcases by the front door when I got home from school. One evening Dad cried through the whole of dinner while we just sat there eating in silence. I don't think he had any idea how to cope with Mam's pain. He'd been brought up by Lala, who was all about having a stiff upper lip and being worried what the neighbours thought. He didn't have the tools to deal with this emotional maelstrom.

What my parents needed was professional marriage counselling, but there was no question of that. Back then – as it still is today - such problems were kept firmly within the congregation and dealt with by the elders, the unofficial (and unqualified) carers of the flock, even though they had zero specialist training to guide a couple struggling with something like this.

The day the elders came to talk to my parents I stood listening at the top of the stairs. By now I was an expert eavesdropper, as it was the only way I could find out what was going on. The elders were as gentle and patient as ever, but they went heavy on the shame and embarrassment divorce would bring to the community. The religion could exert a powerful pressure on a couple by reminding them that marriage is a God-given gift, like blood, and as such is sacred. My parents would never have wanted to break the rules set down in the Bible or bring reproach on the name of Jehovah, which is why by the end of the meeting they had agreed to stay together.*

Somehow, remarkably, they managed to make it work. I know my father made an effort to change, as he genuinely didn't want to lose my mam, though for a long time she warned him she would leave if things went back to the way they were. And now, in their sixties, they adore each other to the point that I'm terrified when something happens to one of them, because they are literally inseparable. It's an extraordinary success story of two people who under any other circumstances wouldn't have stayed together, yet stuck with it, and from the ruins of a relationship managed to build something rock solid and absolutely beautiful. I am so very proud of them.

---

* Interestingly, there are loads of divorced couples in the religion today. Almost half of the people I grew up with are now divorced.

9

It was at secondary school that things got really dark. Overnight I went from a cosy village school with Mam waiting on the other side of the yard to a sprawling comprehensive a bus ride away, with hundreds of new, much older faces from all over the Valleys, including the big brothers of the bullies from junior school. If I'd hoped I might be able to reinvent myself at Bedwellty Comprehensive, to move on from being the weird kid with a target – or a Garfield bag - on his back and make new friends, then I was very wrong.

An undercurrent of aggression flowed through those corridors. Looking back, I'm sure a lot of those kids came from deprived, unhappy homes. They probably didn't have the sort of loving parents who would take them to swimming lessons or to a theme park during the holidays; they may well have been living with abuse themselves. If you're dealing with violence at home, it's hardly surprising if your instincts turn primal – and the way those kids dealt with anything alien to them (a soft-spoken, skinny Jehovah's Witness boy, for instance) was to attack.

I remember the first time I got punched. I was with my friend Carla and we were walking back to her house from the park when two boys started taunting me. I ignored them – my usual method of dealing with bullies – but they followed us. We walked a bit faster. God knows why they picked me – they must have just sensed something in me, in the same way a lion knows exactly which gazelle to attack – but as we hurried down the alley behind Carla's house, my heart racing as I heard their footsteps grow closer, they closed in on us and punched me hard in the ear. My head was ringing and my eyes were watering, but I didn't react or try to fight back; I just picked myself up and kept walking, my hand clutching my throbbing ear. I was deeply ashamed; I wanted to pretend it hadn't happened. I don't think Carla and I even talked about it, let alone told our parents.

I became savvy in dealing with the bullies by finding ways not to be around them. On the bus to school I would sit as close to the driver as possible. I joined every extracurricular club going so that I was out of the yard during breaktime and lunch, and I volunteered to work in the school tuck shop along with the other Jehovah's Witness kids. The teachers were happy to let us be in charge, because they knew we were respectable and wouldn't be siphoning off money or stealing Monster Munch or Cola Bottles. It was tempting though. They never acknowledged the bullying or intervened, though I don't blame them for that. In those days it was so rife that if they focused on one instance they'd have to deal with dozens; half the school would have needed to be expelled.

I was scared of the bullies, but I was also very angry: at myself, for not having the bravery to stand up to them, but also at my dad. It wasn't his fault – he didn't even know what was going on – but what I needed was someone who could tell me how to fight back. Even if I had been able to talk to him about what was happening, I knew his advice would be to walk away, and experience had taught me that if you tried to walk away from a bully they usually just kept following you. It didn't help that I was so different from my dad. He was a bit of a loner and didn't have that need to be around people, whereas I was much more sociable and outgoing, like Mam. I wanted to be everyone's friend, and when you're that sort of child, and nobody likes you – well, it's a very tough thing to deal with.

I just stuck with my Witness friends as much as possible: Emma and Debbie from junior school and their cousin Laurie who had now joined us for secondary school. *Girls are so much nicer than boys,*

I remember thinking. They were kinder, funnier, more accepting and happier with themselves, and they didn't automatically respond to situations with violence. My only male friend at secondary school wasn't a Witness, but he was very clever and a little chubby, so was also an easy target for the bullies. We probably migrated towards each other as we were going through the same ordeal, though we never discussed it; too ashamed, I guess. We're still friends to this day. He's now a headmaster of a school, which I find extraordinary. Of all the paths he could have taken, he returned to the institution where we spent the worst years of our lives! I have palpitations and PTSD if I even set a foot inside a school nowadays, although I do still go to them to give talks.

10

I grew up in a house that was full of music. My dad's record collection had a strong early influence on me: The Beatles, Bowie, The Bay City Rollers, Petula Clarke and Cliff Richard. I got my own stereo at the age of twelve – one of those stack systems with a record player at the top – and the first album I bought was Kylie Minogue's debut LP (an early hint about my future identity!). Stock Aitken Waterman were dominating the charts at the time, so the likes of Rick Astley, Hazell Dean and Pepsi & Shirlie became my music. My tastes moved on after I bought my first CD, *Now 19*, which had a more rock-heavy, nineties sound, and which I played almost continuously through my early teenage years, primarily because I didn't have the money to buy more than one album at a time. There was a song on there by Oleta Adams, 'Get Here', which first sparked my love of women's voices. I would try to mimic the way she sang, her vibrato and phrasing. One day I was digging through the £1 bargain bin in the music section of Woolworths in Bargoed, which sold everything from sweets to school uniforms, and I found a CD in a cracked case with a grainy picture of a black woman's face on it. The artist's name was Roberta Flack: I'd never heard of her, but I was keen to expand my musical horizons, so I bought it. The first song on the album was 'The First Time Ever I Saw Your Face'. It had a profound effect on me from the very first listen. Obviously at the age of thirteen I couldn't relate to what Roberta was singing about, but what I could relate to was the emotion in her voice. It connected to something deep inside me that I needed to express, but wasn't able to. I would listen to that song whenever I was feeling lost and alone and it was like a release for me. It taught me about the power of music, and to this day if you ask anyone who knows me they'll tell you it's my favourite song and I even recorded it for my first album.

While I'd loved listening to music since I was small and had enjoyed singing with the congregation at the Kingdom Hall, it wasn't until I started proper music lessons at Bedwellty Comprehensive that I realised I actually had a voice. On this particular day we were learning the harmonies to 'You Are My Sunshine'. I was standing next to a girl who could really sing, and as our voices mingled and soared together I remember my arms prickling with goosebumps.

I had felt those goosebumps before. When I was younger we had two Jehovah's Witness sisters, Tracy and Amanda, living in our caravan in the garden for a year because they were having trouble at home with their non-believing father. I didn't enjoy spending a week in that thing, so how those poor buggers managed for that long I'll never know. The sisters made wedding dresses for a living, and you'd open the door to that shitty little van and clouds of white satin and crystal-sprinkled tulle would come billowing out. As an only child it was wonderful to have these beautiful, sweet-natured girls living with us, like two perfect big sisters, and I grew very close to them.

One day Amanda went to London to see the new musical *The Phantom of the Opera*, starring Michael Crawford and Sarah Brightman, and returned home with the double LP. I'd never been to a musical, so that night we listened to the album together and I sat on her lap while she talked me through the photos on the sleeve. When we got to the scene in which the Phantom and Christine sing a duet as he takes her on a boat through the underground labyrinth – dozens of candles rising up as mist billowed across the stage – I remember living every second of it. I was spellbound. *Goosebumps*.

That harmony class planted a seed: I had found something I enjoyed and wanted to do more of, although there was little opportunity for me at school, because it was usually either Christmas carols or hymns, neither of which I was allowed to join in with. Then, when I was thirteen, the drama department put on a production of *Bugsy Malone*. The biggest roles naturally went to the older years, but I auditioned and got the part of Snake Eyes, one of the goons in Fat Sam's gang. We even got one of the best songs in the show: 'We Could Have Been Anything'. I was the first Jehovah's Witness to be in a show in our school.

After joining the cast, my day-to-day experience of school was transformed. On a practical level, I now had somewhere to go to avoid the bullies during lunch break, thanks to rehearsals. More importantly, though, I discovered how much I enjoyed being on stage. I'd always loved re-enacting Bible scenes at home for Mam or performing sketches with Dean, but this was the first real production I'd been involved in – and I was actually good at it! I knew I had something to offer, which gave my confidence such a boost. For the first time in school, I felt a sense of belonging: I was part of a gang and accepted for who I was and what I could offer.

Even today, the smell of Brylcreem takes me straight back to the opening night of *Bugsy Malone*, slicking my hair back before our first number. I was the sharpest dressed gangster in the cast, as we were told to wear suits – and obviously I had plenty of those in my Jehovah's Witness wardrobe. Our dressing room was the Religious Education classroom, which backed onto the assembly room where the show was being staged. For a school performance it was a big deal, running for several nights. We had a professional band, led by our music teacher Mr Shepherd, and the whole of the Valleys came to see the show. As I listened to the sound of hundreds of people filling the room next door, the butterflies in my stomach whipped into a storm. These days I know how to handle my nerves – you just have to learn to wrangle that energy and channel it into your performance – but back then the achy, fluttery feeling was almost overwhelming.

That first night passed in a blur, but I can remember standing on the stage for the curtain call, the sound of the applause literally vibrating through me, and being swept up in a surge of exhilaration. *Wow, they're clapping for us! They're clapping for ME!*

From that moment on, I was hooked.

Next year's school production was *Annie*. This time I had my own solo song, 'You're Never Fully Dressed Without a Smile', and was playing the role of radio announcer Bert Healy. I wore a boater and stripy jacket and had three girls dancing behind me while I sang. I loved every minute and certainly wasn't disappointed I didn't get one of the leads; as with *Bugsy*, it was Bedwellty's golden boy, Jason Musgrave, who always got the lead role. Handsome and charming, he was loved by pupils and teachers alike.

At fifteen, *The Sound of Music* was my final school production, as I would be busy with GCSEs the following year. Maria was being played by a girl called Lisa, who was two years older than me and doing her A levels. Jason Musgrave was obviously on course for the male lead, Captain von Trapp, but by now I had a reputation for being a strong singer and a decent performer, so I decided to audition myself. To my delight, I got the part, leaving Jason with the less glitzy role of Rolf, the Nazi delivery boy.

I will never forget the moment I sang my big song – 'Edelweiss' – on opening night. I was standing on the stage in my army captain's uniform; the lights went down until everything was dark and I was lit up in the beam of a single spotlight. The hall was silent apart from the rustling and murmurs of the 300-strong audience. My stomach was churning, but I remember thinking: *You know how to do this*. My voice was the source of all my bravado, strength and courage – it still is to this day. I can be as nervous as hell, but the instant I open my mouth a sense of calm comes over me. As the first notes of the song rang out, I looked out into the darkness and I noticed that I could see the top of everyone's head in the audience, because they'd all been lit up from behind by this giant spotlight at the back of the auditorium that was trained on me.

All these lit-up heads were moving around, looking for their sweets or chatting to each other, but when I started to sing all the movement just … stopped. The heads grew perfectly still. And it occurred to me, with a sense of absolute wonder, that this was because of something that *I* was doing. I might not be able to kick a ball into the net or scrum down with the boys on a rugby pitch, but I could capture everyone's attention with my voice. I had that power.

After I sung the last note there was a moment of silence – and then thunderous applause. It was so overwhelming; I was almost in tears. It wasn't just about the acknowledgement of my performance that got me. It was about being recognised. At the start of that song neither the kids nor their parents had any idea who Luke Evans was. I was a faceless person; utterly anonymous. Then I opened my mouth and out came this pure voice with a strong vibrato (that I'd been perfecting via *The Phantom of the Opera* album) and suddenly I was *someone*. I had an identity. It was the most extraordinary feeling.

They put on the show for an extra few nights that year because it was such a success. My whole family still talks about how incredible that show was for all of us. Yet at no point during this production, or any of the others, did I think about performing as a future career. Not once; it didn't even cross my mind. As I've said, you didn't have those sort of ambitions as a Jehovah's Witness, and the Valleys certainly wasn't a place that encouraged crazy dreams. You think you'll become an *actor*? Don't be daft … Besides, at that age my ambitions lay in a very different direction. I wanted to be a forensic pathologist.

I blame Patricia Cornwell. One day I borrowed one of her books from Bargoed Library and that was it – I was hooked. I read everything she wrote. Her stories tended to follow a formula: there was a murder, the police couldn't solve it, so it was up to the forensic pathologist to piece together the evidence in her lab, working out the victim's last moments and then identifying the killer. It was the same fascination

I'd had watching *Crimewatch*: the thrill of the murder – my heart rate rocketing at the sense of danger – countered by a feeling of comfort and reassurance from the expertise of the pathologist, who had the knowledge and ability to catch the bad guys and make the world a safer place.

Our biology lessons at school didn't satisfy my curiosity, so I asked Mam to get a pig's heart from the butcher so I could dissect it at home. She happily obliged; she loved my enthusiasm and always embraced whatever mad scheme I came up with. Unlike at school, I never felt as if I'd be shut down or made to feel weird for my ideas. And, by the way, Mam was just as fascinated as I was. If she'd been given the opportunities and help with her dyslexia I really think she could have achieved something spectacular – although she's won gold every year of my life for being the best mother ever.

After the heart, it was on to a pig's head. This was surprisingly massive; poor Mam, having to lug it home from the shops along with Sunday's leg of lamb. We laid out a plastic tablecloth on the kitchen counter and plonked down the head on a tray. It sat there, pale, enormous and fleshy, staring back at us with sinister blank eyes. I obviously didn't have the correct tools, so I borrowed a Stanley knife from Dad's toolbox for the procedure. First, I went straight for the eyeball. Once I'd removed that, I moved onto the teeth. It was absolutely fascinating. Patricia Cornwell's protagonist often had to remove the scalp to check for trauma to the brain, so I had a go at slicing away the flap of skin to see how easy it would be (not at all). I then cut open an ear to try to locate the cochlea (I couldn't). I clearly didn't have a clue what I was doing, but I took it all very seriously.

I knew that getting work experience could be a route into your chosen career, but as I didn't know any forensic pathologists, I had to think laterally. Which is why, in the summer holidays aged fourteen, I knocked at the door of our local chapel of rest. For those who don't know, this is basically where bodies are kept, dressed and put in a coffin before making their final journey to church, then either the oven or the ground.

A grey-haired man in a grey suit answered the door.

'Yes? Can I help you?'

'Hello! My name is Luke, I'm at Bedwellty Comprehensive and I want to become a forensic pathologist when I'm older and I'm going to study to become one, but in the meantime I'd love the opportunity to be around some dead bodies so I can get more comfortable with them.'

The man looked at me as though I was dancing flamenco. I'd prepared my speech carefully beforehand – but perhaps I hadn't made myself clear enough?

'What I mean is, could I please help you with your dead bodies?'

'My dead bodies?' he repeated, the crease between his brows deepening.

'Yes! I don't want to be paid,' I added quickly, 'I'd just like some work experience.'

There was a long pause. 'Nobody's ever come here asking for work experience before.'

'Great! I'd be happy to help you, like, clean the bodies, too. So … can I come in?'

The man scratched his head. 'Um – Luke, is it? I'm sorry, I'd love to say yes, but I'm afraid I can't. It wouldn't be allowed. You're far too young.'

I was mortified. I'd really had to work up the courage to knock on the door, and it hadn't even occurred to me that it might be a no.

'Oh, okay, no problem. Thank you very much! Bye then.'

Before he could say anything else, I hurried away. I should have been used to rejection after the years of Jehovah's Witness door work, but I felt like an idiot for even asking.

The following year, however, I got another shot at work experience. We had to fill out a questionnaire at school that was fed into a computer to calculate our ideal career, which would then be followed by a relevant work placement. There was no direct mention of forensic pathology on the form, but I made sure I ticked all the boxes that had anything to do with hospitals, doctors, medicine or psychology. When I got my results back, however, the top suggestion was 'interior designer'. I couldn't believe it. It was about as far from a forensic pathologist as it was possible to be. There was no arguing with the computer though, so I ended up spending two weeks in a beautiful little interior design shop in Cardiff with two upper-class Welsh ladies, going through wallpaper sample books and material swatches – and do you know what? I loved every single second of it. My forensic pathology ambitions dwindled soon after.

· · ·

The only person who ever gave me even a hint of a suggestion that I should consider performing as a career was a substitute teacher who taught us music while Mr Shepherd was off for a term. Her name was Ros Phillips, and she had very black, tightly permed hair and a full face of make-up. When she asked me to stay behind one day after class my first thought was: *Uh-oh, what have I done?* When she came to talk to me, though, she was smiling.

'It's about your singing,' she said. 'You do realise you have a very lovely voice?'

'Oh! Thank you, Miss.'

'I think you should have lessons, Luke. You have real talent.'

'I don't think my parents would be able to afford that, I'm afraid …'

'Well, I'm going to give you the contact details of a singing teacher I know in Cardiff. Her name's Louise Ryan.'

She handed me a piece of paper with a phone number, but as I put it in my pocket I was thinking: *Cardiff's miles away. We don't have the money. It's never going to happen.*

Yet for some reason, I held onto that scrap of paper.

11

Being on stage was an escape for me. I could be someone else; not the character I was playing, but a better, shinier version of my real self. The Witness kids didn't tend to excel at anything – we kept a low profile and then went off to start our real work, spreading the word of Jehovah – but I knew I could sing, so this was an opportunity for me to stand out.

Yet as much as I felt like I was reinventing myself, as far as the bullies were concerned nothing had changed. They wouldn't let me escape the box they'd shoved me into back in junior school. One day I was making my way to a lunchtime rehearsal of *The Sound of Music* in the assembly hall and found some older kids hanging round the entrance, smoking. As I approached, one of them stepped in front of me. Edwin, his name was. If you had to draw a picture of a dangerous kid it would be Edwin. He had an older brother, too: think Edwin on steroids.

'What are you doing, bender?'

'I'm going to rehearse.'

'Rehearse?' He spat the word back at me.

I knew there was no point trying to reason with him, so I tried to walk around him. If I could just get inside the door, I knew I'd be safe ... but then suddenly Edwin drew back his fist and punched me hard in the head. I staggered in pain and shock, but managed to stay on my feet. My vision was blurry, but I could hear Edwin and his mates laughing at me. My only thought was to get the hell out of there as fast as possible, so I just turned and walked away. It wasn't the last time I had to miss rehearsals because of them.

• • •

I still hadn't told my parents about the bullying, because I didn't have the words, strength or processing skills to tell them that not only was I being called gay, but also that I *was* gay. It was something I'd been sure of since the age of ten or eleven, having started puberty early. The evidence felt conclusive: I'd never been interested in having a girlfriend and my crushes were only ever on men, such as the young mechanic who often came to our house to fix my dad's car. At eleven I saw an episode of the BBC's *Omnibus* series about a writer called Mary Renault, whose historical novels were set in Ancient Greece at a time when men would have male lovers as well as wives, and the next day I went to Bargoed Library and took out her novel *The Persian Boy*. I knew that homosexual relationships had happened in the past because of those terrifying images of Sodom and Gomorrah, but Mary Renault's writing presented same-sex relationships in a wholly positive, beautiful light. I was a slow reader, so I'd have to keep going back to the library to check it out, but it was an eye-opener to discover that at one point in history how I was feeling was considered completely normal.

Not that this historical context helped with my current dilemma. Even though I now knew what I was, I still wasn't ready or able to process that fact, because I had absolutely no idea how to live as a young gay man.

It's shocking to remember how isolated you were growing up gay in a small town in the eighties and early nineties. There were no mainstream role models on television. The only gay men you'd see on screen were people like Larry Grayson, Kenneth Williams and John Inman in *Are you being Served?* Camp clowns. Jokers, but also a joke themselves. You might laugh at them from the sofa, but you certainly wouldn't have had their kind round your house for tea. My family loved Michael Barrymore, the presenter who ruled primetime with *Strike it Lucky* and *My Kind of People*, but when he came out in the mid-nineties he was destroyed by the press. Soon after I was at my nan's house – the TV was on as usual – and when Barrymore came on she immediately switched it off. 'Ugh, dirty bugger,' she muttered. It was one of the only times the television in that house went off. I remember sitting there in silent horror. *Is that what she'll think of me too?*

The only person I knew living as an openly gay man was a very effeminate hairdresser who lived in our village. All the women had their hair cut by him, but they didn't socialise with him. He was a very lonely man who died alone in his bed. There were whispers that he had been having an affair with a married member of the constabulary, which was rumoured to be the reason all his private papers and diaries mysteriously disappeared after his death. Apparently the police were first on the scene and cleaned up any incriminating evidence. Whether or not this was true, it was another instance of how gay men were treated at the time: as subjects of gossip, scandal and entertainment. Not quite fully human, and certainly not proper men.

It was against this landscape that I had to come to terms with my own sexuality. I had no doubt that how I was feeling was somehow wrong. Even though being gay appeared to have been acceptable in Mary Renault's vision of Ancient Greece, I'd grown up with our religion insisting loudly and repeatedly that it was perverted. I longed to talk to someone about it, to get some help dealing with the battle that was raging inside me, but I couldn't tell my parents or even my best friends, Emma, Debbie and Laurie, because I was terrified I would lose all of them or that they would tell the elders and our parents. We knew of a Witness family in our congregation who had an openly gay adult son and it was like he was dead. Incredibly, he still lived in the Valleys, not far away – can you imagine? People he'd grown up with, his own family, deliberately avoiding him every day. He'd been completely ostracised, and I knew this would be the fate that awaited me too, so I had no choice but to stay silent. Jehovah knew, though, and I would pray to him every night, begging him to make the sinful thoughts go away.

Yet even though the religion still exerted a magnetic pull over me at this stage, I was already preparing myself for the fact that as soon as I was legally allowed to leave home at sixteen then I would probably have to. At that young age it was terrifying to consider a life without my parents, or friends, or support of any kind at all. I was so close to my parents that the thought of losing them broke my heart, but that never felt like a reason not to leave. I reasoned that they had been able to make choices about their lives, so I needed to do the same. I still believed that being gay was a death sentence – I knew I would die at Armageddon with the rest of the sinners – but by this point I already felt it would be preferable to get a couple of years living as who I really was, than spend a lifetime hiding away. I knew just how unhappy I would be if I stayed in Aberbargoed, living a lie. I had no idea how I would do it and what it would really be like to lose everything and everyone I knew, but as soon as I could leave school I planned to go somewhere I could introduce myself as the person I really was, make new friends and build a future outside the religion. Looking back, it's quite remarkable how much confidence I had in this plan, but by my early teens I had already started to plot my escape – and even then I knew my final destination would be London.

. . .

I got my first tantalising taste of the city when we became friends with a Jehovah's Witness family who lived in Hemel Hempstead. We would visit them every year and while staying with them would always fit in a day trip to London. Even now, I can remember the thrill of catching the train from sleepy St Albans, switching to the underground, then emerging at Piccadilly Circus into this incredible city, vibrant with noise and energy and a dazzling variety of people. From early on, London was cemented in my mind as a place where you could be anything or anyone you wanted to be.

I'd been desperate to see a musical since being introduced to *The Phantom of the Opera* by Amanda, the girl who lived in the caravan in our garden, so in my early teens Mam and I joined a coach party of local, non-Witness women who made regular excursions to the West End. We'd be up at 6am, arrive in London by midday, have a bit of time for a look round before heading to a matinee – *Starlight Express, Sunset Boulevard, Joseph and the Amazing Technicolor Dreamcoat* – and then back on the bus home. It was on one of these trips that I spotted my first celebrity. Mam and I instantly recognised the tall, handsome man striding along the backstreets of the West End, a scarf elegantly thrown over his shoulder – although it took us a little while to work out that it was the actor Charles Dance, who we'd loved in Merchant Ivory films. I can't begin to imagine how I would have reacted if you'd have told me that twenty years later I would be starring opposite Charles in my movie *Dracula Untold*!

On the bus to London, Mam and I always sat with an older lady called Pam, who was a veteran of these theatre trips. Pam always knew where to find the cheapest tickets and the best spot for a pre-show cup of tea and cake. On the coach mid-morning, like clockwork, Pam would unpack her sandwiches, take out her teeth and wrap them in a piece of tissue, then sit there gumming her way through her cheese and pickle. I would watch, equal parts horrified and amused, while Mam muttered under her breath: 'Just don't look, Luke …' Pam didn't care though, and I loved her for that. I was just relieved my cousin Dean wasn't on the bus. It would have been disastrous!

As I got older, Mam would let me go on these trips by myself with Pam as my guardian. By now I knew London was where I wanted to be, so I lived for the two hours of free time I would get before the 2.30pm matinee, when I could explore the city. I'd be on the coach next to Pam – teeth out, sandwiches in – trembling with excitement as I checked off the landmarks on the approach to London. First there would be the planes coming into Heathrow, looking as if they were hanging, stationary, in the sky as we drove by, then you'd get to the flyover at Hammersmith, past the Cromwell Hospital, then Harrods – my eyes would be on stalks by now – then we'd drive down Piccadilly and finally we'd park in one of the side streets near Leicester Square. I would immediately sprint off the bus, map in hand, my plan in place.

First, though, I had to deal with Pam.

'Right,' she would say, 'we're all going for a lovely coffee in—'

'You know what? I think I'll just go for a walk.'

Pam frowned. 'Really? Do you know where you're going, Luke?'

'Yep!' I waved the map at her.

'Right … but do you know where the theatre is?'

'I know *exactly* where it is and I'll see you there at 2.15. Okay?'

A long pause. 'Are you quite sure, love? Is your mam alright with this?'

'She's absolutely fine with it!' *Come on, come on …*

'Well, okay, then …'

I was off into Soho like a rat up a drainpipe. At first I just wandered around, soaking in the atmosphere and the wonder of being among so many gay people. Everyone seemed relaxed and at ease with themselves. Some were dressed to stand out; there was zero sense of hiding away or being apologetic for who they were. It was intoxicating. I sat in a coffee shop with a large front window open to the street, watching this new, miraculous world go by. I must have drunk about five coffees – as soon as I'd finished one, I'd order another – because I was worried they were going to ask me to leave. After a couple of hours, my heart racing from all the caffeine, I made my way to the theatre, but when I got on the bus home later that afternoon I made a vow: *I'm going to live here one day.* It was just a little glimpse of the life I might have, but I now knew there was a world out there that would accept me for myself. So as much as I was scared, there was also excitement about my future. I would be losing something, but at the same time I would be gaining a life. I just knew it was going to be okay. For some reason, I had that conviction.

. . .

With all this going on, you might imagine I'd lose interest in the religion – especially one that hated who I was – but it actually had the opposite effect. Teenagers are never simple, and I suppose I was still hanging onto the hope that Jehovah might save me from the life of sin I seemed to be plummeting towards. On top of that, as I've mentioned before, I loved learning, and to me the religion was just another subject, like English or Art, that I could immerse myself in. I was already giving talks in front of hundreds of people at the Kingdom Hall; I knew the elders were impressed with my attitude. So I made a decision. Until I could get out of there, I was going to attempt be the best Jehovah's Witness they'd ever had.

12

I stood in front of my bedroom mirror, feeling like a rock star who's about to headline Glastonbury. My suit was brand new, bought for the occasion so it fitted me perfectly, and my hair was behaving itself for once. Early morning sunlight streamed through the window, lighting me up as if I had been chosen – which, at that moment, was exactly how I felt. Today I was to be baptised at the Jehovah's Witness convention, the biggest and glitziest event in the religion's calendar. Not only that, but at thirteen I was one of the youngest of our congregation ever to make such a serious commitment. My parents had been worried I wasn't old enough, but I stood a little straighter as I remember the elders reassuring them that I was most definitely ready.

Mam called up from the foot of the stairs. 'Are you ready love? We don't want to be late.'

I took a last look in the mirror, holding my gaze. *You're doing the right thing,* I told my reflection. In the religion, baptism is a public declaration that you are dedicating yourself to serving Jehovah for your entire life. It's a huge deal and can't be entered into lightly. This would be a big enough gesture to put a stop to the shameful thoughts that continued to plague me every night. It had to be.

'Coming, Mam,' I said, and turned towards the door.

It had taken me months of preparation to get ready for this day, yet I had zero concept of the magnitude of the commitment I was about to make, or the lifelong consequences I would face for doing so.

...

I should explain that before being considered for baptism you had to have lived as a Jehovah's Witness for years. You needed to have attended all the Kingdom Hall meetings and Bible study groups, and to have been an active participant in both; you couldn't just sit there and never put your hand up. Only once you'd proven your dedication could you approach the elders to discuss the possibility of baptism, although even then it wasn't a done deal. You would have to go through six months of study with one of the elders, during which time it would be explained to you that by committing yourself to the religion you have to abide by the rules and standards set out in the Bible and prioritise being a Jehovah's Witness above all else. You must agree to spend as much time as possible working for the religion (for free, naturally): knocking doors, building reputation and privileges in the congregation and ultimately, hopefully, ending up as an elder or maybe even a member of Bethel, the religion's headquarters, the peak of achievement. It's effectively like committing yourself to an unpaid internship that you can never get out of.

I'm sure an adult would have a more nuanced understanding of the seriousness of all this, but as a naive thirteen-year-old I was just like: *Sure, sounds good – where do I sign?* And I can see why the elders thought I was a suitable candidate: I had been a Witness since birth and was fully involved in spreading the word, knocking on doors every week and giving talks to the entire congregation. Since word of my impending baptism got out I was getting a lot of buzz in the Kingdom Hall – 'Wow, Luke's getting baptised? Amazing! He's so young!' – which, of course, I enjoyed. Everyone seemed to think it was the most wonderful thing. My confusion over my identity hadn't gone away, but if all these grown-ups believed baptism was the right course, then perhaps it might somehow convert me from feeling gay?

Jehovah's Witness conventions take place in stadiums around the world, attended by millions, and when I was a child the closest to us took place just down the road at Cardiff Arms Park, today known as the Principality Stadium. Tens of thousands of Jehovah's Witnesses converged on Cardiff every summer for three days of Bible readings, performances and speeches, and I looked forward to it in the way other kids breathlessly awaited Christmas.

On the morning of the convention we would get up early, make sandwiches, a flask of coffee and a bottle of squash, and then drive to Cardiff: Mam in a new summer dress with a little sun parasol, me and Dad in suits. We'd always take a blanket or camping chairs, because back then one end of Cardiff Arms Park was standing stalls with no canopy, so you'd be sitting in the spot that, two days earlier, boozed-up rugby fans had been spilling pints of beer and pissing on during the big match.

It was always a thrill emerging from the subterranean corridors into that magnificent stadium. Excitement in the auditorium would be at World Cup Final levels. There would be a stage in the middle of the pitch, which was the focus for the day's events, but it was the sight of all those thousands of people in the stands that gave me goosebumps. During the lunch break my friends and I would climb up as far as we could in the stadium – so high and steep it took your breath away – and then gaze down on all the tiny people. I often felt isolated in our little village in the Valleys, but the convention reminded me that I was part of this huge global community.

For me, the highlight of the events was always the dramatic re-enactment of a Bible story, such as Moses leading the Israelites from Egypt. The soundtrack was provided by the Bethel in New York (the religion's headquarters) and production values were impressively high, with music and special effects like Jehovah's thunder and lighting, but the performers would be Witnesses from local congregations. I'm sure my interest in performing was sparked by watching these annual productions and thinking (or knowing) I could have done a better job. My dad took part on a couple of occasions, but as only adults were eligible I never got the chance, which frustrated me hugely. I had to make do with recreating these productions at home, a tea towel on my head, with cousin Dean as my baffled co-star: 'So who's this Abraham bloke again …?'

* * *

When we arrived at Cardiff Arms Park on the morning of my baptism I was directed to a different part of the stadium from my parents where I would sit with the other candidates, all of us immaculately turned out with neat hair and shining, happy faces. We looked like perfect Witnesses; as far as everyone else was concerned, we *were* perfect Witnesses. From the stage there was a talk about the commitment we were about to make and how wonderful it was, the hopeful, joyous words reverberating around the stadium and into my soul, chasing out any lingering doubts. At one point we were asked to stand up and everyone gave us a round of applause. All those thousands of people! I loved it.

The baptism itself took place during the convention's lunch break. Rather than taking care of formalities at the stadium, they hired a nearby swimming pool to perform the ceremony; after all, Jesus baptised his disciples in water. It was an ancient rite that underlined the seriousness of the commitment we were about to make. I filed out of the stadium with the rest of the candidates to make the short walk to the pool with our families, who were permitted to come and watch.

After getting changed into our baptism gear we trooped out onto the pool's edge to await our turn. The smell of chlorine and littering of armbands and old verruca plasters slightly took the edge off the solemn mood; it's a little odd having a life-defining experience under a sign that reads: NO BOMBING, NO RUNNING, NO HEAVY PETTING. Still, it felt like a real moment, and I was certainly ready for my close-up. More than ready. This was going to cleanse me of my sinful thoughts, I was sure of it.

When it was my turn, I climbed into the shallow end where two white-clad elders were waiting. I stepped between them, held my nose as I'd watched the other candidates do before me and in one swift movement I was tipped back into the waist-deep water and out again. The elders said a few kind words and patted me on the back, then I climbed out of the pool, my clothes heavy with water. It was over in a matter of seconds.

We dried off, got our suits back on and returned to the stadium. Mam and Dad watched, glowing with pride, as the brothers and sisters from our congregation gathered around to congratulate me, thrilled that I had officially joined the fold. Yet all the time I was shaking people's hands, my face aching with smiling, I was trying to ignore the treacherous little voice inside my head that was whispering: *Is that it?*

...

When I look back at my baptism today, I see a naive kid who was swept away on a tidal wave of enthusiasm. At a time when I was drowning in confusion, the religion held out a hand to a future that sounded appealingly simple and straightforward. *You'll be committing yourself to a life of being a good servant to Jehovah! You're going to spread the word! It's all going to be wonderful!* Despite my doubts I trusted what the elders were telling me – they had always been part of my life, after all – but there was never any mention of what would happen if I changed my mind about the whole dedicating-your-entire-life-to-Jehovah business. The fact is, if I hadn't been baptised, then when I left the religion I would have been allowed to stay in contact with my family and friends. Instead, because of a commitment I'd made while barely into my teens, they were obliged to cut me out of their lives. How can this crucial piece of information never have been explained to me? The lack of transparency feels brutal, almost an abuse of power and care.

Unsurprisingly, within a few weeks I realised the feelings and fantasies weren't going away. I'd been banking on the baptism to 'cure' me, and now that it hadn't there was no Plan B. There was no one I could talk to about my confusion, no internet to give answers or reassure me that how I was feeling was completely normal. From that point on, my faith in the religion rapidly dwindled. They had failed me as authority figures. I needed someone – or something – else to steer my path.

13

On Saturdays, after we'd finished knocking doors, Mam and I would often go shopping in Cardiff. She'd head to Howells department store while I'd revel in the freedom of exploring the city alone without a destination in mind. Cardiff is famous for its maze of Edwardian and Victorian indoor shopping arcades, and one day I found myself in front of the entrance to a pretty arcade that I'd never visited before. The shops still had their original wooden facades, with ornate Venetian-style windows along the first floor and leaded Victorian lamps hung at intervals from the glass ceiling, adding to the feeling that you'd been whisked back a hundred years in time.

It was at the end of this arcade that I discovered the bookshop. It was called Chapter and Verse and was a charmingly quirky-looking place, the antithesis of bland corporate chains. Still, I couldn't have imagined the impact this little shop was about to have on my life.

There was an older guy behind the counter, who I assumed was the owner, and he smiled and said hello as I came in, then went back to whatever he was doing, leaving me free to look around. I worked my way along the shelves, past alphabetised fiction, cookery, memoirs – and then in the far corner I came upon a display of books that literally made me freeze. It was the LGBT section, although that term wouldn't have been used back then. (In those days it was basically all just 'G'.) My heart racing, I selected a book at random: it was *Maurice* by E.M. Forster, one of the most celebrated literary gay novels, though I had no idea about any of that at the time. Turning it over with trembling hands, I read the blurb on the back cover: *astonishingly frank account of homo-*

sexual relationships ... profound emotional and sexual awakening ... intimate tale of one man's erotic self-discovery.

Oh my God. I shoved it back on the shelf, guilt and shame pummelling my growing excitement, and glanced back at the counter. To my relief, the owner was busy elsewhere, so I picked up the book again and started to read. My eyes grew wider with every page I turned. After that, I chose another book at random, and then another. There was a vast photographic book dedicated to the perfect male physique and I lost myself in the pictures inside. I was feverish, torn between triumph and terror. I had an incredible feeling of excitement: I knew I had found my place, somewhere I could learn more about the life I would have to lead one day, but what if somebody saw me in here? And, more importantly, how was I going to get these books home with me?

I was going to have to play the long game, I decided. I made a mental note of the books I wanted to buy and how much they cost and hurried towards the door. 'Thank you!' I called to the man at the counter. 'I'll be back!'

My plan was going to take patience, nerves of steel and a very roomy pair of trousers. From then on, every time I went to Cardiff with Mam I would go straight to Chapter and Verse to buy a book. I could only get one at a time, partly because I needed to save up, but also because there was the tricky issue of getting it home without Mam finding out. The prospect of her seeing some of those books ... well, it didn't bear thinking about. I couldn't carry my purchases in a bag, as she was bound to ask to see what I'd bought, so instead I would hide my new book down the back of my trousers, tie my jumper around my waist for added security and then sit very uncomfortably on the train next to Mam for the hour's journey back to the Valleys. The final hurdle would be walking up the hill from the station, all the time desperately hoping the book wouldn't drop out, and then – success! – I was home. Mission accomplished.

My plan worked brilliantly for the more slender volumes, but once I moved onto the heftier, pictorial books it became more of a challenge. My biggest prize, both literally and figuratively, was a retrospective of the homoerotic artwork of Tom of Finland. You can Google it if you're not familiar with his work. The drawings are a famous part of queer history, an expression of a certain part of gay subculture, and to me they represented the perfect idealistic fantasy.

This book was enormous, yet somehow I managed to smuggle it home. I had to sit there on the train, listening to Mam telling me about the neighbours up the road who were building a conservatory, while a book full of gigantic penises burned a hole in the back of my trousers.

At home I kept my stash of gay literature in a Kwik Save carrier bag, hidden in the lining of an armchair in my bedroom that had once been part of our old three-piece suite. Looking at my collection always brought a thrill, but there was also a lingering undercurrent of fear. I could still sense Jehovah's disapproving eye on me, though the relief of knowing that I wasn't on my own in the world outweighed any shame I might feel. Thanks to my chance discovery of that bookshop, I finally had a source of information about gay culture. Chapter and Verse isn't there any more – it's now an organic beauty shop – but I'll be forever grateful to the owner for throwing this confused thirteen-year-old boy a lifeline.

By the age of fifteen I'd built up quite a collection of books, then one day I slid one hand inside the lining of the armchair to retrieve the Kwik Save bag and it wasn't there. A brief moment of confusion was swiftly followed by crushing panic and horror. I hadn't moved it, and the only other people who ever came into my room were my parents. The truth dawned on me with sickening certainty. Mam or Dad must have found the bag – and if one of them knew about it, the other would as well. I sat down heavily on the bed, dropping my head in my hands.

I must have stayed sitting there for about an hour. Even today, reliving this incident makes my heart rate shoot up. I cycled through shock, terror and shame, until finally survival mode kicked in. I got up and packed a bag, because I knew that as soon as I went downstairs and addressed this with my parents (because I had to, I wouldn't be able to sleep that night without knowing what had happened), I would probably have to leave home.

Feeling like a condemned man, I went downstairs. Dad was busy in the garage as usual, but Mam was watching TV. I took the seat opposite, so I could look her in the eye.

'Where is it, then?'

'Where's what?'

'Just tell me where it is.'

'I don't know what you're talking about,' she said, although her eyes told me otherwise.

'Please don't make this any harder than it is already. Where's the literature that was in my bedroom?'

Her entire body stiffened. 'If you're talking about the items your father found a couple of weeks ago, he's got rid of them, and we don't want to talk about it.'

I gawped at her. This was not how this was supposed to play out. As much as the prospect of coming out to my parents was terrifying, it would also be the moment I could finally stop hiding.

I tried again. 'Don't you want to know why I had those books?'

'No, I don't.'

I'm sure my mother's reaction isn't unique. In this situation, I imagine a lot of parents would choose denial. *Let's pretend it isn't happening and he'll grow out of it.* But to me it was a slap in the face. I'd spent so many years coming to terms with the fact I was gay, all the while having to keep it secret, alone, and then suddenly the two people I love most in my life find out the truth – and they refuse to believe it or even talk about it! I had no idea what to say, how to deal with Mam's stonewalling.

'So where's my stuff?' I eventually demanded. 'What did Dad do with it?'

'He took it all out into the garden, lit a bonfire, tore out every page and burned it. He sat out there for hours crying.'

And despite all this, the heartbreaking situation, my father's tears, I just thought: *Every page? Oh my God, I hope he didn't see page 62 …*

. . .

Mam and I can laugh about it now – 'he could have just put the whole book on the fire, but no, he had to go through every single page and have a good old look!' – but at the time my parents must have been terrified. Their only child, who they had lovingly raised to follow in their footsteps in their religion, was going to die. There would be no paradise on earth waiting for me. To a Jehovah's Witness it's that simple: if you are gay, you will be thrown out of the congregation, lose every contact you've ever known and then die at Armageddon. That's it. No wonder my parents wanted to tell themselves it was just a phase.

14

I didn't get much sleep after confronting Mam that night. When I got into bed, the bag that I'd packed before going downstairs to speak to her was still sitting at my bedroom door, all that was left of an alternative future that now wasn't going to happen. I would have almost preferred it if she'd thrown me out of the house, because at least then we would have had to have an honest conversation. Instead I just lay there, staring at the ceiling, endlessly turning things over in my mind. My parents knew I was gay – *they finally knew!* – but they refused to talk about it. In a way it was the worst possible outcome. They clearly had no interest in knowing the real me.

That was the moment I realised: *I'm done.* I wasn't going to be able to get them to accept my true identity; the religion's hold on them was too strong. It didn't make it any easier knowing they were only trying to protect me. They would have been well aware that if they'd engaged with this as a reality they would have to involve the elders, and as I'd been baptised there was a real danger I might be disfellowshipped. This basically means being cast out of the flock and is the punishment for a whole list of offences, from minor transgressions such as smoking or swearing to having an affair, right through to murder. You can repent, which allows you to attend meetings at Kingdom Hall, but nobody in the congregation is permitted to speak to you until the elders announce you're forgiven. If you choose not to repent, however, then you'll be disfellowshipped, after which all those people you've spent your whole life with, your friends and family, have to pretend you don't exist.

From that day on I became intolerable to live with. I hated my parents; I hated my life. I was locked into a religion that hated me, yet I was still bound by their ridiculous rules. One night a few months after Dad burned my books I remember sitting in my bedroom feeling so angry, miserable and helpless that I couldn't bear to stay in the house a moment longer. It was dark and raining and I had no idea where I was going; I just knew I had to get out. I walked down my road to the bottom of the hill and stood on the bridge over the Rhymney River and as I stared into the rushing water, my hands gripping the wet railings, I remember thinking: *Maybe it would be easier if I jumped.* I was going to lose everything anyway, because once I'd been disfellowshipped my family and friends wouldn't be allowed to have anything to do with me. I must have stayed out there in the rain for about an hour, but in the end I forced myself to go home. That was the point I knew I had to speak to someone, because I was terrified that next time I might not have the strength to turn away.

. . .

I decided to confide in Katie, a Witness friend who was a few years older than me. She was going out with my mate and I often acted as chaperone for them on dates, as the religion didn't permit a couple to be alone before marriage (although I'd often get out of the car and leave them to it). When I told Katie about the feelings I'd been having I could see she was shocked, but at least she didn't try to shut me down. At her suggestion, I found a psychiatrist in the Yellow Pages and made an appointment to go and see them. It was in Cardiff, and Katie offered to drive me there. She picked me up after school and I could tell she was hoping that this person was going to be able to 'cure' me. As for me, I just desperately needed someone to tell me it was all going to be okay.

The psychiatrist's office was in her home, a smart Victorian villa lined with books and artwork. I perched on the edge of the couch and explained that I was gay, but that I came from a very religious family who refused to talk about it and I was struggling to deal with the feelings on my own. I spoke for twenty minutes and when I finally ran out of words the psychiatrist said: 'I'm sure I'll be able to help you with this.'

Honestly, I could have hugged her. 'Thank you so much!'

'So I'd initially recommend a fourteen-week course of sessions ...'

Fourteen weeks? 'Is there nothing you can do today?'

'I'm afraid not. These things take time.'

'But I can't afford to come back again.' This one appointment had cost me my savings.

Slightly annoyed that her new business pitch had failed, the woman thought for a moment. 'Well, you could always try the Samaritans,' she said.

Katie drove me to a phone box. I called the number for the Samaritans and the man who answered told me he was about to close the office for the evening, but if I could come right now he would see me. Thankfully, the address he gave was only a short drive away.

The door was answered by a middle-aged man with a kind face. By this point I was desperate; after all the effort it had taken to get me here, I needed to go home with *something*. I told the Samaritan the same story I'd given the psychiatrist and when I finished he looked me in the eye and said: 'I can tell you now, Luke: there's nothing wrong with you.'

It was the first time I had heard those words. I can't describe my relief.

'There's a whole world of people like you out there,' he went on. 'I'm gay, I've got lots of friends and a wonderful life. Once you've left school you'll be able to get a job and meet new people, but in the meantime, I promise – you're not alone.'

I sat with that man for an hour and when we finished I dried my eyes, because of course I'd cried – this was the first openly gay man I had spoken to, and he had given me a future – and when I walked out of his office I knew that I was leaving with something: I was leaving with hope.

Katie was waiting in the car outside.

'Well? Did it work?'

'Yeah,' I said, smiling. 'I think it did.'

I couldn't tell her what had been said, because to Katie it would have been a failure. She was banking on my gay feelings being 'fixed' so I'd go back to normal and carry on being an obedient Witness, because she was a good friend and didn't want me to die at Armageddon. For me, though, the meeting with the Samaritan had given me the strength to keep going until I could leave home and start a new life as the person I was meant to be. I now knew there was nothing wrong with the way I was feeling. He had changed my whole perspective.

The Samaritan told me to call if I ever needed to talk again, but I never did. That hour – a chance meeting that nearly didn't happen – had made all the difference. I knew the finishing line was in sight. *You're almost there, Luke. Just keep going.*

. . .

A few weeks later I answered the door to find three elders standing on the doorstep, their faces grave. My heart sank. Clearly, I hadn't convinced Katie that our little road trip had really fixed me, so she'd called in the cavalry. I don't blame her for telling the elders – as a devout Jehovah's Witness she really had no choice – but it was a very serious thing to do, to reveal that a baptised member of the congregation was having such dangerous feelings.

Thankfully, my parents were out. I showed the elders into the living room and we all sat awkwardly together.

'We understand you've been struggling with certain feelings,' they said. 'Luke, these are temptations sent by the world. You do know that to pursue these thoughts would be against the religion?'

I nodded, trying to look appropriately penitent.

One of them got out a Bible. 'Let's look at the scripture together.'

It took all my effort not to roll my eyes. *You can say what you like,* I thought, *but nothing in that book is going to change who I am.*

The elders were kind and dealt with the matter as sensitively as they could, but by now I was confident they didn't have a clue what they were talking about. I had known these men all my life. One of them was the father of my friend, Debbie, and ran the corner shop down the road: he might be qualified to discuss the price of baked beans, but the issue of my sexuality and how it's possible to change the very essence of who I am? Not so much.

They didn't threaten me outright with being disfellowshipped, but the warning – that if I kept going down this road I would lose everything – was implicit in everything they said. I was nodding politely and making the right noises, but it didn't matter how many times they told me I was going to die at Armageddon, if I couldn't live as my true self then I would die anyway, because I'd be too unhappy to go on living.

'I appreciate you coming to talk to me,' I said, when they had finally finished. 'I think it's really going to help.'

I told them what they wanted to hear, but I knew that I no longer believed a word of it.

15

'Do you still pray, Luke?'

It wasn't surprising that Laurie and Emma, my oldest and closest Jehovah's Witness friends, were asking me this. When you're baptised, praying is a daily routine. You do it all the time: before meals, during the day, privately before bed. It's as fundamental as attending Kingdom Hall – which is probably why the girls had brought it up, because over the past year I'd been going to meetings less and less frequently. Emma and Laurie were still committed to the religion and it must have been obvious that I was drifting away.

'No,' I admitted. 'I don't pray any more.'

The girls looked stunned. 'You need to start again, Luke,' said Laurie. 'It'll help you work things out, I'm sure of it.'

Needless to say, I ignored her advice. I was venturing out into the world that the religion had tried to keep me away from and was discovering how much happier a 'worldly' life could be. I had begun to feel less like a Jehovah's Witness and more like an entirely new person; I wasn't sure exactly who that was yet, but something exciting was bubbling inside me. On Friday nights I would secretly watch *The Word* and *Eurotrash* – the surreal, sexy Channel 4 show featuring gay icons like porn star Jeff Stryker – on the small black-and-white telly in my bedroom with the sound turned right down and socks stuffed in the space under my door, so the light wouldn't spill out into the hallway and give me away. I was starting to experiment with my appearance, rebelling against the religion's diktats on always looking modest and respectable. I got my ear pierced and one weekend I bleached my hair.

I'd been hoping for an icy blonde, but it ended up Big Bird yellow. My parents weren't around, so in a panic I called my nan (who remember wasn't a Witness) who said she'd fix it with a purple rinse. One hour and two long, bumpy bus journeys later, my custard-coloured hair hidden under a beanie hat, I arrived at my grandparents' house in Trinant.

Nan answered the door, fag in hand.

'Go on then, let's see it,' she said.

I took off my cap; Nan grimaced.

'Well, bugger me.* You look like a canary's arse.'

. . .

At school I'd always stuck with the other Witness kids, but I was starting to reach out beyond this small group. I became friends with a girl called Joanne Thomas, who was a total tomboy and absolutely hilarious. Her mam, Trudy, dabbled in the Truth, as the religion is known, but Joanne wasn't a Witness herself. Whenever I sat next to her in class you knew for a fact I'd be doing nothing apart from giggling at her getting away with murder. I remember once we had a spitting match and Joanne launched the biggest gob of spit I've ever seen at my face. It landed on my cheek and just clung there, while we both peed ourselves laughing. As I've mentioned, Bedwellty Comprehensive took pupils from all over the Valleys, many of whom had difficult home lives and all sorts of behavioural issues. It wasn't an easy school in which to be a good student, because the teachers were constantly distracted by the ones running riot. Perhaps that was why I increasingly found myself drawn to naughty kids like Joanne (not the bullies, but the ones who played up a bit). I was fun at heart and wanted to be liked, and I realised that if I was naughty too – throwing chalk, winding up the teachers – then I fitted right in.

---

* 'Bugger' and 'little sod' are used in almost every other sentence in my grandparents' house to this day. Ironic, really.

I was finding new friends outside school as well. I had started hanging out with two brothers, Craig and Mike, who were in their late teens. They'd been raised as Jehovah's Witnesses, but were very different to others I had known, bending the rules as much as possible, and like me would eventually go on to leave the religion.

Craig and Mike had no idea that I was being bullied at school and didn't see me as anything other than just one of the gang. Mike worked as a groundsman at the local bowling green and was dating Katie, the girl who drove me to Samaritans. He would take me bowling or on fishing trips: the sort of things boys often do with their dads, but I never did. Where Mike was sweet and kind, Craig was hard as nails, built like a brick shithouse. I started going to the gym with him and would often come home with bruises as he was very physical, wrestling me to the ground and encouraging me to fight back. He brought me out of myself and allowed me to become – for want of a better word – a lad.

By the age of fourteen I was going out with Craig and Mike most weekends. One of their friends, Steve, had a pimped-up Vauxhall Nova with a boombox in the boot and we'd drive through the centre of Bargoed on a Friday night, music blasting, while I sat safely in the back, hidden behind tinted windows. We would go to pubs at the edge of the Valleys or in Cardiff, where there was no danger of us being seen by anyone from the congregation, and as I looked older than I was I could buy rounds of pints and nobody ever stopped me.

I first discovered alcohol at the age of thirteen when Gransha took me and Dean on a very boozy day trip to Tiverton with the Trinant rugby team. We started on the Guinness and Caffrey's at 9am, on the bus there, and by the time we were driving home I was so drunk that I had to grab one of the rugby player's kit bags to puke in. One weekend my parents were away and I invited Craig and his mates over to my house on the Friday night. I have a hazy memory of luminous-coloured bottles of MD 20/20 and drinking vodka through a straw, then downing Newcastle

Brown Ale. The next morning I was so violently ill I think I must have given myself alcohol poisoning. I couldn't even move, because whenever I did I'd throw up. I knew this was serious and that I should get help, but there was no way I could phone my parents and tell them what had happened, so instead, with the wisdom of an epically hungover fourteen-year-old, I phoned Helen Thomas, the old lady at the bottom of our street whose house we went to for Bible study meetings on a Tuesday.

'Hello Auntie Helen, it's Luke Evans here. Mam and Dad are away and I'm really not at all well. I think I might have – um – food poisoning.'

'Oh dear, that doesn't sound good. Don't worry my love, I'll be with you in just a minute.'

Well, forty-five agonising minutes later, she finally arrived. We lived on a steep hill and Helen had to use a mobility scooter, because she couldn't walk unaided. I remember sitting in our front bay window, hugging my mother's dressing gown around me and feeling like death would be a blissful release, watching as this little dot at the bottom of the hill got bigger and bigger, agonisingly slowly, until her scooter finally reached the house, then waiting another few tortuous minutes for her to struggle to the front door with the aid of her two walking sticks.

Helen made me a pot of peppermint oil tea.

'Just drink that down, my love,' she said, handing me the mug.

I drank it and threw it straight back up.

She made me another; this time it seemed to be staying put. Mrs Thomas seemed satisfied.

'You'll be fine now,' she said, as she hobbled back to the front door. 'And we won't tell your mam and dad about any of this, because we both know what happened here.'

She had three boys of her own; of course she knew what had happened. Within an hour I was back to normal. I've sworn by Helen Thomas' peppermint tea trick ever since.

· · ·

My parents weren't happy when I started going out with Craig and Mike, although it was less of an issue when Mike was going out with Katie, because she was very respectable and they trusted her. It was after they broke up that my parents became increasingly concerned. I'd come home smelling of booze; they would beg me to change my behaviour and we'd always end up arguing. Nobody was being honest and we made no attempts to understand each other's perspective. My parents were worried I was going off the rails (drinking too much was also a disfellowshipping offence), while I resented their small-minded attitude and the box they were trying to put me in that I knew would never fit me.

I was now confident there was a life waiting for me outside the Jehovah's Witness bubble. I still had another year of school to go, but I was looking ahead and had already started to earn my own money. Craig worked for an insulation company that had a government contract to fit subsidised draughtproofing in homes all over the Valleys and they needed people to go around the streets, knocking on doors, signing people up for the scheme – and if there was one thing I knew how to do, it was knocking on doors. This time, however, I'd be on the doorstep with something people would actually want! Winter lasts forever in the Valleys and central heating bills can be crippling, so I was basically going to be offering them free money. And for every person I signed up to the draughtproofing scheme, I would get commission.

On my first day of work they dropped me in Llanelli, a good hour from Aberbargoed, and said they'd be back for me at the end of the afternoon. I was fifteen and on my own. The first street I tried wasn't a great success. I needed to make the pitch more sexy, I decided: you'd be *crazy* not to sign up for this! By the end of that first day I'd nailed it: over 200 people signed up for the scheme, earning me a small fortune in the process. After a week they reduced the commission rate significantly so I wasn't earning so much from sign-ups, then soon after the company moved me from sales to another part of the business because I

My dad with Lala. Lala was in her late sixties when she took on my dad as a newborn baby.

Mam holding me as a baby outside Nana and Gransha's house.

Me with my parents in one of the only two outfits I seemed to have been photographed in as a baby.

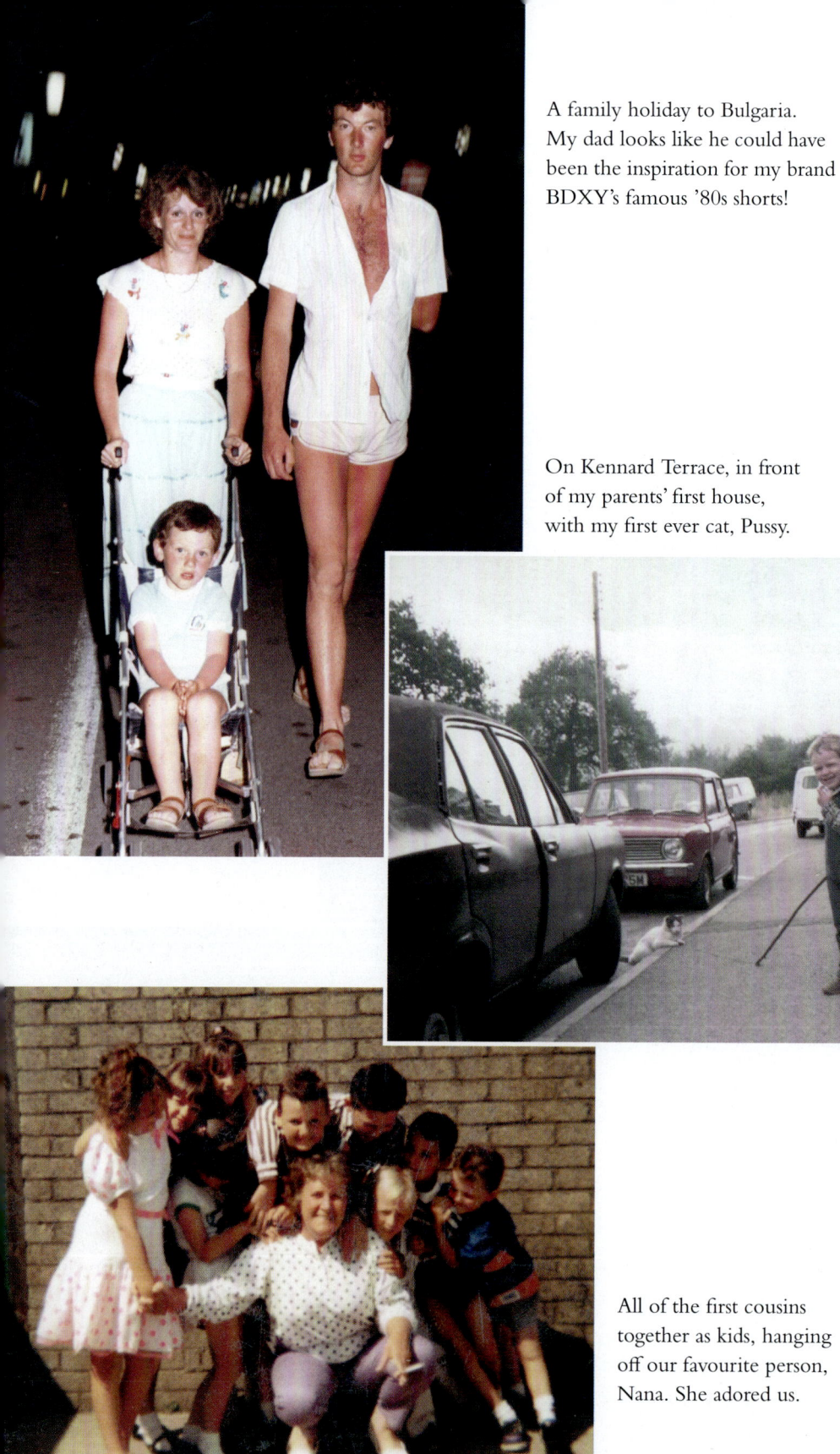

A family holiday to Bulgaria. My dad looks like he could have been the inspiration for my brand BDXY's famous '80s shorts!

On Kennard Terrace, in front of my parents' first house, with my first ever cat, Pussy.

All of the first cousins together as kids, hanging off our favourite person, Nana. She adored us.

Me and my cousin Dean. There are only six months between us and we've always been as thick as thieves. This was the start of it all.

Me and Lala. I was the apple of her eye.

With my Jehovah's Witness friends (from left: Debbie, Sarah, Emma). I used to walk around that mountain after school to avoid the bullies, rather than taking the main road home.

With my parents at a wedding. This is generally how we looked publicly as Jehovah's Witnesses (minus the buttonhole flower).

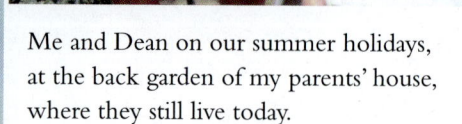

Me and Dean on our summer holidays, at the back garden of my parents' house, where they still live today.

Me with the dreaded cowslick in the dreaded Bedwellty Comprehensive School uniform.

Playing Captain Von Trapp in our school production of *The Sound of Music*. Notice the painted-on grey hair!

Me and my friend Carly at 18 years old. We paid for a photoshoot in edgy black and white, trying to be cool. This was the time of Take That and the Spice Girls!

On a visit back from London to see my parents and Polly the cat.

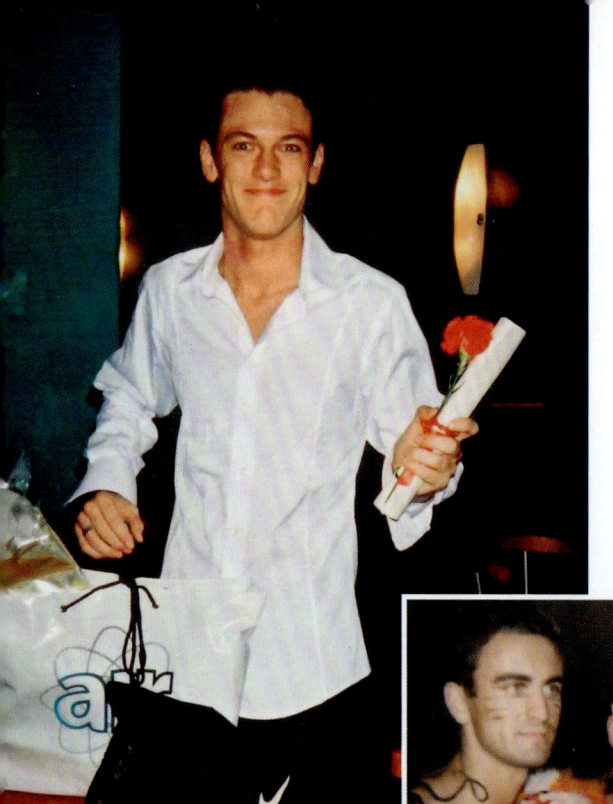

Receiving my (fake) diploma at the awards ceremony at the end of my three years at the London Studio Centre. Still waiting for the real one!

At Mardi Gras in London with Scott, my friend from college, on the left and my best friend Olly to my right, as well as AJ, another college friend. We were giving out the final batch of flyers for my friend's club, still dressed up.

Trying my best to be a New Romantic rebel, backstage at *Taboo*, with Philip Salon's famous wig on the shelf behind.

Me and the inimitable Boy George in the dressing room after a performance of *Taboo*.

Kylie sent me a signed picture of us, taken during her performance of 'Tears on My Pillow' on *The Kylie Show*, where I played her love interest.

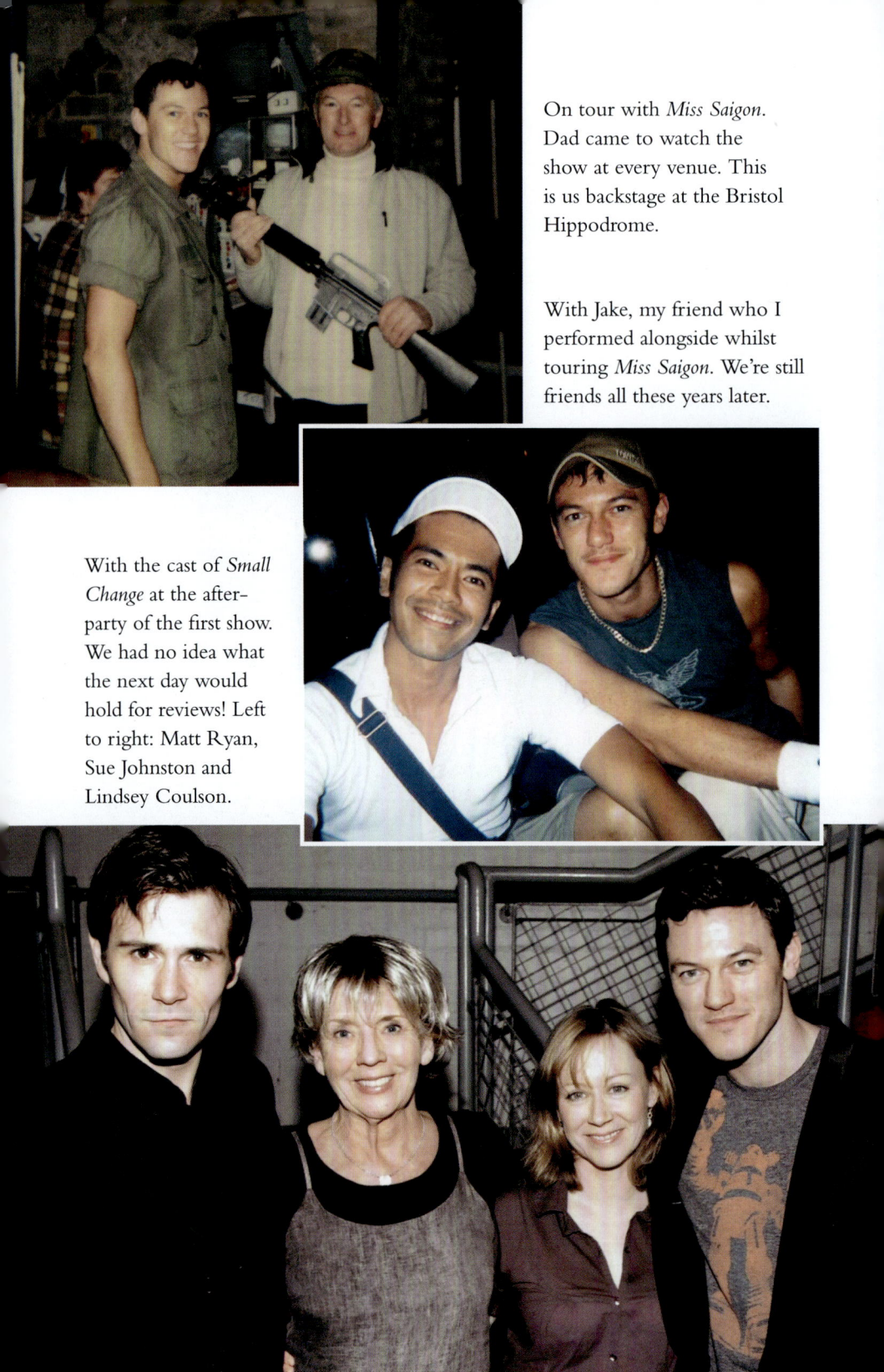

On tour with *Miss Saigon*. Dad came to watch the show at every venue. This is us backstage at the Bristol Hippodrome.

With Jake, my friend who I performed alongside whilst touring *Miss Saigon*. We're still friends all these years later.

With the cast of *Small Change* at the after-party of the first show. We had no idea what the next day would hold for reviews! Left to right: Matt Ryan, Sue Johnston and Lindsey Coulson.

was making more money than the professionals who actually fitted the draughtproofing.

* * *

I still hadn't met another gay person, but spreading my wings and building a life outside school was instilling in me a sense that it was all going to be okay, just as the Samaritan had told me. I could see the finishing line: as soon as my GCSE exams were over I could get a job and leave the Valleys. Even though I still hadn't come out, I felt I was living in a much more authentic way. Craig and Mike treated me more like an adult and because they were very masculine, butch guys, I was picking up on that and slowly changing who I was. It really helped me; maybe a little too much, because rather than wanting to do my best in the exams, my attitude by this point was: *fuck GCSEs*.

* * *

I finished my final exam before anyone else. While the rest of the students were still writing, I put down my pen, walked out of the exam hall and down the driveway towards the gate. Freedom was just seconds away, but before I could escape I heard my form teacher, Mr Cormack, call my name.

I reluctantly turned to face him.

'So you're off then, Luke?' he said.

'Yes sir.'

He nodded slowly. 'I'm telling you now, if you don't take what you're doing seriously you are never going to achieve anything. You have thrown these GCSEs away, and I think you're going to regret it. Please don't waste your life, Luke. You have ability and potential; you could really be something if you just applied yourself.'

I looked at him. I didn't want to be rude, but he knew nothing about the turmoil I'd been going through.

'Thank you very much, sir,' I said, then turned and walked away.

I knew Mr Cormack liked me and my lack of focus must have been frustrating for him, but in that moment he was a symbol of the last ten years of misery. As I headed down the school drive towards the gates I remember thinking: *I'm going to prove you wrong. Whatever I end up doing, I'm going to make a success of my life.*

I've been asked many times if I wonder what those bullies might think about me now. Honestly? Beyond writing this book, I never think about them. Over the years people from my old school have occasionally reached out, some of whom may well have stood by and allowed the bullying to happen, and invariably I don't have a clue who they are. I remember four or five people from school, but that's about it. On the day I walked out of those gates for the final time, I closed that chapter in my mind and never looked back.

16

The weekend after I finished school I was on a train to Cardiff, armed with copies of a largely blank CV. I wasn't worried that I hadn't had much experience. I was confident that I could pick things up quickly and work hard until I was good at something, if not the best. It's the way I've approached at a lot of things in my life. I got a job as a Christmas temp in the shoe department of River Island, starting work in the September after my GCSEs. While I didn't do badly in my exams, I could have done a lot better if I'd tried, but even without straight As I was already well on the way to achieving my ambition: getting a job and then hopefully getting out of the Valleys.

River Island's shoe department was in the basement, so every time someone wanted a different size I'd have to leg it up two floors to go to the stockroom. This was the domain of a lovely guy called Max, who was the first person to accept me as gay before I'd told him. He was straight, but just made the assumption, as if it was as natural and unremarkable a fact as having brown hair. After years of hiding away, it was quite a moment to be instantly and unquestioningly accepted.

'I've got some gay friends you should meet,' he told me. 'Come out for a drink with us this weekend.'

Max's friends, Simon and Dom, were a few years older than me, but they took me under their wing. It was the first time I'd hung out with other gay people, and the first time since I was little that I'd been able to be in the moment without worrying about how I was coming across. Up until then, I'd been forced to fake it. It's a skill that a lot of gay kids of my generation and those before me had to learn to survive:

we observed, adapted and fitted in, like chameleons. Boys were meant to be into football and *Star Wars* toys, so I learned what to say and how to behave to match that profile. I would be watching a rugby match with my cousin Dean, not having a fucking clue what was going on, but making sure I was acting in the same way as all the other boys.* Now, though, I realised that I didn't have to do this any more. Nobody was expecting me to behave or sound or dress or speak a certain way. I can't tell you how liberating that felt.

After meeting at the pub we went back to Simon and Dom's very grotty house-share in Roath. It was a cold and rainy winter's night and as we approached the door I saw a girl sitting on the front step, hunched and miserable. As soon as she saw us, she jumped up and started screaming. I took a step back from this wild woman. *Whoa.* It turned out that she lived there too and one of the boys had taken her keys to work, so she was locked out. 'This is not the normal me,' she muttered apologetically as we went in. 'I'm very tired and cold, and I'm on my period.'

She was right: in reality Ruth was sweet, kind and softly spoken, and we're friends to this day. She lived on the top floor with her two chinchillas, while the boys were on the floor below. The house felt like a squat because it was such a hole, but they did pay rent. Simon and Dom partied hard and the place was always full of Cardiff's most colourful people. There was a beautiful girl who made these incredible outfits: one night she came clubbing with us in a Thunderbirds-style cap, boob tube and miniskirt, all made out of KitKat wrappers. She had a very handsome boyfriend whose bare chest she'd cover in glitter for a night out at a gay club.

Soon I was hanging out with the boys most weekends and would often stay the night rather than get the train back to Aberbargeod.

---

* Nowadays, as an adult, I love watching rugby. I've learned to enjoy it and appreciate it on my terms.

Although I was much younger I was a buzzy, fun-loving kid, and they were always happy for me to tag along. We'd go to a gay bar or a club, then go back to the squat and smoke pot. The living room would be littered with bodies and hazy with smoke, then someone would get me to sing 'The First Time Ever I Saw Your Face' and all these party people, completely off their faces, would be sprawled out weeping. Ruth rarely came out, but she would often come down and smoke a joint with us once we were back. She always looked out for me, as I was so young. 'Luke, I think it's time for bed,' she would say, then I would go and sleep in her room. There were always random hangers-on who came back to the squat after an evening out, and one night someone slipped into Ruth's bedroom while we were sleeping and stole our wallets. The chinchillas were clearly useless as guard dogs.

* * *

As well as the money I now had in my pocket there was something else in there as well: the phone number of the singing teacher Ros Phillips had given me at school. I had kept it, hoping that one day I might be able to afford to have lessons – not because I was thinking about singing as a career, but because it was something I loved to do. I phoned the teacher, Louise Ryan, and booked my first lesson for the following week after my shift at River Island.

It was one stop on the train from Cardiff to Cathays, where Louise lived. The front door was opened by a large-bosomed woman with lots of eyeliner and an explosion of dark hair. She was holding a giant cup of coffee; I would soon realise that she was rarely without it.

'Come on in, I'm just finishing up,' she said, disappearing off again.

As I waited in the corridor I heard a perfect, clear soprano coming from inside the room. It was the most beautiful voice – 'the voice of an angel' is how it would come to be described. A few minutes later a smiley little scrap of a girl walked out the room with her mam. She can't have been more than ten; I was stunned this voice had come from this child. We nodded hello, unaware of how our lives would soon be intricately entwined.

Louise showed me into her room and took a seat at the piano.

'Right, let's see what you can do,' she said.

Most of that first lesson was spent on exercises. She took me through my scales to see where my voice sat – I was a lyric tenor, apparently – and at the end of our time she said: 'Great, when do you want to come again?'

I started to have lessons with Louise every week. Her agenda was to get me competition-ready for Eisteddfods, which are Welsh music and poetry festivals, and within a few months I was travelling to Bristol with Mam and Dad to compete in my first contest. I invited my parents to come because I wanted them to see I was doing something productive with my life. They were hesitant at first, as it was all so unfamiliar to them, but they were soon loving it – especially when I started to win. Louise had entered me into a number of different categories – German lieder, Italian aria, Welsh hymns, pop ballads – and when I returned home that night it was with an armful of trophies engraved with my name. It was mad: the first time I'd ever been in an Eisteddfod and I'd won across the board. The only person who didn't seem surprised was Louise.

'Of course, I knew you'd do it,' she said, matter-of-factly.

I competed in a number of Eisteddfods over the following months and among the prizes I took home was Most Promising Voice in Wales. For someone who had never been any good at sport or won anything at school it was incredibly validating. Sometimes Louise would push her luck and enter me in an older class, and if I won that (which I often did) there would be a lot of people furious at this skinny whippersnapper with a mature ability and naturally strong vibrato. I had been born with a good instrument, but Louise was an excellent teacher and showed me how to use it, plus she always made sure I had the right material to suit my voice.

When my contract at River Island finished, however, so did the singing lessons. I'd have loved to have kept seeing Louise, but I couldn't afford to without a full-time job. So I signed up with a recruitment agency and while I was waiting for something permanent to come up my dad suggested I work for him. As a builder he was always in demand: super-polite and highly skilled, nobody ever had a bad word to say about David Evans when he worked for them. I accepted Dad's offer with mixed emotions. I'd often worked for him during the school holidays — stacking bricks or carrying the compo, which is what they called mortar — and while I was always happy to get paid I'd never been very good at taking orders from him, plus the work was dirty and dull and we'd always have the same disappointing lunch: a Pot Noodle, jam sandwiches and a flask of scalding, sweet coffee.

My attitude to working with Dad began to change as I got older and started to notice the other labourers in their tight jeans and vests. Suddenly there was more to building sites than mud and bad coffee: I could dress up and feel sexy around these other lads. For his latest job, though, it was going to be just me and him, building a wall around a playground in Cardiff. At least we were going to be in the city, so perhaps my new cargo pants and tight T-shirt wouldn't go to waste after all.

17

We hadn't been working there long when I noticed a good-looking man walk past the building site most days. It turned out that he lived in the corner house by the playground where we were working, and soon he would stop to chat to us. One day Dad asked what he did for a living and he told us he was a singer on a cruise ship, which pretty much blew my mind. You could sing on a cruise ship as an actual *paid job*? That had to be a better way to earn a living than stacking bricks.

I was intrigued and wanted to hear more about how he got into singing as a career, but also, judging by the number of attractive men I saw going in and out of his house, I got the strong impression he was gay. I decided to write him a letter. It wasn't a sexual thing; it was just an attempt to expand my horizons and meet more gay people. I wrote that I was the labourer from the playground and told him I'd been having lessons and was interested in becoming a singer. This was in those awkward pre-mobile phone days, so I put in my parents' landline number and then dropped the letter through his door after work on a Friday before heading out for a drink.

When I came downstairs next morning Mam told me I'd had a phone call.

'Your father said it's the man who lives in the house by the building site,' she said. 'Apparently you left him a letter asking for advice on becoming a performer?'

'That's right.'

There was a long pause. 'Your father thinks he might be a homosexual.'

'So? I'm interested in what he does for a living.'

'We just think you should be careful,' she said.
'Of course I will be, Mam. Don't worry.'

. . .

We arranged to meet at a bar in central Cardiff. I told my parents I was going to meet him for a drink and that Max from River Island was coming with me, and I'd stay the night with him after. They'd met Max and liked him, plus they were leaving for a week's holiday the following day so were pleased that I'd have company. I was excited about my plan, even though it had one glaring flaw: Max wasn't coming with me, so if I missed the last train back to the Valleys I wouldn't have anywhere to stay. Still, with the blithe confidence of a sixteen-year-old, I figured it would all work out.

I met up with the cruise ship singer and his mates, who seemed nice enough, and I bought the first round of drinks at the bar, then they invited me along to Club X, Cardiff's famous gay club. Within half an hour of arriving at the club, I had lost them all. I wandered around, shouldering my way through the sea of bodies, but there was no sign of any of them. I was sure they wouldn't have left without me, so I sat on a sofa in the lounge area and figured they'd come looking for me. I was also hoping Simon, Dom and some of their friends might be in the club that night, as I'd been there with that group before, but I didn't see a single familiar face. In the end, I sat there on my own for the entire night. I didn't even have a drink, as I'd spent all my money on that first round in the bar. It wasn't until the lights came up at 2am and I reluctantly joined the flood of people heading for the exit that I finally thought: *What the hell do I do now?*

I hung around outside the club, listening to other people making plans for the rest of the night. I knew the trains weren't going to start again for another four hours and I had started to wonder if I'd have to find a park bench to sleep on when two men came up to me.

'Are you okay?'

They were attractive, probably in their early thirties, one with a shaved head and the other a quiff of black hair.

'Yeah, I'm fine, it's just … I was with some people, but they've disappeared.'

'So where are you going now?' one of them asked. He had a strong Northern accent.

'I'm not sure. I live in the Valleys and the trains are finished.'

'Well, if you like you can come to our place. We live close to the station, so you can get the train home first thing in the morning.'

'Really? That would be great, thank you!'

I don't think it even crossed my mind that this could all go terribly wrong.

Their names were Jack and Ian and they told me they had been a couple for a long time. It was summer and still warm outside, so when we got back to their house they put on some music and opened the living room doors to a lovely little patio garden with a fountain, a silver dome with water trickling over it into a pool. A cat padded inside and wound itself around my legs. We had a few drinks, then one thing led to another and that night I ended up having my first sexual experience with those two sweet guys.

I'd had a kiss with one of the boys from the squat before, but that was the extent of my prior experience. I was so nervous my whole body was trembling, but they were very sensitive. They didn't pressure me at all; I wanted to do it. I knew all my cousins were having sex, so why shouldn't I? I think they must have realised I was a virgin, though they had no idea exactly how young I was. At the time the age of homosexual consent was eighteen, but it didn't even occur to me that what we were doing was illegal.

Afterwards the three of us snuggled up in bed together and went to sleep, and the next morning they made me breakfast. There was nobody expecting me back in Aberbargoed because my parents had gone on holiday, so I hung out with Jack and Ian in their garden and then later we hopped into their little Cinquecento and went to the supermarket to get some food for dinner. It was all very chilled.

    I ended up staying with them for three days and then after I got back to Aberbargoed I invited them to my parents' house for dinner to say thank you. I cooked a three-course meal (my parents were obviously still away) and over dessert felt the need to come clean about my age. When I told them I was sixteen they both went pale, but I promised I wouldn't tell anyone and we parted on good terms. I never spoke to them again, but this was a key experience for me. The gay men I had met through Max were massive party animals: they would go shopping for outrageous outfits on a Friday, party until Monday morning and then crawl into work to earn money for the following weekend. They were great fun, but even at that age I knew there was more to being gay than just partying. Jack and Ian had good jobs, a nice car, a beautiful house. They were content and settled in their lives together as a couple. I needed to see a more balanced view of what my future life could be, and Jack and Ian gave me my first glimpse of that.

18

I had given the recruitment agency the phone number of the telephone box next to the playground where Dad and I were working. We wedged the door open so we'd hear the phone and I'd sprint the length of the building site every time it rang. One day they called to say that I had an interview for the position of mail boy at a large company. The following morning I went for an interview at their imposing headquarters in Cardiff and that evening I told Dad he'd need to find someone else to stack his bricks.

My job was to collect the hire purchase application forms from the mailroom in the morning and then take them up to my desk on the first floor, where I'd stamp the forms with the date and distribute them to the bank of phone operators, known as power diallers, who would then ring the customers who'd applied to buy a sofa or washing machine on HP and go through their credit rating. Coincidentally, one of the power diallers was Ruth, my friend from the Roath house-share, and we'd meet up for cigarette breaks.

My desk was directly opposite the head of the admin team. Helen was strikingly tall and glamorous and had so much thick, blonde, bum-length hair that rather than flick it casually over her shoulder she'd have to gather it up in both hands and haul it over like a sack of coal. You didn't mess with Helen – or her dog, Tyson, the nippiest Chihuahua I've met in my life. She was a few years older than me, but we instantly became friends.

Our boss, Tom, was a smartly dressed man in his late thirties who drove a Mercedes. I still remember my astonishment when Helen told me he was gay. You mean gay people don't just work in bars or on aeroplanes, or at the front of House of Fraser handing out perfume samples? Deprived of role models while I was growing up, I was gradually expanding my understanding of what gay men could be – and, as a result, who I could potentially be.

. . .

I'd been working at the company for a couple of months when Helen and I decided to start looking for a flat together. By now we were as thick as thieves, and both keen to leave home. Now I just had to find a way to tell my parents that I was moving out.

I knew it was not going to be an easy conversation. I could imagine how sad and worried they'd be, but I hoped they would understand that I was leaving for them as much as for myself. I was now living a very different life to the one they had hoped I would lead, not abiding by their rules or those of the religion, yet I was still living under their roof. I could see how hurt they were when they left for meetings at the Kingdom Hall and I didn't go with them, and I was tired of the difficult conversations this was causing.

At this point I was banking on the fact that I could leave the religion but still keep seeing my parents. If you were a baptised Jehovah's Witness they'd permit you to walk away as long as you didn't do anything to bring the religion into disrepute, in which case you'd be disfellowshipped and your loved ones would have to pretend you didn't exist. So that was my plan: keep my sexuality a secret, avoid being disfellowshipped and continue to see my parents and friends. As far as I was concerned, my parents *never* needed to find out I was gay. I figured I could still introduce them to my friends without causing suspicion; most of them were girls, after all.

Before breaking the news to my parents, I told two of my aunties – Elaine, my mam's twin sister, and Helen – that I was going to move out.

It felt safer testing the water by talking to Elaine first, because she wasn't a Witness and I knew she wouldn't try to talk me out of it.

'Ooh, that's a big step,' said Elaine. 'You know your mam's not going to be happy.'

'I do, but I'm not comfortable in that house anymore. I don't want to live as a Jehovah's Witness.'

She nodded. 'It's your life, Luke, you must do what you need to do.'

. . .

Within a week Helen and I had signed a lease on a two-bedroom flat in Roath. It was a Thursday, and that same evening I went home and told my parents I was moving out that weekend.

It was a horrible conversation. As I had feared, they were devastated. I can't imagine how traumatic it must be for a parent to learn your only child is leaving home at sixteen – especially for my mother, as we were so close. Mam later told me that she had even considered involving the police because I was so young.

I have no memory of the day I left, of packing up my clothes and possessions or saying goodbye to my parents. Over the years I've lost little pockets of my life, certain painful moments and memories I've blocked out, which I think can only be down to PTSD – because how can I not have suffered it to some degree? I was dealing with the loss and grief of having to leave home at such a young age, of not being able to be honest with the only two people in my life who really mattered to me. Helen was waiting for me in the car outside, but my parents wouldn't come out. They had decided that if I was set on leaving, they weren't going to help me. Mam says she can still hear the front door closing behind me to this day.

The flat wasn't particularly great, but it was ours. It was on the first floor of a house overlooking Roath Park, with big bay windows and a fire escape out back that caught the sun in the evening, where Helen and I would sit and chat after work.

This was all still to come, though. On that first day I felt lost. I remember unpacking my bags in my bedroom and crying when I found an envelope of cash that Mam had tucked in there before I'd left.

That evening Helen and I sat in the living room and talked about our plans for the future. She told me about a guy she was seeing, who she really liked. I talked about maybe buying a bike, so I wouldn't need to take the bus (which I ended up doing, then dislocated my shoulder after riding home from work in the pouring rain and crashing into the back of a transit van that didn't even stop to check if I was okay). Helen had brought her sound system with her and put on 'Killing Me Softly' by the Fugees. Even today, when I hear that song it takes me straight back to that night: the feeling of loss, mingled with a thrilling new sense of freedom and independence.

We opened a couple of Hooch Lemon and drank to new beginnings.

ACT TWO

19

Soon after we'd moved in together, Helen and I had an impromptu flat-warming party. We were at the pub, drinking with the gang from the office, when she suddenly announced that everyone was invited back to our place.

'They can't all come over,' I hissed. 'The flat's a tip!'

Helen was, to put it generously, a little messy. You could barely see her bedroom floor under the sea of clothes, hair products and make-up.

'Who cares?' she said, already heading for the door. Helen was always up for a party; that girl could drink me under the table any night of the week.

I was probably more aware of the state of our flat because our boss, Tom, was out with us that night, and I didn't want him thinking we lived like pigs. I'd never really spoken to him before because he didn't come out with us very often, but we started chatting back at the flat and once I'd got over the fact that he was my boss I began to relax. Time passed, and while everyone else got drunker and rowdier around us we became locked in conversation in the corner of the living room. I noticed the fresh scent of Tom's cologne, his wickedly infectious laugh. I was aware of a spark between us and realised, with a mixture of excitement and disbelief, that something was about happen.

By the early hours the guests had gone home and Helen went to bed, leaving Tom and I on our own. At some point we moved to my bedroom.

He left early the next morning before Helen woke up. A few days later he invited me out for lunch at a restaurant outside town, where there was no danger of us being spotted, and within a few weeks we were discussing booking a holiday so we could spend time together without worrying who might see us. Everyone had been so drunk the night at our flat that they hadn't noticed us chatting, and since then we'd been meticulously cloak-and-dagger about meeting up. We had to be; not only because Tom was my boss, but because I was still below the legal age of gay consent. The only people I'd told about our relationship were Helen and Ruth, and they'd both been sworn to secrecy.

Tom suggested we go to Mexico. I'd never been abroad without my parents, and our last family holiday had been Crete when I was fourteen. A week in an all-inclusive resort in Cancún, with this handsome older man? Yes please.

We would have to book the same period off work, but we figured it wouldn't raise suspicions. My cover story was that I was going to London for a week to stay with friends. There were a few jokey comments in the office – 'Ooh, you and Tom are going away at the same time!' – but, as expected, nobody seriously questioned it.

It was a joyous holiday: sunbathing by the pool, beach volleyball and a night out at this truly awful club called Señor Frog's. Tom and I returned home with matching tans, but the only person to notice that I was suspiciously sun-kissed after a week in the UK was my mam.

'Tanning beds, Mam!' I told her. 'They're everywhere in London!'

. . .

And so began my first ever relationship. It may have looked unlikely on paper, but I was attracted to Tom on many different levels. There was the physical side of things, obviously, but my Jehovah's Witness upbringing placed high value on respectability, of being well-dressed and having good manners, and Tom ticked all those boxes. The age gap wasn't an issue; in fact, for me it was probably part of the appeal. I had lost my support network on leaving home and at times had felt a little lost, but now here was a handsome, successful and knowledgeable man who could guide me as I built my new life. Although I was mature for my age in some respects, I had lived a sheltered life in the Valleys: I knew how to breed finches and canaries and build a brick wall, but had little knowledge of culture, politics or current affairs. The TV news was only on at home when Dad needed to watch the weather to find out whether he would be able to dig the footings for a wall or not. I had a lot to learn about the world; Tom was patient and kind, and happy to help me fill in those gaps.

We hadn't been seeing each other for long when Tom said he wanted to introduce me to an old friend from his hometown. Karl used to be a model, but was now in a committed, long-term relationship with a guy called William and the couple lived together in Chelsea. I loved London beyond all description, so when Tom suggested we go to their house for lunch I didn't need further encouragement.

I'd never been to Chelsea and my eyes grew wide as Tom drove us past a row of Georgian mansions overlooking the Thames, pointing out the homes of various celebrities. We took a left onto a street lined with elegant townhouses and Victorian streetlights, which was where Tom stopped the car.

'Your friends live here?' I asked.

He nodded, smiling at my stunned expression.

I looked up at the building next to where we were parked. 'That's their house?'

'Yup, the whole thing.'

'Oh my God.'

We got out with our overnight bags – because we had been invited to stay – and walked up to the steps to the front door. I was a little nervous, but mainly excited: I had never been in such a beautiful house before.

Karl opened the door. He was extremely handsome – prime trophy-boyfriend material – and dressed in a cashmere sweater, chinos and leather moccasins, a look of understated luxury which I would come to recognise as the uniform of the truly rich.

'It's so lovely to meet you,' said Karl, in a beautifully cultured voice.

William was just as charming: warm, witty and clearly very intelligent. I learned that he came from a very wealthy family who had made their money in the construction industry. Among his various projects, William had set up a charitable foundation with a portion of his inheritance.

I stood in the hallway, marvelling at the decor and all these beautiful things around me. This was a completely new world, but I didn't feel intimidated. William and Karl were so welcoming they instantly put me at ease: they were aware that Tom and I had to hide our relationship in Cardiff and wanted to give us a safe place where we could relax and be ourselves.

Tom would later tell me that Karl's elegant tones were a complete affectation. I think one of the reasons Karl loved Tom was that he was a reminder of his roots, but he'd wanted something better for his life, an ambition I could strongly relate to. I had realised when I was very young that I had dreams far beyond the working-class Valley life I'd been raised in. Television and movies gave me a glimpse into an alternative world that sparked my imagination. While I was still living at home I would sometimes buy the *Sunday Times* and croissants at the weekend, because that's what middle-class families seemed to do. This desire for a nicer life had been bubbling away inside me for years, but meeting Karl and William gave me my first real introduction into this world. There was a sense of calm and ease surrounding the couple, which to me came down to the fact that they weren't on the hamster wheel of chaos that most of us are on just to pay the bills. Yet it wasn't just their money – the beautiful house and expensive clothes – I aspired to; it was how cultured they were, and their good taste.

I spent much of that first day listening: absorbing the rhythm of the conversation, noting which subjects did (or didn't) come up, registering the pronunciation of certain words and then adapting my own speech accordingly. It was a trick I used many years later in my first few experiences on film sets: watch, listen, learn, adapt. In a way, my whole life has been preparing me for making movies. This wasn't about changing my accent – I'm very proud of being Welsh and have never wanted to erase my identity – but I was fascinated by the differences in the way William and Karl structured their speech and the richness of the language they used. They could make a boring sentence sound almost poetic (to my ears) by using words that weren't even in my vocabulary. Up until this point, the way I spoke had largely been influenced by my parents, neither of whom were particularly educated, but I quickly realised that if I answered William and Karl's questions in my usual way it would stick out in this environment. I became aware of my limited vocabulary and was keen to improve it; I even bought myself a thesaurus to expand my choice of words. I knew I wouldn't be able to go to university, but I felt that being around successful, educated people like William, Karl and Tom would give me an opportunity to learn from them and hopefully better myself.

Over lunch I watched William and Karl – their table manners, which cutlery they were using – and copied them; partly because I didn't want to embarrass Tom, but also because as a Jehovah's Witness the importance of always leaving a good impression had been drilled into me. Since leaving home I hadn't needed to draw on the skills valued by the religion, but now it all came back into play. I didn't feel out of my depth. It was a case of: *Right, I know what to do here.*

After that first visit we met up with Karl and William regularly in London. There was lunch at Bibendum, a beautiful restaurant in Kensington in an old Michelin garage, which had a stained-glass window of a giant Michelin man watching over you as you ate your lobster. Another favourite restaurant of theirs was Maggie Jones's, which was named after the pseudonym Princess Margaret used whenever she called up.

'Oh, hello, it's Maggie Jones, may I please book a table for 32?'
'Certainly, Your Highness – I mean, Maggie.'

. . .

Six months after Helen and I moved in together, she suddenly quit her job. She stormed out of the office one afternoon and when I got home later that day, she tearfully confessed she had a personal problem and planned to move back home with her parents.

Moving back to Aberbargoed wasn't an option, so I either had to find a new flatmate or another place to live, but before I had even started looking Tom said: 'Why don't you move in with me?'

. . .

We took out a lease on a smart two-bedroom apartment in Cardiff's newly cool docklands area. It was in a new-build block on a wharf, a world away from my and Helen's grotty Roath flat and even further away from my parents' home in the Valleys, and I loved it instantly. Even at that age I knew I wanted a nicer life than the one I'd come from. I'd always been frustrated that Dad worked so hard, yet refused to consider expanding his business so he was able to buy a better car or extend the house. 'We don't need to show off,' he would always say. My parents never had any big ambitions or dreams and although the religion definitely played a part in that, I think it was also in their nature. They were perfectly happy with their lives in a small village, surrounded by their friends, and it wasn't until many years after I'd left home that I realised my parents' contentment was actually something to admire. My horizons were always far broader. I was driven by a need to better myself, to see the world and be something more than just a Jehovah's Witness in the Valleys, and if that wasn't something I could achieve by myself then I'd already figured I might meet someone who could help me. I hope that doesn't sound like I was using Tom, because it wasn't like that at all. I certainly wasn't planning to lock him down and get a ring on his finger. Like most sixteen-year-olds, I was just enjoying the moment.

Yet while I was gradually disentangling myself from my past, the web of lies I'd had to tell my parents since leaving home kept dragging me back. I now had to come up with a plausible explanation as to why I was moving into an expensive apartment with an older man. The only solution was yet more lies.

'You'll never believe it,' I told Mam. 'I was looking through the paper for a room to rent and I've found one in Cardiff Bay for the exact same price as I was paying with Helen in Roath.'

'Ooh, that's fantastic!' said Mam. 'Whose flat is it?'

'It's a businessman who travels a lot and wants the apartment to be occupied while he's away, so he's looking for a tenant to rent his spare room.'

'Have you met him? Is he nice?'

'He's lovely,' I said. The only true words in the entire conversation.

My parents were obviously keen to meet the stranger their son was now living with, so a month after we'd moved in they came to visit. Tom was understandably uncomfortable about lying to them, but I asked him to stick around to say hello before he made his excuses.

The meeting went amazingly well; of course it did, you couldn't not like Tom. He had a down-to-earth charm that my parents instantly responded to. He told them they must visit whenever they wanted: 'Luke's probably going to be on his own here anyway!'

Mam and Dad couldn't believe how lucky I was. A gorgeous flat in one of the smartest new developments in Cardiff, together with the loveliest of landlords. The whole family came to marvel at my good fortune.

'Look how he's living!' said Nana. 'You've landed on your feet here, love.'

They were dazzled by this shiny image I had created, though if they'd looked a little closer around the hazy edges of this seemingly perfect reality they might have realised that it was all too good to be true.

I was now living a very different life to when I first moved to Cardiff, one probably more suited to a thirty-something than a sixteen-year-old, but as much as I enjoyed partying with the guys from the squat, the Jehovah's Witness in me was drawn to order and respectability and Tom offered that in spades. The flat was always spotless and he was a stickler for routine: a roast on a Sunday; steak, potatoes and peas every Thursday. There wasn't much room for spontaneity, but I felt secure, and that meant a lot to me at this time.

That year I celebrated my first ever Christmas. I remember putting up the tree in our apartment, choosing the baubles and piling on the tinsel, while Christmas songs played at high volume. There was excitement and wonder, but also an undercurrent of guilt. I'd had a lifetime of being told Christmas was wrong, so while it was a thrill to taste this festive forbidden fruit, I was fighting years of conditioning. In a way, it felt like a betrayal of my parents. They'd worked so hard to bring me up a certain way and live by the religion's rules and now I was trampling all over them. The lure of the fairy lights was stronger than the guilt, though. We cooked Christmas lunch for friends and I loved every second of it.

Life was good. I was living in a beautiful flat with my boyfriend, I'd resumed my singing lessons with Louise Ryan, I had a job I enjoyed, new friends and my parents were happy for me. The lies were holding up – or so I believed.

20

It was a Thursday morning and I was sitting at my desk in the office as usual, date-stamping the morning's mail. Outside the window, Cardiff was doing its best to be as grey and uninspiring as possible, but Tom and I had been talking about planning a holiday the night before, so my mind was off on a tropical beach somewhere.

I'd nearly finished the pile of post and reckoned I was due a cigarette break, but as I was getting up from my desk the phone rang. It was an external call, so I answered it formally. There was a pause on the other end of the line, then a man's voice asked: 'Is this Luke Evans?'

That was odd: callers didn't usually ask for the mail boy by name.

'Yes, this is Luke speaking.'

'This is South Wales Police. We've been informed you've been having underage homosexual relations.'

I froze. My first thought was: *Is this a joke?* But no, of course it couldn't be; nobody would be cruel enough to find that funny. Which meant that this was actually the police and they somehow knew about my relationship with Tom.

'Mr Evans? You do know that it is illegal to have gay sex at sixteen?'

His words hit me like physical blows. I knew I needed to answer but I couldn't breathe, let alone find the right words to stop this rapidly unfolding car crash. My mind was darting around, desperately trying to find a solution, a way to stop this from going any further. Perhaps if I told him how happy Tom and I were together, how much we loved each other – surely they would understand we had done nothing wrong?

'We're in a car outside your office,' the officer went on. 'If you don't come out to speak to us, we'll have to come in and accompany you to the police station for an interview.'

Well, that was enough to snap me into action.

'I understand,' I said quietly. 'I'll be out in two minutes.'

As soon as they had hung up, I called Tom at his desk. Every part of me wanted to keep this from him – to protect him – but whether I liked it or not he was part of this.

'The police are outside,' I told him. 'I think someone's reported me, assuming I'm having underage sex.'

I heard his sudden, sharp inhale. 'Are you okay?'

'Yes … No. I don't know.' I was close to tears. I was so young, and the situation was terrifying. 'What should I do?'

'Just go,' he said. 'I'll cover for you here.'

As I stood up I felt my legs trembling, just as they had all those years ago when I cowered on the landing listening to my parents fight. I gripped the edge of the desk to steady myself.

'I'm just going for a smoking break,' I announced to my colleagues as breezily as possible.

I still remember climbing in the back of that unmarked police car, smiling at the two grave-faced officers in the front seats, wondering if the next time I got out of there it would be at the police station, hoping I wouldn't throw up out of sheer terror. The police told me they'd had an anonymous letter saying that I'd been having underage sex and asked me lots of questions. I told them it must be someone on the gay scene spreading malicious rumours and the officers quickly agreed this was the most likely explanation. 'When we get anonymous tip-offs it's usually someone out to cause trouble,' they said. They thanked me for my time and let me go, but I was seriously shaken – Tom and I both were. Who could have tipped them off about our relationship? We'd been so careful to keep it hidden. Besides, we couldn't think of anyone who hated us so much they would report us to the police simply for being together.

. . .

For the next few weeks Tom and I were in a state of high alert, imagining danger round every corner. We stopped going out together; we couldn't even let our guard down in our apartment building, because it was entirely possible one of our neighbours had reported us. As the days passed, however, and nothing further happened, we slowly began to relax. Until, one day, I was at my desk when Tom called me on the internal phone system.

'I've just been asked to a meeting with the head of the company,' he said, his voice low. 'I've been told I probably won't be coming back to my desk afterwards.'

I looked across the room to where he was sitting. 'Is it about us?'

'I think so, yes.'

I felt as if the ceiling was falling in on me. 'What do you want me to do?'

'You can't do anything, I'm afraid. We'll talk at home later.'

I watched Tom pick up his papers, put on his jacket and walk out of the office. Sure enough, he never came back again.

. . .

We never did find out who tried to destroy our relationship, but though they hadn't succeeded, our future was looking bleak. Tom's reputation had been seriously damaged, and without his income we couldn't stay in the flat. We had no idea what we were going to do.

It was in the middle of this crisis that Karl and William invited us to their country house in Dartmoor, which was where they often spent the weekend. They had heard what had happened and rallied round. With everything that was going on, we were just glad to be able to get out of Cardiff for the weekend.

We arrived in Devon on a stormy Friday night. It felt as if we were driving into the middle of nowhere, when our headlights flashed over the grey stone walls of a house looming up from the moor. Though it was too dark to see the scale of the place, you could sense how vast it was.

The front door was opened by Sion the butler. It was late and Karl and William had already gone to bed, so he showed us through the maze of corridors to our room.

Next morning we went downstairs to meet Karl and William at breakfast. From the dining room window you could see an immaculate stretch of lawn that rolled down to a river, on the other side of which was the moor itself. I could have quite happily spent the day just staring at that view, but after breakfast Karl suggested we check out the pool.

Between swims, playing with their two red setters and reading the papers, the day slipped easily by. William and Karl were such gracious hosts that when they asked if I would sing for them after dinner I was more than happy to oblige. I sang 'Danny Boy', everyone clapped politely and off we went to bed.

When we woke next morning the weather was still terrible; the sky so heavy with clouds it looked like the middle of the night. Karl and William were already at the breakfast table. Sion came in with a fresh pot of tea and as he put it down, I noticed him shoot William a very deliberate look.

'Ah, yes …' said William. 'Tom, we have a proposal for you. We'd like to offer you the job of chairman of our charitable foundation. It would mean you moving to London, but we think you'd be perfect for the role.'

I was stunned, and I could see Tom was too. Before he could answer, though, William turned to me.

'We think you have something very special, Luke, so we'd like to offer you a bursary to attend a musical theatre college in London. Our foundation already sponsors two performers, so it would be a pleasure to help you too – if you'd be interested, that is?'

I had woken up that morning expecting nothing more than maybe a compliment for my singing, but instead I was being handed the most incredible opportunity. I wanted to jump up and scream: *Yes! One thousand per cent YES!* But I knew William was only offering me the bursary because of my relationship with Tom, so I needed to wait for him to reply first. He was obviously as overwhelmed as I was, but as soon as he gratefully accepted William's offer, then I did too.

It was a moment that would change the course of both our lives. Tom would go on to run the foundation for the next thirty years, while I would build a career in musical theatre and beyond. Who knows, perhaps I would have become an actor without his help, but William certainly sped up the process.

That afternoon, Tom, Karl and I took the dogs for a blustery walk on Dartmoor. I have a memory of standing on the top of a giant rock that afternoon, leaning into the wind at an almost 45-degree angle. That moment takes me straight back to the day my new life began. It's like I'd just been given a set of wings and this was the moment the wind lifted me up – and now I was able to fly.

21

I knew nothing about colleges, but Louise Ryan suggested I apply to the London Studio Centre for a three-year diploma in Musical Theatre. I was confident in my singing ability but had minimal acting experience and had never had a single dance class. Louise waved away my doubts.

'You've been given this incredible opportunity, so just run with it,' she said. 'Absorb everything and see where it takes you.'

My nerves didn't improve when I was sent the list of items I would need for the audition. Ballet shoes, jazz shoes, tights, leotard, jazz trousers … Apart from the jockstrap, a staple of most gay men's wardrobes, I wasn't even sure what half the stuff was. The suggested stockist was a dance shop in Covent Garden, so I got the train up to London. The shop had pink walls and draped velvet curtains and was full of willowy girls in buns trying on pointe shoes. Completely out of my depth, I gave my list to one of the assistants; she took my measurements and handed me a surprisingly small bag in return. I remember looking inside at my purchases and thinking: *Where's the rest of the material?*

On the morning of my audition, I arrived at the London Studio Centre in Kings Cross, where I would be spending the day in classes watched by a panel of teachers who would assess the candidates' ability (or lack of). I was struck by the fact that many of the other kids waiting to audition had been accompanied by their parents. I'd been living such an independent life for over a year it was almost a shock to be reminded that most people of my age were still living at home. I remember watching a boy's mother fuss over him and couldn't help imagining what it would be like to have Mam here with me. Since leaving home I'd had to grow a tough shell to protect myself, but at moments like this, when I let myself wonder what might have been if I hadn't been forced to leave my parents' care at such a young age, the sense of sadness and loss was always close to the surface. It was safer, I'd learned, to keep that door closed.

We were shown to the changing rooms to get ready for ballet class, which would then be followed by jazz, contemporary dance and finally singing. I glanced around at the other boys as I wriggled into my tights. I was a skinny, gangly kid, lacking the poise and confidence of the more experienced dancers, and felt painfully self-conscious in the skin-tight dancewear. Some of the boys were chatting, others were expertly warming up; they appeared completely at home in what for me was an alien environment. My new ballet shoes stood out from the scuffed, well-worn shoes of the others, marking me out as the complete novice that I was. Some even had holes in their tights, no doubt worn through by hours of expert pliés and relevés. My hands were so clammy that I struggled to pull up my leotard. *What the hell am I doing here?* It wasn't the last time that day I would ask myself this.

In the ballet studio, the teacher instructed us to line up along the barre. Across the other side of the room, a table of five or six people sat watching us, pens poised.

'Okay everyone, first position please.'

I didn't know what this meant. The only dancing I'd ever done was at Club X, and you couldn't really call that dancing. I glanced around and saw the other boys bring their heels together, so I did the same.

'And now second position,' said the teacher.

Again, I just copied what the others were doing.

At third position, however, the wheels started to come off, and by fifth position the teacher came over to me and said, not unkindly: 'Perhaps you should go to the back of the group so you can follow what the other boys are doing?'

I tried my best, but I must have looked ridiculous. The others moved as naturally as if they'd been doing ballet all their lives (which many of them probably had) while I flailed around at the back, constantly tugging at my leotard to stop it riding up my arse crack. I was burning with embarrassment, but I knew there were people who believed in me enough to get me in this room and I owed it to them to stick it out. I was doing it for William, Karl, Tom and Louise as much as myself. Besides, if I walked out of this audition, what did I have to go to?

The jazz class was equally painful, though I quite enjoyed the contemporary dance class, because it allowed you to move in a more interpretive way. And then, finally, it was time for the singing audition. I was relieved to at least be finishing the day with something I knew I could do.

I walked into the room to face the same panel of teachers who'd been watching me all day.

'I bet you're happy you've got to this part of the day,' one of them said.

I laughed. 'Yes, actually, I am.'

'Well, off you go then.'

I sang 'Bring Him Home' from *Les Misérables*, a song I'd performed many times at Eisteddfods. When the last note died away I looked at the panel, hoping for maybe a smile or word of approval, some sign that I wasn't a total no-hoper, but they all had their heads down writing notes. After a moment one of them looked up, thanked me for my time and that was it: I was dismissed.

On the train home to Cardiff, I stared out of the window, replaying the day's disasters in my head. I was doubtful that my voice, as strong as it was, would be enough to make up for my total lack of dance talent, and if I'd failed this audition (and I must have failed, I thought, as the memory of my tragic attempt at a pirouette had me cringing all over again) then what future did I have? I felt as if I had let everyone down.

• • •

The next day I went into the office as usual. I'd always been happy in my job, but now that I'd had a glimpse of an alternate future, I found myself bored and irritable: compared to a career on stage, processing finance applications seemed dull beyond belief. Yet as the weeks went by without any word from the London Studio Centre I began to resign myself to the unhappy fact that I hadn't got a place, and would have to find something else to do with my life.

. . .

'Luke, stop what you're doing. I have news.'

It was Louise on the phone. There was an energy to her voice that made me instantly put down the paperwork I had been dealing with and pay attention.

'What is it?' I asked.

'You've got in.'

My breath caught in my chest. Did she mean …?

'The London Studio Centre have offered you a place,' she said.

'Oh my God …' I slumped back in my office chair, then my face slowly stretched into the widest grin. 'This is amazing!'

I could hear the smile in Louise's voice. 'Didn't I tell you that you could do this?'

'I can't believe it … So what do I do now?'

'You hand in your notice.'

Louise was blunt. She didn't suggest I take time to discuss it with my parents or consider my options, because we both knew this was the only one I had. Although I was sure Mam and Dad would be thrilled to hear I'd got into college because they knew it would make me happy, I was also well aware that what they really wanted, deep down, was for me to come home and rejoin the religion, even though I'm sure by this point they'd accepted it wasn't ever going to happen. I knew they wouldn't have been able to relate to my drive to better myself and build a career, because the only ambition you were encouraged to have as a Jehovah's Witness was to be a better Jehovah's Witness. Any decisions about my future were solely down to me. So I did what Louise told me, handed in my notice and a few weeks later Tom and I said goodbye to Cardiff.

. . .

The month before I started college, we moved into an apartment on Tower Street in Covent Garden, which was owned by William and Karl but had never been lived in. It was the penthouse flat, with stripped wood floors and a spiral staircase that led from the living room to the master bedroom. It was just a few stops on the tube to the London Studio Centre and close to Tom's new office in Chelsea. After all the years of wishing and dreaming, I had done it: I was seventeen and living in London. And not just anywhere; in the heart of the West End. I remember, the morning after we moved in, pouring some cereal into a bowl for breakfast when I glanced out the window at the opposite building and looked straight into the eyes of Andrew Lloyd Webber. In an instant I was whisked back to that grotty little caravan in our garden, sitting on Amanda's knee, listening to *The Phantom of the Opera* on repeat – and here I was, face to face with the man who wrote the music I loved so much! I instantly ducked down out of sight, embarrassed I might shriek or otherwise embarrass myself. I later discovered that his company, The Really Useful Group, had their headquarters in the building opposite, but coming face to face with the godfather of British musical theatre on my first day in London – days before starting a course in musical theatre – felt very much like a sign.

I told my parents that Tom had got a job in London so was moving to a flat in the city and had asked if I'd like to rent his spare room again. They were already thrilled that I'd got a place at college (I told them I'd won a scholarship, which is the same story I've told everyone until now) and in a monumental stroke of luck, my landlord was moving to

London at exactly the same time! As my Auntie Elaine said: 'I don't know how you do it Luke, but you fall in shit and come up smelling of roses every single time.'

You might wonder why my parents so easily accepted this explanation, but people will believe the narrative that best suits them. Their son was happy, healthy and getting opportunities they could never have provided for him. And perhaps, deep down, they knew that if they prodded this house of cards even slightly it would collapse, and they would then have to face up to some very uncomfortable truths. No wonder they preferred to take my version of events at face value.

Now I was living in London I couldn't wait to wake up in the morning so I could get out to explore the city. I would walk to the South Bank, then up through Covent Garden, check out the galleries round Trafalgar Square, walk along Oxford Street into Fitzrovia and then up to St Paul's, where I'd jump on a bus back to the West End. Pretty soon I knew the city so well I could have got a job as a tour guide. When I was back at the flat I would lean out of the kitchen window and watch the world go by, as mesmerised as that kid who sat for hours in the window of the cafe on Old Compton Street, soaking in the city when he was supposed to be having a slice of Battenberg with Pam and the other theatre ladies. I walked down Tower Street the other day and looked up at my old window. It would be a very cool place to have a flat even now – imagine living there as a seventeen-year-old! But I knew how lucky I was and didn't take a moment of it for granted. Now, I just had to prove myself at college.

22

These days the London Studio Centre is based in North London, but when I was a student in the late nineties it was on York Way, just around the corner from Kings Cross station. Let me tell you, this was nothing like the Kings Cross of today, which is home to high-end boutiques, restaurants and the headquarters of Google and the *Guardian* newspaper. Back then York Way was the sort of street you'd take a lengthy detour to avoid walking down. Every morning you'd see these little dancers in legwarmers and new Buffalo shoes they'd bought that weekend, picking their way through the shit and rubbish to get to college. Standing by the entrance, a few steps away from a half-naked tramp scratching his balls, there would be a couple of ballet dancers, hair scraped into the tight bun we called a 'Croydon facelift', smoking a cigarette. You passed through that door and suddenly you were in a different world. You'd hear echoes of people warming up, laughter, bursts of piano from one of the dance studios. It was full of light and colour, a magical place that only felt normal when you were inside those walls. The second you stepped outside that rarefied environment you were like: *Oh yeah, that wasn't real life.*

I remember feeling very conscious of being an outsider on my first day at college. I arrived early and went down to the canteen in the basement to wait. This was where everyone came for lunch during the one break in the college's very strict daily timetable. It was run by a lovely Spanish couple; I didn't realise until years later that the delicious potato thing I had for lunch every single day during college with ketchup and coleslaw was actually a traditional Spanish tortilla.

That first morning the canteen was full of people – Brazilian dancers, Northern kids, Londoners, contemporary dancers from Argentina, Russian ballerinas – and they all seemed to know each other. Intimidated by their easy confidence and poise, I stayed quiet and fell into my usual role of the observer. It was the first time I'd been in an educational environment since leaving Bedwellty Comprehensive and I couldn't help looking around at all these new faces and wondering if there were any bullies among them. This place felt very different from school, though. Everyone seemed happy and positive; there was none of the lurking sense of menace I'd been so horribly familiar with at Bedwellty. Besides, *I* was different now; I had life experience and I had a voice. I was confident that I could stand up for myself if I needed to.

In those early days at college I was very much on the back foot. As a musical theatre performer you need to be able to do everything: dance, sing and act. Some of the students in my year were true all-rounders, such as Scarlett Strallen, the niece of musical legend Bonnie Langford, who was an amazing singer, dancer and actor with magnetic stage presence and would go on to star as Mary Poppins in the West End. I knew that I could sing, but that was just one string to my bow, whereas I needed at least seven. Everything else I would have to pick up from scratch – and fast. This was when I first started to suffer with imposter syndrome. I would question myself constantly: *Am I worthy of being here, or just lucky?* Most of the other students had been planning a career in musical theatre for years, but this opportunity had appeared for me out of the blue. I hadn't thought about it until William and Karl offered me the bursary. This sense that I wasn't quite good enough and that the bubble could burst at any minute would follow me well into my future movie career.

We were divided up into four or five different grades for each of our classes, so at least I wasn't having to try to keep up with kids who'd been in ballet shoes since the age of two. Unsurprisingly, I started in the bottom grade for all the dance disciplines, but I approached everything with the mindset of working hard, doing my best and then seeing how good I could become. I'm sure leaving home at a young age was the reason I was so focused. A lot of the other students had come here straight from school, so they'd gone from living at home into digs arranged and paid for by their parents. I knew far more about the world than they did; I also knew what it was like to *have* to work. I would listen to their conversations about clothes or music or shows they'd seen and would realise just how different my life had been from theirs. While they'd been having a carefree teenage existence, I'd been working out a way to leave home and survive on my own. If this didn't work out, they had a safety net; I knew this was my only shot.

. . .

As much as I loved the London Studio Centre, with hindsight it was completely the wrong college for me, because it was so dance orientated. We started every morning with ballet. Our teacher, Anita Young, tried her hardest with me, but the only positive thing I can say about my technique is that I could point my feet really well. 'Look at that arch!' the class would gasp. Anita once told me that if my pointe was on any other boy in the school she'd have the next Nureyev on her hands – 'but sadly it's on you, dear.'

I was excited to try tap, but my ability wasn't a match for my enthusiasm. The teacher, Alison DuBois, was the most amazing dancer and extremely patient, but I just never managed to master it. Still, that little Witness kid who'd badgered his parents for metal plates on his shoes, so he could go tip-tapping down the street while knocking doors in New Tredegar, absolutely loved it.

Contemporary was the only style of dance that I actually became rather good at. As I mentioned, it involved a degree of improvisation and I just seemed to have an instinct for it. Our teacher, Sue Goodman, would pull me up in front of everyone and get me to demonstrate what she had just asked the class to do.

'Do you know why Luke can do this without any problem?' she'd tell the class. 'It's because you lot have all been trained by terrible teachers and picked up bad habits. Luke hasn't got any, because he'd never had a single class before he came here and he's now learning correctly from me!'

As with all the other dance classes, I started contemporary in the bottom grade, but by the end of three years I'd been moved into the second highest. I even performed in one of our end-of-year shows, which for a novice dancer like me was quite an achievement.

Dance was such a focus that the acting classes always felt like an afterthought, which was frustrating because I felt I had much more to offer as an actor. It was something I knew I could do – and had loved – from taking part in school productions, and I wanted to build on that initial spark of interest and develop my technique, but there were far fewer acting classes compared to dance and we would learn something different every week, so there was never a chance to progress. I'd always leave class wishing it could have been longer.

Drama was taught by Ian Dewar, a lovely guy and quite an eccentric character. I remember him going through the register in our first class and destroying everyone's names. 'Who's Katie Clark? You? Well, you'll obviously have to change your name. You'll never work with a name like that – terrible!'

We would grow accustomed to Ian's manner, but it was quite the introduction.

The class I lived for was singing. It was my joy. I would always be the first outside the classroom waiting for it to begin. Philip Foster, our singing teacher, still remembers me asking if could stay behind to talk to him after our first class. I wanted him to know that I'd already had a year of singing lessons – not because I thought I knew everything (although

Philip jokes that I did seem a little too sure of myself) but because I was desperate to progress. I didn't want to waste time going over stuff that I already knew. Thanks to the lessons with Louise and my natural ability I felt I'd already mastered things like breath control: Philip would get us to hold a note as long as possible and I was able to keep going for twice as long as everyone else. What I didn't realise on that first day, however, was that while I might have a strong technique, Philip would help me understand how to use my voice to emote and tell a story. He taught me a great deal and has played a big role in my life and career.

* * *

For the first six months of college I didn't really fit in. Many of the other kids were so loud and colourful, extrovert peacocks to my quiet little sparrow. I became friends with a girl called Carly who was very sweet and funny and seemed – for want of a better word – normal, like me. We both came from similarly humble beginnings. She had been raised by a single mum and worked in a burger van in Camberley market at weekends, and like me, she needed to make her money last. Carly always knew about the best discounts and where you could find a half-price lunch.

    I gained more friends as the months went by. Once word got around college that I was a strong singer, people would come up and talk to me about it. It gave me an identity in this fantastical bubble of larger-than-life characters. I still felt as if I was never going to catch up with everyone else, but I was so happy. I loved every single minute of college. It was such a celebratory and positive place. I'd been nervous about going back to education after my experience at school, but I never encountered even a hint of bitchiness, which validated my assumption that the bullying I'd gone through as a child wasn't because of who I was, but the place I'd been in. I'd always hoped that the rest of the world wasn't like that and it was joyous to have been proved right.

23

The week before Tom and I moved to London, I had a leaving party at Minsky's Showbar, a drag cabaret in Cardiff. All the friends I'd made since leaving Aberbargoed came to say goodbye: Helen, Ruth, Max, the boys from the squat. Louise Ryan was there too, and she brought a friend with her. This woman had dark hair, dark lipstick, big boobs and was wearing high heels and tight jeans that put a wiggle in her walk. She looked familiar, but I couldn't place her until she came over to introduce herself.

'Hi, I'm Maria Church,' she said, while behind us on stage Miss Kitty belted out 'Hey Big Spender'. 'I'm Charlotte's mother – we met at Louise's house?'

Of course! The little girl with the big voice. We chatted for a while and Maria told me they might be coming to London in a few weeks. I told her to get in touch if they did; sure enough, in typical Church fashion, two weeks later Maria was on the blower asking if they could come and stay with us in Covent Garden.

Who knows why you click with certain people? Charlotte was only eleven at that time, five years younger than me, but even then she had a mature head on her shoulders and would process things in the way of someone twice her age. That weekend the four of us instantly hit it off. I would later realise that the thing about the Churches is that you very quickly feel part of their gang.

Charlotte and Maria were in London because Maria's sister Caroline, who was also a singer, was going to be appearing on *The Big, Big Talent Show* with Jonathan Ross, a sort of nineties precursor to *Britain's Got*

Talent. Each week the show introduced five new entertainment acts that would then be put to the public vote. Jonathan interviewed a friend or relative of the performer before each act and Charlotte (who was then completely unknown) had been chosen to introduce her aunt.

Tom and I went to watch the show being filmed. You can still find the clip online: Charlotte is so small she's dwarfed by the armchair she's sitting in, but she has this dazzling smile and not even a hint of nerves. Jonathan mentions that he's heard Charlotte sing too and asks if she'd like to give the audience a little burst, so she stands up – cool as you like – requests a 'C' from the orchestra and sings a few lines of 'Pie Jesu'.

Well, the audience went mad. Hearing this gigantic mezzo-soprano come out of this little girl's mouth – it made no sense at all! It was a disaster for her poor aunt, because how on earth do you follow something like that? Two weeks later Caroline had gone back to cabaret and Charlotte had signed a deal with Sony's Epic Records.

From that point on, the ball rolled very fast. Two days after their first visit, the Churches were back with us again for meetings with music executives and managers. I'm sure they would have put her up in the Dorchester if she wanted, but she preferred our spare room. I don't think they ever stayed in a hotel again. At one point, Charlotte and Maria were staying with us for at least a few days every week.

It was a lovely time in our lives. Every evening Tom would cook dinner for the four of us and Charlotte would tell us about meeting Richard and Judy on *This Morning* or recording her album at Abbey Road studios. She did so many amazing things in those early days, and it was wonderful to be a small part of it. I got to know a few of Charlotte's team at Sony, including Paul McGhie, marketing manager of Epic Records, who later became a good friend. One day Charlotte had a meeting with the big boss of Sony Epic – the guy who had signed Celine Dion – and to my excitement she said I could come with her. I sprinted out of college that day, jumped on the tube and met Charlotte and Maria at Sony's offices in Soho. I remember looking at the framed discs on the walls, imagining all the legendary artists who had passed through these doors. It was an extraordinary feeling for an aspiring singer. Was I envious of what Charlotte was doing? Oh, absolutely – 100 per cent! I might have been training for a career in musical theatre, but I would have dropped everything to become a recording artist. I never for a moment begrudged her success, but it certainly crossed my mind that once I'd graduated I might have a foot in the door at Sony because I'd already made these connections.*

I remember going to watch Charlotte perform on *Top of the Pops* when she was still very young, probably no more than thirteen. Ricky Martin was also appearing on the show and he stopped by her dressing room to say hello.

'Hey, Charlotte, great to meet you,' he said.

Maria and I glanced at each other, wide-eyed – *it's Ricky fucking Martin!* – but Charlotte was unfazed.

'Hiya, Ricky,' she trilled. 'How ya doin' love?'

'I just wanted to say how amazing you are. That voice! Wow.'

'Aww, thanks love,' she said.

I was just sitting there open-mouthed. Here was Ricky Martin, probably the hottest man on the planet at that point, talking to this chirpy little sprog. Madness!

• • •

Looking back, there was an element of Charlotte and Maria acting as the cement in my relationship with Tom. Our lives were now very different from when we'd been living and working together in Cardiff: I would spend the day at college with other people of my age, while Tom would be working at his office in Chelsea. I didn't socialise much

---

* It didn't happen – and that was okay.

with the other students in those first months, because I knew Tom would be waiting for me back at the apartment. I didn't resent that at all: I was still finding my feet, so I valued his support and the stability he provided. Yet we were now conscious of the age gap in a way we had never been at the start and deep down I think we both knew that once I went to college the clock had started ticking on our relationship. Even if we didn't want to admit it, our lives were heading in very different directions. For now, though, the Churches were a reason for us to stay together. We had become like this weird little family. Tom doted on Charlotte as the daughter he never had, making her bacon sandwiches just the way she liked them with the fat trimmed and crusts cut off, while she adored him right back, to the point that when she made her millions the only person she trusted to manage her money was Tom.

As Charlotte's star continued to rise we didn't see her and Maria quite as much, though we kept in touch and I'd often stay with them when I went back to Wales. Within a couple of years Charlotte had become world-famous and was never out of the papers. God only knows how she coped with the harassment; she even had her mobile phone tapped by journalists. Not that anyone deserves it, but Charlotte did absolutely nothing to invite the constant press intrusion. She didn't move to London and work her way round the showbiz parties; she didn't have any celebrity friends. She just wanted to be a normal teenager, go out in Cardiff and get drunk with her mates. Unlike a normal teenager, however, if she was hanging around the bus stop with her friends, having a fag and a Cheeky Vimto, you can bet there would be a gang of paparazzi at the bus stop on the opposite side of the street taking photos. I can't imagine how you can go through that as a kid, being stalked and harassed by packs of grown men, and not let it screw you up, but then Charlotte has always been incredibly strong.

24

I didn't know what gay was until I started at the London Studio Centre, or at least I didn't know that it came in a fabulous spectrum of colours. That place celebrated anything and everything: you could be whatever you wanted and would be instantly accepted by your peers. I was now meeting gay people from all over the world with their own unique dreams, style and personalities. Some were quiet and thoughtful; others made the drag queens back at Minsky's Showbar look like Mother Teresa. There was a ballet dancer called Simon in my year who was the gayest, most screaming queen that I'd ever met. He was so flamboyant that he made me look like a rugby player in comparison. Simon was very tall, with slicked-back hair, and would suddenly drop into box splits in the middle of the corridor; when he started pirouetting you better move out of the way or else he'd have your head off mid-spin. Everybody loved Simon because he was so entertaining and didn't give a shit about anything. As much as I knew that I would never be as flamboyant as he was, seeing how comfortable he was with his sexuality and how embraced he was by everyone allowed me to relax and become more of who I wanted to be.

Looking at photos of myself from this time I see a skinny kid, clean-shaven (I could never grow anything more than stubble) with a massive cow's lick hairdo. I had tried experimenting with my look at school and been bullied for it; now I found myself in a place where the crazier you dressed, the better you fitted in. I was hanging out with dancers and would steal a little bit of each of their looks to find out what suited me. One day I'd wear extremely baggy tracksuit bottoms and no shoes, just socks, the next it might be jeans and a hoodie. Another day it could be a very tight top with flared jazz pants. I never stuck to one look, and this magpie approach to dressing – picking things up here and there that catch my eye – has continued throughout my life. With age I've accepted certain things look better on me, but back then I would try anything. I would go to army surplus stores and buy parachute trousers to wear with big sneakers. I even found a scarf on the street one day, took it home and washed it; I wear that scarf to this day. And I still loved the way a suit looked on me. The wonderful thing about college – and London itself – is that you could wear whatever you wanted and nobody said a word.

After six months living at Tower Street, Tom decided he wanted his own place and bought an apartment on London's South Bank, right next to where the Millennium Wheel (aka the London Eye) stands today. It was in the old Shell office building, now rechristened the Whitehouse, and was one of the first residential developments in that area. The South Bank was still a bit rough in those days: kids would skateboard in the graffitied concrete vaults under the Royal Festival Hall and there were none of the smart shops and restaurants you find there today.

As much as I had loved Tower Street, the Whitehouse certainly didn't feel like a step down. Our apartment had views of the Thames, and there was a gym and pool for residents. Cilla Black was one of our neighbours, though I never saw her. This was around the time that London became a property hot spot for overseas investors and I remember when we moved in being struck by the fact that the number four was missing from the apartment numbers as it's considered unlucky in China.

My mam made the curtains for the two bedrooms, one of which was Charlotte and Maria's and the other mine and Tom's (or one was mine and the other was Tom's, depending on who was asking). I wasn't seeing much of my parents at this time, but they were proud I'd made it to college – though if I'd told them I was moving back to Aberbargoed I know they would have been even happier. They'd occasionally ask if I thought about the religion, clearly hoping I might change my mind at some point, but they didn't push it down my throat. The distance between us suited me; I still felt I needed to detach from them and grow into the version of myself I wanted to be.

...

Tom and I didn't have a very 'gay' life before we came to London. We didn't go to gay bars together and we mainly socialised with women. Now, all of a sudden, I was surrounded by handsome gay boys of the same generation. Ridiculous as it sounds, this was something of a revelation to me: *Oh my God, there are people of my age who are gay?* There was a German guy called Laurence in the year above who I had a crush on, a strapping giant of a man and an amazing dancer, and I still remember my astonishment at discovering that he was gay.

As the months went by, I became friends with two gay boys in my year, Matthew and Nuno. They opened my eyes to the fact that there was a whole lifestyle that came with being gay. I would hear them talking about their Friday nights out at the bars and clubs and begin to feel that I was somehow missing out. Was there a part of my life I should be living but I wasn't, because I was with someone so much older than me? If an opportunity for a night out came up I wanted to be able to grab it, but I was always aware that I needed to get home to Tom. What had been a comfort at the start of college now felt like a weight around my neck.

We didn't talk about it, but Tom must have been aware of all this. I started to not come home straight after finishing college. Nuno, who was a flamenco dancer, might take us to a Spanish bar, or we'd go to see a show with discounted student tickets. Tom never once came out with my college friends; our lives were increasingly separate. As the end of my first year approached, I came to a decision. While the thought of leaving him terrified me, it had reached the point where I knew I had to go.

Tom didn't try to change my mind when I told him it was over, but we were both very sad. There were a lot of tears that day and on those that followed. He told me he'd been expecting it to happen since we left Cardiff, which was hard to hear. Clearly, though, Tom had far more life experience and knew that an eighteen-year-old was going to want to spread his wings – which, of course, is exactly what happened. I was very proud of our relationship. We had helped each other through a difficult period in both our lives, standing by each other when either one of us might reasonably have decided it was all too messy and thrown in the towel, but I think we both knew it had run its course.

Our split was as amicable as these things can be. We moved to separate bedrooms for the final days of term and I immediately put a notice on the board at college asking if anybody was looking for a flatmate for next year. Tom reassured me that I wouldn't lose my bursary from William, which was the most selfless thing anybody could do when their heart was being broken. Yet I felt no relief about having made the decision to end our relationship. I felt selfish and stupid, and for a time wondered if I'd made a terrible mistake. I'd had an incredible partner who had supported me in every respect – I'd never had to think about paying for food, clothes or holidays – and I'd thrown it all in the bin, all because I was a bit envious of my friends' social lives.

25

I arrived back in Wales for the long summer holiday with few possessions, but weighed down with anxiety and depression. As much as I love my parents' house, to this day going back to Aberbargoed reminds me of those early years of unhappiness – and if it's bad now, imagine how much worse it was back then, fresh from my split with Tom. I thought I'd managed to escape, but as soon as I set foot back in my bedroom I instantly reverted back to the confused, angry kid of three years previous.

The weeks were bleak and unending. I was desperately missing Tom. I didn't have anyone to hang out with, because I was distanced from my Witness friends, Laurie and Emma, because of the years that had passed and my life in London. I visited Helen and Ruth in Cardiff, but then I always had to come back to my bedroom again, where I would endlessly dwell on my fears about the future. Where was I going to live in London? How would I pay the rent? And what compounded it all was the fact that I couldn't talk to anybody about how I was feeling. Once again, I was having to cope with it all on my own.

One night it all felt too much, so I took myself off to bed very early. Better to be on my own and lick my wounds than have to fake a smile and pretend I was fine. I remember feeling particularly desperate and lonely that night. My parents didn't know anything about what I'd been through; they knew nothing about my entire life! It was their fault that I'd been forced to lie about who I was and all that had happened to me since I left home.

As I lay on my bed, a storm of terror and blame thundering away inside of me, there was a tap at the door.

When I didn't answer, Mam's head appeared. 'Are you okay, Luke?'

I nearly laughed. 'No, not really,' I said, turning to face the wall.

'What's wrong, love? You haven't been yourself since you got back.'

'I'm just dealing with a lot right now,' I said, hoping she'd get the hint and leave. Instead she came over and sat on the bed.

'Talk to me about it. I'm your mother.' She put her hand on my arm. 'Please, Luke, I'm worried about you.'

I could tell by the tone of her voice that she wasn't going to be fobbed off.

Christ, I thought, *what do I do now? Is she going to force this out of me?*

I turned to look at her. 'Mam, there are a lot of things you don't know.'

'Well, tell me then! What on earth's going on?'

From outside I could hear the dull thudding sound of Dad chopping wood.

'There's so much I need to tell you,' I said, 'but I either tell you everything or nothing at all. And you won't like a lot of it, but I'm not going to beat about the bush or tell you half a story. If I open my mouth, I'm not going to stop until all of it's out. So make your choice and I'll respect whatever you decide.'

She held my gaze. 'I've never seen you so unhappy Luke, so you're going to have to tell me. All of it.'

'Okay.' I took a breath, not quite believing what I was about to say. 'Mam, I'm gay.'

. . .

She listened in silence as I told her that I'd known I was gay for years, that it was the reason I left home and that I'd been living as a gay man ever since. She was calm – at this point there were no tears or denials – but when I paused to take a breath she stood up.

'We're going out for a walk,' she said.

That was the moment when I let myself hope this might all be okay.

She wasn't shutting me down or refusing to listen like she'd done before; she wanted to hear me out.

We put on our coats and slipped out the front door – 'We're just popping to the chip shop!' she called to Dad – then we headed down the hill and kept walking as the whole story flooded out of me. I told her everything I've written in this book, holding nothing back. I just needed Mam to know the truth, whatever the consequences might be.

I had mentally prepared myself for this moment several times throughout my life, once when my parents found my stash of books and again after Katie involved the elders, but on both occasions it hadn't happened. Now, all of a sudden, here it was and I was very well-rehearsed, because I'd already run through all the scenarios in my head. The only difference was that I'd always assumed it would be me who instigated the conversation, but this time it was Mam who had started it. I'd never even considered that as a possibility.

The relief in finally telling her the truth … well, you can't begin to imagine. I don't remember being hugely emotional as I spoke; my job was to unroll all that had happened as honestly as possible. Despite her initial calm, Mam was terribly upset. When I told her that I had been bullied for years at school but couldn't talk to her about it, she sobbed uncontrollably. It must have been such a horrible, painful thing for a mother to hear.

She flatly refused to believe some parts of the story. When I told her about me and Tom I could tell from the look on her face that it was not computing.

'Mam, it's true,' I said. 'He wasn't just a nice man with a spare room to rent. We had to tell you that about him, because I couldn't be honest about who I am.'

'No, that can't be right,' she said again.

My parents were not cynical people; they had taken my story at face value and believed Tom was my landlord. I had to pull the story apart bit by bit to try to convince her of the truth.

'Remember when I said I'd been to London and came back with a tan? I'd actually gone on holiday to Mexico with Tom.'

She was shaking her head. 'No, that's not true, you said it was sunbeds.'

It was a huge wrecking ball of a revelation, and clearly too much for Mam. My parents had loved and trusted Tom, and she was now being forced to rethink everything she thought she knew about him. No wonder she struggled to accept it.

...

After wandering for over an hour we eventually ended up in the park at the bottom of our street. It was past 9pm by now and we sat on the swings, side by side, staring out across the valley into the darkness. I was painfully aware that to my mother, what I'd just told her was effectively like handing her my suicide note. I was gay, so I would die at Armageddon; to her, it was as simple as that. I knew she wasn't upset about the fact I liked men, but because being gay meant that while she and Dad got to live in paradise on earth, they were going to lose me. It's something my parents still believe to this day. The religion has brought them an amazing community and many wonderful things, yet it's also given them this terrible cloud that hangs over them everywhere they go. *Don't forget, you're going to lose your son at Armageddon and then you'll never see him again.* I can't imagine what that's like. It's brutal.

Mam did try to bring up religion during our conversation. As a Jehovah's Witness, her duty was to protect the flock from any rotten apples – and as an openly gay man, I was right up there with the worst of humanity.

'But God hates gay people,' she began.

'I don't want to hear it,' I said. 'I'm not a Jehovah's Witness any more. There's nothing I can do about being gay – there's nothing I *want* to do about it. I'm perfectly happy with who I am.' Part of me still feared my mother might turn her back on me now she knew the truth, but during the course of that conversation I was beginning to believe that she wouldn't. After all, my parents had already dealt with me leaving the religion to live a 'worldly' life and had seen how well I was doing. I hadn't gone off the rails or acted shamefully: I was respectable, working hard at college and had good friends. She'd met Ruth and Helen, who she had liked – plus, of course, she adored Tom. As hard as it must have been to imagine us together in that way, I think the fact she liked him so much must have softened the blow when I came out to her. And when I explained what he'd done for me, helping me to get a bursary to college and supporting me, she was able to consider the situation with clear eyes, put her religious views to one side, and see that it was a good thing. It says a lot about the sort of person my mother is: you can't teach someone that kind of emotional intelligence.

As we walked back up the hill towards the house, I said: 'I suppose we ought to tell Dad now.'

Mam stopped. 'Oh no, not yet. He doesn't have the tools to deal with this. I need to get my head around everything and then we'll decide how to deal with your father.'

When we got back to the house, Mam took me in her arms and I felt so much love and acceptance in that hug that I started to cry.

'Get some sleep, love,' she said. 'We'll talk more in the morning.'

Lying in bed that night, my overwhelming emotion was one of relief. Finally, one of the two people I loved most in the world knew the real me. Mam now understood the trauma I'd suffered over the years; I no longer needed to lie or hide who I really was. And now that door had been unlocked, I was determined to wedge it open. I vowed it would never close again.

26

At the start of my second year, I moved into a maisonette in East London with two friends from college, Gianni and Gavin. My parents drove up to London to help me move in; we had told Dad that Tom was buying a new place and no longer had a spare room available. We went shopping at the Indian stores on Poplar High Street with their bewildering range of herbs and spices – food we'd never even seen before – and shops that sold everything from hamster cages to Hindu statues. I'd gone from a Thames-view apartment with Cilla Black living upstairs to a cramped ex-council maisonette in the East End, but I was happy to be standing on my own feet.

Now that I had rent to pay, I got myself two jobs: working weeknights at the Lincoln Arms, a pub next to school, and on weekends as a Christmas temp at Harrods. My parents couldn't believe it: their son working at the world's poshest department store!

I arrived on my first morning excited to find out which department I'd been assigned to. Would it be men's fashion? The room with all the giant TVs? No, it was bedroom furniture. The dullest department in the entire store.

It's not every day you need to buy a bed – not even every year – so most customers were just passing through on their way to a more interesting destination. If I wasn't helping pregnant rich women choose nursery furniture, I was giving people directions to the technology department, which was on the same floor as us. My bedroom furniture colleagues were nice enough, but they were a lot older than me, and every now and then Mohamed Al-Fayed would make his rounds of the store and it was like awaiting a visit from the headmaster. You'd stand there, back straight and mouth shut, praying everything looked perfect.

There were some memorable moments during my time at the store. I sold Jeremy Clarkson a Ferrari bed for his son, and one morning I was loitering by the mattresses when I realised the familiar-looking young couple browsing the beds were David Beckham and Posh Spice (aka Victoria Adams), who had just started dating at the time and were all over the press.

I glanced over at my manager, wondering if I should approach them, and she nodded at me to go ahead.

I sidled up to the future Mr and Mrs Beckham. 'Hi, can I help you?'

'Yeah, we're looking to buy a bed,' said Victoria.

'Of course,' I said, in my best Harrods-sales-associate voice. 'How about this model?'

They were very sweet; they were only a couple of years older than me, after all. They listened while I rambled on about the mattress, with its sixty-five layers and air pockets and titanium alloy springs and Hungarian goose down, and I can't have done a terrible job, because I ended up selling the couple what I assumed was their very first bed (which was, of course, the most expensive bed in the store).

. . .

After splitting from Tom there was nothing to stop me having no-strings fun. I was young, living in London and surrounded by people like me: for the next two years I was like a kid in a gigantic sweet shop. I wasn't interested in a relationship, but had the occasional one-night stand and dated a bit, including Laurence, the German dancer I'd had such a crush on in my first year. If I wasn't in college or at work, I'd be out with Nuno, Matthew and Simon, the flamboyant dancer who'd now become a close friend. On Fridays we'd start at the Rupert Street Bar, work our way around Soho and then finish the night at Heaven, to see Kylie or

Madonna or whoever was appearing that week. Simon was friends with a lot of very well-connected people, so he'd often manage to get us into the best clubs and parties. I was living as a free, happy gay man, with the campest dude I'd ever met as my wingman; it was an exciting time.

As young gay men, we are all searching for our own tribe. Those of us who grew up in small towns, in particular, often don't have a clear sense of our identity, so we need to experiment until we find a vibe that feels right – and during this period that's exactly what I was doing. I knew I was never going to be as flamboyant as Simon because I'd never fancied extremely camp men and in the gay world it's very much a case of like attracting like. I knew I would have to cultivate a strong, masculine image, because that was what I found attractive, though at that age I was still very skinny and boyish.

It's a little strange that even as a minority, one still feels the need to find a clique within that minority. I flitted between all the different groups – the muscle gays, the elitist gays, the twinks, the professional gays in their suits, the party gays – but despite my best efforts I never felt part of any of them. I had moments of sadness that I hadn't found a tribe, until I realised that the fact I didn't fit into any one of them also meant that I was never confined to one. The different groups never really mixed with each other, but I could be friends with them all. I guess that explains why the men I've dated over the years have all been so different.

· · ·

Now that I was living the life of a gay man it made things more complicated when friends and family from home came to visit. Mam, of course, now knew the truth, and it had made our relationship fifty times stronger, but the rest of them had no idea, and when Dean told me he was coming to stay for the weekend I was worried how my cousin, who'd been raised in a very traditional environment, would take the news that I was gay.

I arranged to meet him and his girlfriend, Rachel, (who is now his wife) in a bar in Covent Garden. I was already there drinking with friends and had warned them that my cousin had no idea I was gay, but that I was planning to tell him that night. Everyone was cool about it and said they would just follow my lead. Dean and Rachel arrived; everyone was getting on brilliantly and we were all getting a bit merry, so I decided it was time to break the news. Dean was like a brother to me, we had grown up together, and I knew it would be a huge shock. I went to the bathroom to prepare myself for dropping this bombshell on him, but when I got back to the table I discovered that one of my friends had jumped the gun and told him! And, of course, it turned out that Dean already knew; he had known for years, he said. He and Rachel held my hands in this very crowded bar and told me how much they loved me while my tears flowed – not just out of happiness, but for the younger Luke who'd been so ashamed of his identity he had hidden away, when all the time Dean had known exactly who I was and had loved me anyway.

...

Although I had lost touch with most of my childhood friends, I had managed to keep in contact with Laurie and Emma, the Witness girls. At this stage I hadn't been disfellowshipped, because as far as the elders were concerned I'd done nothing to bring shame on the religion, so in theory they were still permitted to be part of my life, even if it wasn't actively encouraged.

They came to stay with me for the weekend when I lived in Poplar and I took them to the Ministry of Sound – quite an eye-opener for two good Jehovah's Witness girls. The club night was called Pink Pushca, so I dyed my hair pink for the occasion. We had such a great time, we missed the last train home, and as we sat at the bus stop in the rain waiting for the night bus I told them I was gay. When we were growing up,

I felt there'd been a sort of unspoken assumption that me and Emma would end up together. I loved Emma, but I just assumed she knew – even if it was never made explicit – that I wasn't interested in her in that way. Perhaps I was wrong or perhaps she was simply nostalgic for the childhood friendship.

Laurie would go on to leave the religion in her late thirties, with her husband and three children, which is an incredibly brave thing to do – especially at that age, when you have kids – because you lose your entire support network overnight. Laurie and I are now close, but Emma is still very much part of the religion, to the extent that she can't speak to anybody who isn't a Jehovah's Witness. Laurie was her best friend since childhood; it's just another instance of how brutal a religion that professes to care for people can be. Where's the compassion, the acceptance that we're all different? I find it astonishing that religious dogma can lead people to act so heartlessly.

27

In the third year of college all the students had to join one of the London Studio Centre's theatrical companies. I was clearly only ever going to be in Seedtime, which focused on musical theatre, but there were also companies for contemporary dance, classical ballet and jazz. For the rest of the year, all our lessons were based around our chosen speciality; for those of us in Seedtime that meant learning song and dance routines from the big musicals, often taught by performers from the shows' original casts. We had some classes with Petra Siniawski, who had played Cassie in the 1976 production of *A Chorus Line*. Petra's personal story was the stuff of showbiz legend. She had been an understudy for the lead, but on opening night the actress playing Cassie had taken ill and so she went on instead and instantly became a star. It was an inspiring story for us students and focused our minds on the fact that we too would soon be out in this exciting new world, hoping for our big break.

Our final year of work culminated in a showcase in a London theatre, in which we put everything we had learned at college into a night of performances. It was a chance for our friends and families to see what we'd been up to for the past three years, but more importantly, it was an opportunity for agents to discover the new generation of musical theatre stars.

Without an agent, a performer will struggle to have a career. A good agent knows what productions are coming up, when the auditions will be and what casting directors are looking for. We all knew that if we left college without an agent we'd already be five steps behind everyone else, and this showcase would be our best chance of getting one.

For our Seedtime showcase, our singing teacher, Philip Foster, had written an original musical loosely inspired by the movie *Midnight Cowboy*, in which I took the role of a pre-op trans woman and everyone else in the company played my conscience. All of us, boys and girls, were dressed in minidresses and bright blonde wigs; I remember walking out onto the dark stage to get into position and seeing all these blonde bobs glowing in the darkness around me – knowing this was our one shot, but feeling so ready for it. We also performed an excerpt from *The Rocky Horror Picture Show*, with me as 'transvestite' Frank-N-Furter, and I sang a solo of 'The First Time Ever I Saw Your Face', which was already known as my song.

The audience was full of family and friends, so the applause was rapturous. As well as my parents, Charlotte and Maria came along to support me. By this time, Charlotte was a huge star and I remember a lot of excitement backstage about the fact that *Charlotte Church was in the audience!* It was a bittersweet night: I loved every second on stage, but we all had a sense that this was the finale to our time at college and very soon we would be out in the world looking for work.

The following week I got a letter from a talent agency called Grantham Hazeldine, saying they would like to represent me. I couldn't believe it. I went to meet John Grantham and Caroline Hazeldine at their office on Bond Street and they were utterly delightful. I'll always be grateful that they saw something in me and took that chance. When I started at college, I'd been so far on the back foot that I thought I'd never catch up, yet here I was among the lucky few to have secured an agent from the showcase. We still had a few months left at college, but within weeks the agency had got me an audition for a brand-new West End musical. I was on my way.

28

It's ironic that I've been linked to the role of James Bond throughout my career, because my first ever professional audition took place at EON Productions, the company behind the Bond movies, in front of Dana Broccoli – wife of legendary Bond producer Cubby Broccoli – and their daughter Barbara, who today controls the global movie franchise. It's even more ironic that despite all the chatter linking me to the role of Bond, I've never actually auditioned for it, although I'll forever be grateful that this little gay Welsh kid has been talked about in the same breath as the world's most famous English spy for over a decade.

Of course, this was all way off in my future as I made my way through Mayfair to the address my agent had given me for the audition. I was up for the juvenile lead in a new musical called *La Cava*, which was based on a novel by Dana Broccoli. While accompanying Cubby on a location-scouting trip around southern Spain for his movie *Chitty Chitty Bang Bang*, Dana heard the tale of a girl named Florinda la Cava, whose love triangle with King Roderic of Spain and a North African prince in the eighth century had triggered the Moorish invasion of Spain. I knew little about the project at this stage, but had been given a song to learn for the audition called 'I Stayed Behind', which I'd practised with Philip Foster at college until I was ready to go.

When I arrived at EON House I gazed up at the pillars and arched windows and wondered if I was at the right address, because this place looked more like a six-star hotel. Things were no less intimidating once I'd been buzzed through the imposing front door. I walked into the audition room to be faced by a vast round table, around which sat a worryingly large number of people, including Dana and Barbara Broccoli, the show's director, musical director, choreographer and assorted producers. There was a lot of power in that room; you didn't have to know who everyone was to be able to feel it.

I've seen Barbara many times over the years at industry events and to this day she still talks about my audition. 'You walked in,' she says, 'this skinny little slip of a kid, and then belted out that song and just blew us all away.'

At the time, however, the panel were keeping things very close to their chest. Once I'd sung the song, they conferred in whispers, then the musical director asked if I was able to hit a certain note. I don't remember exactly what it was, but it was high. You'd need to be a strong tenor to be able to hit it consistently for eight shows a week.

The moment I sang that top note and saw their reaction was when I first felt a glimmer of hope that I might be in with a chance. They asked me to sing the song again, this time including the new high note, and I could see how excited they were that I'd been able to pick it up on the spot. Here was a kid with a beautiful voice, who could instantly do what he was asked, and who would undoubtedly bite their arm off for the gig, because he was still at college. I certainly wasn't cocky about my prospects, but I began to think I might just have it in the bag.

After my agent called the following afternoon and uttered the magic words – 'You've got the job' – I sat on the stairs, my head in my hands, struggling to take it all in. *Oh. My. God.* This was the moment my friends and I had spent three years training for – and it was happening to me! I couldn't dial my parents' number fast enough to tell them. At every stage of my college journey they had told me how proud they were of me, but as much as they supported my ambitions, I'm not sure they ever truly believed that a course in musical theatre would lead to actual paid work. It wasn't a world they understood at all, because it was so far removed from their own lives. Now, though, I could tell them I had a job doing something I loved and was going to be paid well for it. I can still hear Mam's shrieks of excitement down the other end of the phone.

I floated into school the next day. I was the first person in my year to get a job. Everybody was thrilled for me, though it was a competitive environment, so for some I'm sure it was through gritted teeth. My friends were genuinely happy, though. 'We knew you were going to do this,' they told me. It was a magical moment.

Within a month of that audition I was in rehearsals for *La Cava*. I never went back to college; I never officially graduated, in fact, although they still consider me an alumnus. Despite three years of never once putting pen to paper, the teachers told me I would need to write a 5,000-word essay about my experience from rehearsals to opening night in order to get my diploma. This made no sense to me. I'd achieved what I came to college to do: I'd got a role in a West End musical – surely that was enough to allow me to graduate? But no, apparently not: they needed that bloody essay. I was allowed to attend the graduation ceremony, where Wayne Sleep presented me with a fake diploma (a rolled-up sheet of blank paper that looked like the real thing), I got my photo taken with him and celebrated with my friends, but I'm afraid they're still waiting for that essay.

29

On the first day of rehearsals for *La Cava*, we stood in a circle and the director introduced each of us. It was a big cast, many of whom had come straight from other West End shows. The lead role of Florinda was played by Julie-Alanah Brighten, who had starred as Belle in the original London stage production of *Beauty and the Beast*, while Oliver Tobias, who starred in the movie *The Stud* with Joan Collins, played the Spanish king. Looking round at all these professionals, I felt the familiar flicker of imposter syndrome, but by the end of that first day, having sung the musical all the way through, I felt as if I was part of the company. I had earned my right to be there and decided to enjoy every minute of it.

We rehearsed for five weeks, Monday to Friday, at rooms in Lambeth. As the show's creator and producer, Dana Broccoli came to every rehearsal. She was in her late seventies, fragile, but always perfectly turned out, like a beautiful piece of china. Dana arrived every morning in her very own London taxi, which had been fitted out by her late husband Cubby. From the outside it looked like a normal black cab, but inside it was as pimped as a private jet: polished wood, leather seats, carpet, heated headrests – the works. Dana was a charming woman, paying for caterers during rehearsals so we never had to buy our own lunch, which is certainly not how it usually works in theatre.

My character, Theodomere, was King Roderic's scribe. In the final scene of the musical, after the epic fight between the Moors and Christians, I climb across the battlefield, stepping over the bodies and flames, and then the lights go down and I sit at the front of the stage and start to write down this legendary story of the Moorish invasion of

Spain. When I first read the script and realised that I sang the last song of the musical – the finale of the entire production – I got goosebumps. What a way to begin my career!

It was an extremely technical show and needed a lot of rehearsals and previews, so the plan was to open at the Churchill Theatre in Bromley in the London suburbs, where it would run for a couple of months to iron out any issues before transferring to the West End. The set was absolutely insane: the stage revolved, there was a huge wall that broke in two, and a castle that collapsed to reveal the battlefield. To this day, I don't think I've ever seen anything like it. It was so complex we had to build up a bible of contingency plans for what to do during a performance if the wall didn't fall over or the stage got stuck.

One of the standout moments of *La Cava* for me was the *Sitzprobe* (a German word literally meaning 'seated rehearsal'), which is when the cast sings with a live orchestra for the first time. I wasn't sure what to expect as I had never sung with an orchestra before, but when we got to the end of the show and I sang my finale song it proved so overwhelming that I felt myself welling up. The electricity in that room was tangible; the emotion almost too much to bear. I still get that intense feeling whenever I sing with a live orchestra, but that first time – well, it was beyond magical.

The show itself wasn't brilliant. I still have a giggle about lyrics like: 'He was a prince, he was a God, I worshipped the ground, on which he trod.' But the producers had money and the audiences came. The official opening night was after we transferred to the Victoria Palace Theatre in London, one of the grande dames of theatres, where *Hamilton* runs today. I remember the excitement and nerves backstage, our dressing rooms packed with flowers, cards and chocolates from well-wishers. The after-party took place in a giant Berber tent with flaming torches that they'd set up in Bedford Square. Mam and Dad came, and I wore a petrol-blue leather suit that I'd had made for the occasion in Camden.

I shared a dressing room with a group of boys – Daniel, Woody, Chris and Paul – and the banter never stopped. Over the run we became as thick as thieves and we're all still friends to this day. We each had our own stations in the dressing room, surrounded by lights, where we did our make-up. Paul played the Spanish queen's eunuch, so had a shaved head, a white face, red lips and eyeliner (and, of course, no genitals). Woody had come straight from a run in *Cats*. He played a warrior, but would put on his make-up like he was still one of Andrew Lloyd Webber's felines. 'Babe,' I'd say, 'you're meant to be a soldier!' After months in the same show, I guess you get into the habit of a certain style of make-up. A few of the dancers in the ensemble had come from the same show and even when they were dressed in their Berber outfits, with headdresses covering everything but their eyes, you could always see which ones had been kitties, because there'd be these warriors with eyes made up like RuPaul.

It was at the Victoria Palace that I had my first experience with autograph hunters. I admit I'd already practised my signature – most of the younger cast members had, as we were all still working things out – but I still wasn't happy with how it looked. I've been through many versions over the years and have now gone back to my original signature, which still looks nothing like my name! Over the years I'd come to realise that you always see the same faces waiting at the stage door; autograph hunters tend to move in packs around the West End, from one theatre to the next. Last year I returned to the London stage for the first time in nearly two decades and there was a girl who I recognised from all those years ago at the stage door. She couldn't believe that I still remembered her name.

After a few months at the Victoria Palace we moved for a third time, to the Piccadilly Theatre, which is quite remarkable because the cost of rebuilding a show that complex is huge. I was now working in Soho and had money in my pocket, so we were out every night, often for a late dinner at Randall & Aubin and then onto a bar or club. One Saturday night after the show, Daniel invited me to meet his friends at Abigail's Party, a bar on Brewer Street that was decked out like an apartment. The group included Peter (a talent agent), his boyfriend and their friend Tim. It was about half ten by the time we arrived and they'd been drinking since seven, so they were all extremely drunk. Tim was clearly the centre of attention. He was tanned, fit and super funny, with a big, roaring laugh. He had been an actor, but now worked in venture capital.

The group asked for the bill and when it arrived – a roll of paper the length of my arm – Tim took one look, shrieked 'Jesus!' and threw it into the middle of the table, where it landed on a candle. In case you didn't know, receipts are highly flammable and this thing went up like it was gunpowder. For a second the entire room was lit up by this explosion of flame. I stared open-mouthed at Tim, who was crying with laughter. He was clearly crazy, but he was also handsome and charming and a completely fun human being. We went to another bar, got even more drunk and I ended up going home with him.

The next morning, he asked me to read the newspaper to him while he took a bath, which felt quite sophisticated, if a little overfamiliar. I stayed all weekend and on Sunday night we went to a little karaoke bar in Kennington and I got up and sang 'Mustang Sally'. While everyone cheered, Tim shouted: 'Oh my God, I *love* this man! He can sing like a lark!' And that was the start of my first proper relationship since Tom.

Over the next few weeks, I just very casually and naturally became part of Tim's life. I'd come out of the theatre after *La Cava*, catch the bus to Camberwell, get off the stop before his street where there was an amazing kebab shop, then walk back to his flat, eat the kebab (every night – can you imagine!) then go to bed. I basically lived with him for a year.

Tim knew so many amazing people from all walks of life and my friendship circle instantly broadened. His friends couldn't believe that our relationship was lasting, because Tim had never stuck with anyone before. 'What have you done to him?' they joked. I had no idea; all I knew was that I really liked him. He was intelligent and articulate, with bags of wit and charm, and he was extremely supportive of my career. He's always said that from the day he met me he knew I would go on to achieve something huge.

Tim and I had a very fun year together and then our relationship fizzled out. I can't remember exactly what happened; Tim loved being around his friends, whereas I wanted to spend time on my own. He loved going out to parties, bars and clubs, but I wanted a bit less of that. It's weird, I know, because I was a good ten years younger. Maybe I was jealous of his friends. Anyway, we split up. For the time being, at least.

. . .

I was very sad when the year-long run of *La Cava* came to an end. I had loved being part of a company and performing to an audience every night, and because I wasn't the main character, I didn't have the stress of carrying the show. While I was confident that I would get another job, I knew it would never feel the same as this one, as it was the first. I had celebrated the Millennium and my twenty-first birthday in that show. It had been the moment all my dreams and hopes and ambitions had become a reality: an actual paid job. Now I knew I could make a living doing something I loved.

I kept one of the giant posters from outside the theatre as a souvenir. It's a photo of me singing my finale song with a quote from a newspaper review: 'It's thoroughly Moorish!' I gave it to my parents, who had it framed, and it's been hanging in their bathroom ever since. This thing is humungous – 4 foot high – and I always smile at the thought of the elders, who would come to my parents' house for weekly Bible meetings, having to sit on the toilet and stare right at me on the opposite wall.

30

Soon after *La Cava* finished, my agent got me an audition for *Crossroads*, the rebooted TV soap. The show was originally based in a motel and had run for twenty years until the late 1980s, but it was being relaunched and updated, with a slightly more upmarket hotel setting. I was up for the role of Shaun, who was the bad-boy mate of Phil, one of the bell-boys. I had zero television acting experience and my look at the time was more 'underfed adolescent' than 'menace to society'. Nevertheless, I got the part.

The show was taking over *Home and Away*'s prestigious lunchtime slot, so they had thrown a lot of money at the production, building an entire hotel inside the studios in Nottingham. I lived up there for a month and had great fun filming my episodes, though I was absolutely awful in it. I've clearly got no idea what I'm doing. My character is supposedly trying to persuade Phil to leave his job so we could go and work in Ibiza for the summer, but I'm woefully miscast. My friend Paul remembers watching an episode while he was running on the treadmill one lunchtime. Apparently, I say the line: 'Come on, Phil, you'll love it in Ibiza. Sun, sea, sand ...' – here I pause for a suggestive smirk – '*ladies.*' Paul laughed so much he fell off the treadmill.

Despite being terrible in it, I did wonder if *Crossroads* would lead to more work on television. I was interviewed by the TV weeklies and Welsh newspapers; it felt like there was momentum building. Unsurprisingly, however, it didn't go anywhere. Shaun was in the show for four or five episodes then off he went, back to the laydeez in Ibiza.

⋯

Back in 2001 there hadn't yet been the explosion in jukebox musicals (shows featuring pop songs rather than original music) that now dominate theatres, so there was a lot of excitement about two new shows that were set to open the following year: *We Will Rock You*, featuring the music of Queen, and *Taboo*, which was based on the story of Culture Club star Boy George. Everyone in the business knew these were going to be special jobs, and, like everyone else, I went up for both shows.

Auditions, by their nature, are a one-shot deal. All you have is that five minutes in the room. Imagine your livelihood being wholly dependent on you opening your mouth and singing one song. You mess it up – that's it! They may be kind enough to let you try again if they think you have something, but that's far from certain. It's quite ruthless, really.

On the morning of an audition I would practise the song at home and then keep my voice warm on the journey there by sirening, a soft vocal exercise which takes you from the lowest to the highest note of your range. I always kept a pack of Vocalzones in my bag, strongly flavoured sweets that keep your voice clear, and would suck on one before going into the room. Years later I met Sir Tom Jones at a concert just before he went on stage and he was sucking on a Vocalzone. Tom actually sings with one in his mouth, which I could never do. I'd be too worried it would shoot out and hit someone in the eye when I went for a high note.

You'd often have to wait in the corridor, so – depending on how good the soundproofing was – you might hear the people who'd gone in before you, which could either be terrifying or brilliant, based on how good they were. Then your name would be called, you'd go into the room – smile! – and give the pianist your music (this would usually be a reassuringly familiar face, as a handful of them did all the auditions) and away you'd go. Sink or swim. It's a process I've been through hundreds of times over the years.

If I had to go back to auditioning now, I would be far better at it. I'd certainly be more confident, because I'd have a body of work to back me up. Back then, however, my toolkit was extremely small: I was up against people with years and years more West End experience than I had. When I walked into that room there was no one saying, 'Oh of course, you were *marvellous* in that show!' I was auditioning for people who didn't know who the hell I was.

With that in mind, I was astonished to make it through to the final round for the lead role in both *We Will Rock You* and *Taboo*. The same director was working on both shows, so I would be performing in front of Brian May and Roger Taylor in the morning and then Boy George in the afternoon.

No pressure, then.

The audition for *We Will Rock You* was at the Dominion Theatre, which is one of the biggest in the West End. I walked onto the stage and gazed out into this cavernous auditorium, which seated over 2,000 people, more than the Victoria Palace where we had performed *La Cava*. It blew me away. *Imagine performing to this every night!* And there were Brian and Roger, these instantly recognisable rock legends, sitting in the middle of the stalls.

I was confident in my choice of song for the audition, Queen's 'Who Wants to Live Forever' (which I actually recorded with the Welsh National Opera a couple of years ago). My voice has quite a raspy nature that works well with contemporary music, which is probably what got me through to that stage. In musical theatre you really need to project and articulate every word, so you're understood by the audience seated in the gods, but that doesn't work so well for rock or pop, which is more about emotion and storytelling. These days, thanks to the popularity of jukebox musicals, it's far more common to hear musical theatre performers singing in a more relaxed way, but back then the training was quite rigid.

I was less sure about my song choice for the *Taboo* audition. I was told I needed something upbeat and pop, but my repertoire didn't include anything that fit the bill, because my training had been in musicals. So I sang 'Wake Me Up Before You Go-Go' by Wham, which, in retrospect, was possibly not the best choice, although in my defence I couldn't have known that Boy George and George Michael weren't exactly best of friends.

George was sitting in the auditorium wearing a baseball cap and a hoodie, smoking a cigarette; it certainly wasn't the Boy George I knew from *Top of the Pops*.

After I finished my song there was a long pause. George took a drag on his cigarette.

'So you came to a Boy George audition,' he said, slowly, 'and sang a George Michael song.'

'Yeah,' I said, my cheeks burning. 'Sorry!'

George subtly lifted one eyebrow, though he might as well have rolled his eyes and told me I was a fucking idiot. In that moment, if a trapdoor had suddenly opened beneath me and sent me plummeting to the basement, I don't think I'd have minded. I couldn't get off that stage fast enough when the director thanked me for my time.

. . .

I can't have pissed George off too badly, though, as a few days later my agent called to tell me I'd got the role of Billy in *Taboo*. Crazy as it sounds – I had one of the leads in a new West End show! – I was initially a little disappointed that it wasn't *We Will Rock You*. Queen had been the soundtrack to my childhood. Along with ABBA, it was the music we'd sing in the car on the way to Aberystwyth for our caravan holidays. Although I'd listen to Culture Club when it was on the radio, it wasn't ever played at home because George was a cross-dresser, which was obviously frowned upon by the religion.* Also, it had been such a thrill

---

* Freddie Mercury was obviously also gay, but somehow that wasn't considered as bad because he (usually) dressed like a man.

standing on that vast stage at the Dominion, whereas *Taboo* would be opening at a new theatre called The Venue, which was tiny in comparison. In this instance, my ego felt very much like size mattered. Within days, however, I had got over myself. The buzz around *Taboo* was such that I realised just how lucky I was to get the part.

I later discovered that it was the show's director who had made the final decision that I would be best in *Taboo*. I was in Germany filming *The Three Musketeers* in 2010 and James Corden, who also appeared in the movie, got us into the opening night party of *We Will Rock You* in Berlin. Brian and Roger were there, and we started chatting.

'You auditioned for us in London, didn't you?' asked Brian.

'He did,' said Roger, before I could answer.

Brian smiled. 'You were my first choice,' he said.

31

On the first day of rehearsals, I was absolutely cacking it. I couldn't even open my mouth to speak to George, because I was in absolute awe of not only what he'd accomplished – the boundaries he had broken, his success in America, the music, bravado and style – but also what he'd survived. And now here he was, standing in front of me. *Working* with me.

Taboo the musical was loosely based on George's personal story and focused on the legendary eighties nightclub of the same name. My character, an aspiring photographer called Billy, was a fictional amalgamation of several people from George's life, but most of the other characters who featured in the show were real, including punk and New Romantic icons Philip Sallon, Leigh Bowery, Marilyn, and Steve Strange. George had known all these figures and we were going to bring them all to life in this new show, featuring Culture Club's biggest hits and original music. We were opening at The Venue, the first new theatre in the West End for seventy years. It was built in the crypt of the Church of Notre Dame de France, just off Leicester Square, and as a Jehovah's Witness boy, the irony was not lost on me that we would be recreating a nightclub, with all these freaks and extroverts from London's underground gay scene, in a church.

Being in *Taboo* was the most insane experience. The show's punk spirit exploded off stage and into our dressing rooms; backstage was always raucous with screaming and laughter. Put it this way: all of us were well aware that we weren't doing *Hamlet*. We were dressing in the craziest outfits with incredible make-up created by George's own make-up artist, Christine Bateman, whose sister had been married to Leigh Bowery, the legendary performance artist who had set up the club Taboo.

On the opening night of *Taboo*, the audience was full of punks and New Romantics – not your usual West End theatre-goers. During my first song I saw the spark of someone lighting up a cigarette in the auditorium. Most of the people who featured in the musical came to see it, which was fascinating. We had got to know them all through the story and the people behind the characters were all pleasingly on-brand. Philip Sallon turned up to opening night wearing a giant wizard's hat made out of corrugated cardboard that he'd pulled out of a skip on the way to the theatre. Anyone who'd been sitting behind him – and a good seven rows behind that – wouldn't have been able to see the stage. He was often in the audience and treated the whole thing like his own personal catwalk. One night he wore a 'hat' of shaving cream squirted all over his head. Philip was eventually banned from speaking to the cast, because he would constantly give notes to the actor who was playing him: 'No, I'd probably have said it more this way ...' Marilyn was so furious at his portrayal in the musical that he stood up mid-show, tore his programme into pieces and dramatically threw it in the air, and then strutted out of the theatre. He made sure everyone knew how much he hated it (although he was back another night, of course).

Appearing in *Taboo* was the first time I had been around so many famous people. So many celebrities came to see the show and they would always come backstage to meet us. All of a sudden I was being treated as an equal by these familiar faces, as though we were on the same level, and it was surprising to discover that they were just normal people. They may have had more interesting things to talk about, because they had achieved remarkable things and lived extraordinary lives, but they were human beings like the rest of us.

I remember my excitement at being introduced to Joan Rivers; I told George the next day, 'I think she was so overwhelmed by the show that she was crying.'

'Darling, that wasn't crying,' he said. 'She's had so many facelifts that her tear ducts are on the outside of her eyelids.'

. . .

After I'd managed to get up the courage to speak to George, we got on very well and he took me under his wing. A few weeks before the show opened, I got a call from him: he'd been at a wake and had lost his house keys, so as I lived closest to him he was on his way over. By this time I had moved to Angel, where my friend Alex ran the Chapel Bar and had a room above that I could rent, along with two other housemates. I loved the area and thought it would be fun to live over a cool bar run by a cool friend.

When George arrived – clearly quite drunk – he looked around my room and instantly zeroed in on my CD collection: 'Okay, let's see what we have here …'

My heart sank. George was a wildly successful house DJ at the time, and I didn't have anything like that amidst the Kylie and Rick Astley – plus he was bound to see my George Michael album. Sure enough, he went through every single CD and assassinated my entire collection while I sat on the bed, cringing into my pillow. We stayed up talking late into that night (*just* talking, thank you) and eventually fell asleep on my bed. The next morning George went down the corridor to use the bathroom; moments later I heard a muffled shriek and then the sounds of footsteps running towards my room. The door flung open to reveal one of my housemates. This guy worked in the toy department at Harrods, reading kids stories, and that morning was dressed in a full ringmaster costume, complete with top hat and tails.

'Is that who I think it is?' he spluttered, wild-eyed.

I said that yes, it probably was.

'Oh my God!'

Apparently he was a huge Culture Club fan; George had been like a god to him when he was growing up, so it must have been a shock to find him in the bathroom. Still, watching the Greatest Showman having a meltdown from my bed while Boy George used my toilet was one of the weirder moments of my life.

* * *

There was something very exciting about being around George's fame. I'd often fantasised about what it would be like to walk into a shop or restaurant and have people turn their heads to look at you, a ripple of whispers trailing in your wake, and to see it for real was just thrilling. I knew it was never going to happen for me as a theatre actor (the odd person would ask, 'Are you Luke Evans from the show?' though that was rare) but I had spent so much of my life as a Jehovah's Witness, having to conform and blend in, that the idea of being the centre of attention, of people knowing who you are and adoring you for it, was very seductive.

* * *

After we finished our run in the West End, the show transferred to Broadway. Rosie O'Donnell had come to see our production in London and loved it so much that she financed the move to New York. They cast an American actor as Billy, but George took over the role of Leigh Bowery and some of the other West End cast went with him.

I happened to be in New York shortly before *Taboo* opened, so I stopped by the theatre to say hello during rehearsals. The moment I walked into the auditorium I felt like something wasn't quite right. Rosie was sitting at a huge spotlit table in the middle of the stalls with her assistants, waving her arms and giving direction to the actors on stage. Rosie is a tour de force and had invested millions into the show, so had clearly taken full control. I was upset not to have been included in the Broadway cast, but when the show was unfortunately savaged by the critics I did breathe a small sigh of relief.

32

While I was in *Taboo* I did my first interview with a gay magazine. I had been featured in a photo shoot in *GAY TIMES* to promote the show and a writer from *The Advocate,* an American gay magazine, had seen it and got in touch. He was interested in me as an openly gay 21-year-old man playing a role in this very famous story of Boy George's life, so he interviewed me about living in London and working in the West End. It was a celebratory article and I was proud of it. Perhaps if I'd known where my career would go in the future, I might have thought twice about being so open about my sexuality, because there certainly wasn't the same candidness among television and movie actors at the time, but I was a musical theatre performer – it felt like everyone in my industry was gay! Besides, nobody knew me in America, so I didn't worry about the reach of the article. The possibility it might be online hadn't even occurred to me, because the internet was so new back then that I barely used it. It was only after the magazine came out that I discovered the interview was also on their website. Suddenly, I was faced with the possibility that someone from back home would see me proudly declaring that I was gay.

I phoned the journalist multiple times, begging him to take the article down from the website, explaining how much trouble it could cause for my family, but he said there was nothing he could do. Although he was obviously right not to censor the article, I just needed an immediate solution to a potential disaster.

It was too late. The following week I got a voicemail from the elders saying they urgently needed to speak to me. At that point I was still a baptised member of their congregation; even though I had left the religion at least six years ago, in their eyes I was still ordained. In the message they said they wanted to know if it was true that I was a 'practising homosexual' and they warned me that if it was, they would disfellowship me. I knew from experience the next step would be to announce in the Kingdom Hall that 'Luke Evans is no longer a member of the Christian congregation', the subtext being that you should therefore never speak to or have anything to do with him. The worst part of all this was that my parents would be sitting in the audience to hear it.

I hadn't spoken to the elders for years. They'd never asked me or my parents how I was doing; I could have been dead for all they knew! And now out of the blue I get this phone call summoning me to Aberbargoed like a naughty child. God, I was angry. I had left home while I was barely into adulthood, moved as far away as possible and built a new life where nobody knew I was a Jehovah's Witness, so as not to bring reproach on them, and now they'd hunted me down after all these years because they were worried something might tarnish the reputation of their precious religion. They cared nothing about me; worse, they didn't care how this would affect my parents, who'd been nothing but the most faithful and devoted of followers.

I didn't call the elders back – they didn't deserve that courtesy – but I phoned Mam and she agreed that we would now have to tell Dad.

* * *

A week later my parents came to see me in London. We were sitting in my bedroom, as it was the only private place in the flat, my parents perched on the bed. I readied myself to break the news to Dad. As hard as it was going to be, I was less nervous than when I'd come out to Mam two years previously. At that point I'd been in a broken relationship with an uncertain future, stuck in the place I'd thought I'd managed to escape from years before. As painful as it was going to be to hear Dad's reaction, I felt like a stronger person.

'Dad, I'm gay,' I said. 'Mam knows already.'

His immediate reaction was to do exactly what he'd been taught by the religion, which was to tell me that homosexuality is filth and hated by God. He tearfully reminded me that I was going to die at Armageddon. Didn't I want to live in paradise on earth? Why would I choose to live in such a sinful way?

Dad was getting more and more upset, but by now I'd had five years living outside the religion. I'd had strong and meaningful relationships, I'd been around inspirational people and had seen gay men with happy, successful lives. I was impervious to the religion's arguments, though his words still stung.

'I don't want to hear it,' I said, cutting him off. 'I'm going to go for a walk. I'll come back when things have calmed down.'

It was only when I was outside in the dark that I let myself cry. Although Mam had been upset when I'd told her, she'd at least been willing to listen. Dad seemed far more rigid in his beliefs and it suddenly occurred to me that he might actually change her mind. Perhaps he'd make her feel guilty for knowing I was gay yet still associating with me. As I walked the streets, I became increasingly worried that my parents might turn their backs on me.

I would have ended up wandering around all night, but then my mobile rang.

It was Dad. 'Come back to the flat, Luke. We need to talk.'

I was expecting the worst, but when I got to my room he beckoned for me to sit next to him on the bed.

'I'm really not happy about this,' he said. 'Homosexuality is expressly forbidden by the Bible, and I've no idea how I'll come to terms with it. But the important thing is that you're my son and I love you. And whatever happens we'll deal with it together, as a family.'

We hugged each other for a long time. I felt weak with relief that Dad had come round, but now worried for my parents. I knew what was going to happen next: the religion would dictate they should cut me off and have nothing more to do with me. It was going to be a tough time for them, but the most important thing was that they loved me – and love is far more powerful than any book or belief system.

. . .

Eight months later Mam and I were having lunch at Wagamama in Cardiff and I asked her what she'd said to Dad that night at my flat.

'Well, your father was inconsolable,' she recalled. 'His only son had just given himself a death sentence – can you imagine? He knew it was going to make things very difficult for us to stay in your life.'

She told me that she had held him for a while as he wept, but then pulled back and looked him in the eyes.

'Dave, listen to me. You and I can go home and deal with this together, but Luke's got nobody to help him through this. He's on his own. We cannot leave him here thinking we've turned our backs on him. As much as this is against the religion, Luke needs to know he still has us.'

I was in awe. Mam had shaken Dad into seeing the reality of the situation, to look beyond the rules and dogma of the religion they still held dear and realise what was at stake. I now understood why she hadn't wanted to tell him when I first came out to her. She'd known that she would need time to process it herself, so she was in a position to support Dad and help him deal with the news when the time came. She's a remarkably strong woman and has always been the one to carry us all.

. . .

A few weeks after our conversation in London, my parents told me that the announcement had been made. I was officially disfellowshipped; an outcast. I asked Mam why they had gone to Kingdom Hall that day.

They had known it was coming; why put themselves through the shame and trauma? She just said they needed to be there.

I think they were relieved the truth was now out in the open, but things weren't easy for them for several years after that. Dad lost all his privileges in the church and was struck off from being a ministerial servant, which is one step below becoming an elder, though he decided it was a sacrifice worth making to stay in his son's life. Some members of the congregation distanced themselves from my parents, as if the shame of my disfellowshipping was somehow contagious, and for a period I didn't often go home, because if my parents were spotted with me then it was immediately reported to the church. As time went by, however, and it became obvious that my parents were standing firm in their decision to stay in my life, people moved on and accepted this, though my dad's privileges were never reinstated.

I should be furious with the elders, that's the truth of it. I should want to burn everything to do with them to the ground. Thanks to their rules, I spent years living with the very real fear that I might lose my parents. I should be sharing my life with my childhood friends, but I can't because the religion has forbidden them from speaking to me. Yet while the elders might refuse to even have an opinion of me, I choose not to be so closed-minded. I'm not angry. I can see that the religion has brought my parents wonderful friends and a supportive community. And it will always be an eternal source of happiness, fascination and pride to me that my parents managed to rise above their beliefs, even though they are still deeply held, and make the decision to remain in my life. Over the years I've introduced them to all sorts of different people and they've been open-minded enough to understand that the 'worldly' aren't bad people, they've just chosen to lead different lives. They realise there's no need to shun anyone who doesn't share their beliefs.

I'm afraid my experience with the Jehovah's Witnesses has burned me for life. I thought one day I might feel the need to rediscover a belief in God, but I don't, and I certainly don't feel my life is missing anything because of it. Sometimes people find God when they're dying, but I find that complete hypocrisy. As far as I'm concerned, we all have the same chance to do something good with our lives, so we should focus on making the best of our precious time while we're here.

33

A friend had opened a gay club in East London and was looking for someone to hand out promotional flyers in Soho. It was summer, I was between theatre jobs and would basically be paid good money for hanging out on Old Compton Street, which is where I'd have been anyway. A guy called Olly was also on board and the two of us arranged to meet at my place early on the Friday evening to get ready.

I'd never met Olly before, but liked him immediately. As the club was jungle themed, we had to dress up as tribesmen, a detail I'd barely given any thought to until I saw the costume: a feather headdress, bamboo chest plate and a tiny pair of camouflaged Speedos.

Olly and I looked at each other. He shrugged. 'Let's just get drunk,' he said.

So we downed a bottle of cheap tequila to give us enough courage to parade around Soho on the busiest night of the week in hot pants with the club's logo painted on our naked backs. We probably got halfway through the night, binned the remaining flyers and then went out for a drink.

Olly and I became solid friends from that day on. He was part of a gang of hardcore clubbers known as the Scoobies (I have no idea why) and over time I became a sort of honorary member. As well as Olly there was Sam and Lorna, friends who'd known each other from childhood, plus a few others. After finishing *Taboo* I had a gap of about two years before my next theatre job and now my weekends were free I'd go clubbing with the Scoobies. We'd start at Atelier on a Thursday might, move onto Fiction on Friday, sleep on Saturday, spend Sunday night at DTPM and then in the early hours of Monday you'd find us crawling out of Orange in Vauxhall. Ballet Simon had already introduced me to cocaine in a toilet in Soho (and what a night that had been) but I was later to discover that ketamine, which was cheaper, and alcohol don't mix: on a couple of occasions I made the mistake of starting the night with a few beers and would later find myself standing in the middle of the dance floor at Fiction while everyone's faces morphed into pigs and rats, then projectile vomiting while attempting a dash to the bathroom.

• • •

A few years after meeting the Scoobies, Sam and I became flatmates. Olly and Lorna had started dating (I would later be best man at their wedding, and am now godfather to all three of their kids) and they had found a flat in a mansion block on Charing Cross Road. The neighbouring flat was also available, so Sam and I took it. I would be back in the West End, which at that time was the epicentre of London's nightlife, the gay universe *and* the theatre world, and would have the joy of living with friends. Plus there had been a, well, *situation* at my place in Angel, which had made me keen to move out.

One of my flatmates was a guy who worked in the bar downstairs. I had come home late one evening and as I walked up the street I remember noticing that my bedroom light was on. I thought nothing of it, but as I walked up the stairs I could hear the sound of the television coming from my room.

I pushed open the door. One of my few (but well-worn) porn videos was playing, while my flatmate was lying on my bed having a wank.

'Get out!' I screeched. 'I'm going to go to the bathroom, and you better be out of my room by the time I get back!'

As you can imagine, things at Angel were never quite the same after that.

• • •

While I was living with Sam on Charing Cross Road I worked on the door of Shadow Lounge, the famous gay club in Soho. Sam worked there too and he stayed on after I left to take a job as a waiter at the Park Plaza in Vauxhall. He was very well connected and one night after Shadow Lounge had closed, he brought a group of people back to our flat, including a businessman in his late forties called Don. I'd never met the guy, but I knew exactly who he was because he'd promised to invest in a production company that Sam was setting up with Lorna. He'd offered Olly a job as well; my impression was of a super-rich dude who enjoyed giving people a leg-up in life.

That night we got talking and Don asked me about my ambitions.

'What's your wildest dream?' he asked. 'Anything at all.'

Like any singer, I would have loved to be a solo recording artist. Even though I trained in musical theatre, I was never really fulfilled by that style of singing. It's very precise: you finish a word as the beat changes, which works perfectly on stage but restricts the emotion you can put into a song. I knew I had more to give than just musical theatre numbers. As I explained to Don, I basically wanted Robbie Williams's career.

'I can help you with that,' he said instantly. 'What do you need?'

'Well, I'd need to find a songwriter, and then record an album …'

'Which songwriter would you want to work with?'

This was the early 2000s and by far the biggest songwriter of the day was Guy Chambers, the man behind Robbie's biggest hits.

'Great, we'll call him up and get him on board,' said Don.

I was stunned: that would take hundreds of thousands of pounds! Realising he must be even wealthier than I'd first thought, I decided to push my luck.

'The thing is, I've got these debts …'

'How much?'

'About five thousand pounds.'

'Give me your bank details and I'll pay that off,' said Don.

'Oh no, I couldn't possibly accept that ...'

He waved away my concerns. 'Luke, I have plenty of money. You're clearly talented and you have dreams, and I genuinely would love to help you achieve them.'

What else do you say to that but 'thank you very much'? Don paid off my debts overnight and the following week he invited me, Sam, Olly and Lorna to spend a week with him on his yacht in Ibiza. The Scoobies used to go there every year, but I'd never been – and none of us had ever stayed on a luxury yacht.

'When we get home, we'll get Guy Chambers booked in and then we'll get started on your album,' he said.

I couldn't believe it. It was as if Don had waved a magic wand and made all my dreams come true. I remember calling Mam to tell her about this man who was going to set me up in a recording studio and pay for me to write an album with Guy Chambers.

'It's madness!' I was still reeling at this opportunity. 'It almost sounds too good to be true!'

Mam paused for a moment. 'I don't want to ruin your big moment, love, but if things sound too good to be true, then most of the time it's because they are.'

I have lived by Mam's wise words ever since, but this time I ignored her. Remember, the other Scoobies had also been promised the world by Don too and fully believed their lives were about to change; it was far easier to let myself be swept up on this wave of excitement rather than question things too deeply. I quit my job at the Park Plaza, because obviously I would need to start working with Guy as soon as we got back, and packed my bags for Ibiza. I mean ... I should have had some idea this was too crazy a plan.

. . .

Olly and I met up with Don at London City Airport. He was flying us to Ibiza by private jet, obviously a brand-new experience for me, and I remember marvelling at his large black car pulling right up alongside the jet on the runway and having our passports checked on the plane, rather than having to battle through airport security.

A car was waiting for us in Ibiza, and as we were driven out of the airport, Don pulled out several bags of white powder and held them up to us with a grin.

'Thank God they didn't check my pockets on the plane,' he said. 'The joy of travelling private!'

Jesus Christ, I thought. *He travelled with that in his pockets! He so easily could have been caught!*

The yacht was as impressive as I'd imagined. The living quarters were spread over three levels, with a huge dance floor on the top deck, an outside dining table that could seat more than twenty, bedrooms for eight, plus the crew's quarters. Don asked if we wanted to invite anyone to join us, because most of the guests wouldn't be arriving for a few days, so I phoned Charlotte. She was dating the rugby player Gavin Henson at the time and they were both up for it, so they came out for our first few nights on the boat (pursued by the ever-present pack of paparazzi). It was all very chilled: we swam and sunbathed during the day, dinner was laid out for us on the boat each evening and then we'd go on to a bar or club.

I remember sitting next to Charlotte at dinner on the yacht one night.

'Isn't this amazing?' I said to her. 'I can't believe Don's going to do all these amazing things for us.'

'Yeah, it's great,' said Charlotte, although she didn't look convinced. I could sense a 'but'.

'What is it?' I asked.

'It's just …' She dropped her voice. 'There's something about his eyes.'

'What do you mean?'

'Take a look at Don's eyes. You can see the whites all round his pupils.'

I glanced over to where he was sitting on the other side of the table.

'Yeah, but that's genetic, isn't it? It's just a bit unfortunate, that's all. He's a really lovely guy, honest.'

Charlotte frowned slightly. 'Okay,' she said, and left it at that.

Once Charlotte and Gavin had left, Don's mates arrived. They had come to take ketamine and dance all night, on boats or at the clubs, all paid for by Don, and the atmosphere on the boat changed instantly. The first evening they were there, Don took Olly and I to one side.

'Do you want to try a little bit of something special?' he asked.

We assumed he was referring to the bags of white powder he'd waved at us in the car from the airport.

He took us down to his huge bedroom on the first floor and offered us each the tiniest little bump of powder on a key. The moment the drug hit my system I experienced the most insane rush. It felt like speed, but at the most monumental level of dialled-up intensity. I'd never felt anything like it. It was stronger than anything we could have imagined trying.

'That wasn't cocaine,' muttered Olly, his eyes wide. 'What was it?'

'I don't know, but I really don't think we should do any more of it.'

Well, from that one tiny bump I was high as a kite for sixteen hours. I didn't need to eat or sleep; I just partied. We danced on the top deck all night and as the sun came up I thought it would be cool to play James Blunt's 'High', so I found the song, turned up the volume, and then turned around to look at everyone, arms and smile spread wide – and discovered I was completely alone. There was nobody else with me up there. In that instant, I came crashing back down.

. . .

Things started getting weirder after that. Don kept to his bedroom and would only come out if we went and fetched him. He seemed strangely preoccupied: you'd have a conversation and could see his mind was elsewhere, though I hadn't met many wealthy people at that stage so I just assumed that was how the super-rich behaved. One day he took me to one side and told me that Olly's girlfriend, Lorna, was a secret lesbian. I laughed and said it wasn't true, but he was insistent, gripping my arm and staring at me with these unsettling eyes. Another time he suddenly clutched his teeth, writhing in agony, and had to leave the boat to find a dentist. Although he was spending so much time in his room, I got the impression that he wasn't sleeping at all. He was clearly doing a bit too much of whatever that crazy drug was he gave us.

Then, one night, there was a huge party on the boat. We were moored out in the bay in front of Cafe del Mar, the bars and restaurants along the shore twinkling in the velvety dark like a string of fairy lights. It was a beautiful night; the boat was packed with people; everyone was dancing and having a good time. Don, however, was completely out of it. I still had no idea what he was on: all I knew was that this drug was having a seriously worrying effect on the man who was meant to be financing my debut album.

Then, at 3am, with the party still raging on the top floor, Don suddenly announced that nobody was allowed off the boat. I was with my friend Leigh and we were sober enough to realise that it was definitely time to leave.

We told the captain we wanted to get off, so they took Leigh and I back to land on a tender boat, then we sat on the beach and over the next two hours we watched this tender going back and forth, bringing everyone from the boat back to shore, as one-by-one they realised their host had gone crazy. As the sun came up, we could see Don pacing up and down across the top deck all by himself.

The next day we went and got our luggage, which had been dumped at the far end of the harbour, then rented a shitty apartment in San Antonio. It only had one bed, so we had to sleep on lilos. I had no job to go back to, my dreams were in tatters and we were stuck in San Antonio, which back then was not at all pleasant, until we could sort out our flights home. I was so scarred by the experience it would take me a good ten years to go back to Ibiza.

34

I'd been auditioning without success for two years after *Taboo*, so when I got cast as the romantic lead in *Miss Saigon* it was a big deal. I was joining the UK tour of the West End production, alternating the lead role of US marine Chris Scott with the actor who'd played him in London. The other guy would end up taking lots of time off, so I appeared in many more performances than the twice-weekly shows I was originally contracted for. Not that I minded at all: of all the musicals I've been in over the years, *Miss Saigon* is the one I enjoyed most. I loved the story, the music was incredible and Chris was a dream of a role.

It was a massive show. They brought it back recently, but the production had been downsized; ours had the staging from the original production, with a helicopter that landed on stage, a giant statue of Ho Chi Minh and scenery that split down the middle to create a black void in the centre of the stage, which cleverly gave the impression that you were watching a movie. And let's not forget the most important element of the production: the Filipino performers who made up the majority of the cast. Incredible singers, but also the kindest and sweetest of people. They were flown over from the Philippines to appear in the production and would earn good money compared to what they could make back home, most of which they sent back to their families. I grew particularly close to a guy called Jake, whose auntie was president of the Philippines and whose grandfather's face appeared on the country's banknotes. He was great fun and would pop ecstasy like it was polo mints.

The set was so immense that the musical could only be staged in the UK's biggest theatres, where we would stop for several months at a time. For me, the main downside of being part of a touring show was having to find a decent place to live in every city we stopped in. I'm not fussy, but actors' digs tend to be pretty grim. We were starting the tour at the Edinburgh Playhouse and as opening night approached I still hadn't found anywhere to stay. Thankfully, my friend Tashi's* mother knew a retired gay couple who lived in the city and would be happy to let me stay while I looked for somewhere more permanent.

David and Phillip lived on Royal Circus in Edinburgh and were the loveliest couple. I've always liked being around older people because of their wisdom and experience and in the end they were happy for me to stay in their spare room for the entire three months of our run.

I spent Christmas in Edinburgh that year. After the show on Christmas Eve, the cast went back to the block of flats where the Filipinos were staying and they cooked us a traditional banquet, including a dish of chicken's feet in a sticky sauce. They filmed me eating it, because they couldn't believe a westerner would try it. I can still remember gagging on some poor bird's knuckle as I tried to swallow it down.

By coincidence, Culture Club were playing a gig in Edinburgh that Hogmanay and I met up with George for a drink the night before. There was a whole gang of us who went out: the band's roadies, friends, my mate Robbie from the ensemble. We all got absolutely rat-arsed and by the time I got home it was already light. At 6pm the following day – New Year's Eve – I got a panicked phone call from George's manager demanding to know where he was. I had no idea – I'd left him at his hotel with everyone else – but for some reason his manager had got the idea I was somehow responsible. He was freaking out.

---

* Tashi was a former Buddhist monk who I met at Gay Pride in Finsbury Park. He was a fascinating character: he'd left his Scottish monastery after deciding he wanted to live as a gay man and went on to become a renowned master of Tibetan calligraphy. Tashi later gave me a painting of my name written with a human-hair brush, which I had scaled down and tattooed on my hand. Luke translates as 'lugg', which means 'sheep' in Tibetan: perfect, as I'm both an Aries and Welsh.

'It's your fault if he doesn't turn up for the show!' he screeched.

They found him in the end, thankfully. And they still put on a brilliant show.

• • •

As well as Edinburgh, *Miss Saigon* went to Birmingham, Southampton and the Bristol Hippodrome, which was magical for me because it was close to home. All of my family came to see the show, including Nan and Gransha. No one in the family had ever done anything like this before, then all of a sudden their grandson was in a West End show – yet I think they'd have been just as proud if I'd been working in a factory.

I arrived at the Hippodrome's stage door one afternoon and there was Mr Cormack, my old form teacher, the man who'd stopped me on my last day of GCSEs and urged me not to throw away my life. I was so pleased to see him. 'You did it, then,' he said with a smile. 'I'm proud of you, Luke.'

While we were in Bristol I lodged with my ex-boyfriend Tim's best friend, Toby, who was a terribly bad influence but a lot of fun. Tim and I had been on and off since we'd split up a couple of years before, but there was clearly still a lot of love between us, and by the time *Miss Saigon* finished, to my deep happiness, we were back together.

• • •

Now that I was free, Tim and I decided to take a couple of months off and backpack around Southeast Asia. I had never gone travelling before and was hugely excited; the only stressful part was trying to fit everything into one bag. I'm not a naturally light packer; I like having options. It wasn't until we got out there that I realised that nobody gives a shit what you look like, plus it's so hot that all you need is vests and cheap flip-flops that you wear until they fall apart.

We arrived in Bangkok in the early evening and by the time we got to the Khaosan Road, which is where all the backpackers go, it was already dark. The road had been taken up for repairs, so instead of tarmac with a sheen, it was a flat jet black. With the lights from bars and restaurants on either side of the road and this black void in between it looked exactly like the opening scene in *Miss Saigon*, which was quite surreal.

It took us a long while to find somewhere to stay. One place had vacancies, but clearly only because it was utterly rancid. 'We are not staying here,' I muttered to Tim, as we smilingly made our escape. Finally we found somewhere that seemed decent and had space for us, but the only available room didn't have windows. It had air conditioning, though, and the bed looked clean, so we took it. It was only 10pm, but we were exhausted after the flight and were asleep as soon as our heads hit the pillow.

Tim and I woke at exactly the same time, fresh as the day and excited to explore the city. We weren't sure exactly what time it was, as we didn't use our phones because it was too expensive, but we were starving and ready for breakfast, so we showered and dressed and then headed downstairs. *What the fuck …?* It was completely dark outside. Surely we hadn't slept through the entire day? No, it was half past midnight: two and a half hours since we'd gone to bed! We were so messed up by jet lag there was little point in trying to get back to sleep, so we went out and got some noodles, visited a few bars and then went to bed. The next day we checked out and made sure the next place we stayed had a window.

After Bangkok we travelled around the islands, enjoyed the beaches and full-moon parties, and then finished up in Phuket. We'd completed our Thailand itinerary but still had weeks left of the trip, so I texted Jake, my Filipino friend from *Miss Saigon*, and he replied almost instantly.

'Come to Manila,' he said. 'I'll sort everything out!'

We arrived in the city in time for Valentine's Day and woke that morning to discover that the streets had been closed to traffic and all the bars and restaurants in central Manila had stages put up in front of them for singers to perform that night. I knew that Filipinos had beautiful voices, but I had no idea the extent to which singing is part of the national culture. Tim and I were watching one of these shows over dinner when the girl on stage performed a song from *Miss Saigon*. Well, I couldn't help myself: during a break I went up and explained that I'd played Chris in the UK and asked if she'd like to sing 'Last Night of the World' together, the famous duet from the musical.

'Do you know the words?' I asked.

She looked at me as if I was mad. 'We *all* know the words!'

Of course she did: Lea Salonga, the first actress to play Kim in *Miss Saigon*, was a goddess in the Philippines. Everyone in the country knew the musical because it had brought Filipino voices to the attention of the world. So we sang the song together and it was a beautiful moment, only slightly ruined by Tim's shrieks as the rats ran over his feet.

Jake arranged for us to visit Boracay, an island famous for its white sand beaches. We flew to the city of Caticlan on a neighbouring island, where Jake had friends who offered to put us up for a couple of nights before we caught a *paraw* (a traditional sailing boat) to Boracay. They picked the three of us up from the airport in their tuk-tuk and we went back to their little house on the beach that was full of kids, dogs and chickens. The family took us to a market to buy fish, then we sailed around the island to a sandy cove. We sunbathed on the beach while they gutted the shrimp and grilled them for lunch. I knew this wasn't an experience you'd find in any of the guidebooks and relished every moment of it.

When it was time for us to leave, the family kindly invited us to a special lunch before driving us to the airport. Back at their house on the beach there were two giant pots bubbling away on the fire. While our hosts tended to lunch, Tim and I sat on chairs by the door enjoying a Filipino beer. I noticed Jake talking to the family and after a minute he walked over holding little shot glasses full of a brownish liquid.

'This is like an amuse-bouche,' he explained. 'It's the stock from the cooking pot. You drink a shot to warm you up before we sit down to eat.'

I reached for the glass, but Jake hesitated.

'There's something I should tell you first. You know that dog you were playing with when we were here last week? It's in that pot.'

'What?'

'They killed it for us to eat, because we're honoured guests.'

I blanched. 'This is dog juice?'

'Luke, stop pulling that face, you don't want to be rude. They have no idea that you're not going to be okay with this.'

'Of course I'm not okay with this!' I hissed. 'They killed their fucking dog for us!'

Jake quietly explained what an honour this was, something they'd usually only do for milestone birthdays and esteemed elderly people. In the circumstances, what else could we do? They'd been so kind to us, the last thing we wanted to do was offend them. So we downed the dog juice, then we ate the meal.

'Mmm, yummy!' I forced a smile, trying not to think about what this tasteless meat I was chewing actually was.

The mother held up another ladleful. 'More?'

'Ooh, no no no! Thank you so much! Full up!'

...

That trip was such an eye-opener for me. I found it remarkable how similar we are as humans, yet at the same time how differently we live. Despite the trauma of eating a family pet, that lunch provided another moment of wonder for me. It certainly didn't make me think, *Christ, I never want to leave Britain again*. Quite the opposite, in fact: it made me greedy to see as much of the world as possible. This had been just one tiny glimpse – imagine what else was waiting for me out there!

I came back home determined to go travelling as often as I could: to meet new people, hear their stories and, yes, to eat their food. To this day, I think it's the best education you can give yourself and anyone around you. Travel as much as you can, wherever you can, whenever you can.

35

Within a week of getting back to the UK, I got a call asking if I could step back into the role of Billy for the touring production of *Taboo*. The current actor, my friend Declan who'd been my understudy in the West End, had been taken ill and they needed me to cover for six weeks while he received treatment. I went with the show to Brighton, Bath and Cardiff, then it was back to London and unemployment.

Whenever I was between theatre work (which was depressingly often) I took whatever jobs I could to cover my bills. I wasn't ashamed; it was a simple matter of survival. My stage work didn't pay enough for me to live off while I was 'resting', as periods of unemployment are euphemistically known in the industry, and I would never have dreamt of asking my parents for money. As a result, I was always trying to top up a very empty pot in any way I could.

I think I probably worked at most of the shops and restaurants in central London at one time or another, but to top up my regular wage I applied to be a mystery shopper. A typical job might be going to Harvey Nichols to enquire about three different products. You'd then fill out a questionnaire, often pages long, about the staff's response and customer service. I'm not sure how effective I was in the role – I don't think I once gave a negative review, because I didn't want to get anyone sacked – but it was £50 a job, and if it involved a restaurant that meant a free lunch.

For a time I worked at a PR firm as assistant to one of the publicists, Cassie, whose job it was to get her showbiz clients featured in the press. Cassie's brother was in S Club 7 and I remember being annoyed that he was out there doing what I wanted to do – singing on *Top of the Pops* – while I was stuck in an office trying to persuade a journalist to mention chef James Martin's new cookbook in their magazine.* Despite my disastrous experience with Don, I still dreamt of becoming a recording artist; I even applied for *The X Factor* but didn't get an audition. Busking was out because I couldn't play an instrument. Then, through a friend, I met a singer called SJ and she suggested we put a band together.

We found some musicians and got a regular Tuesday night gig at the Soho cabaret club Too2Much. It was a nightmare from the start. SJ kept missing rehearsals, so we were always flying by the seat of our pants during performances, and within a few weeks she was gone and the show was renamed 'Up Close and Personal with Luke Evans'. I sang classics like 'Ain't No Sunshine', 'Downtown' and 'Son of a Preacher Man'. 'I've got a bit of a soft spot for this next song,' I'd tell the audience, 'because I actually *am* the son of a preacher man.' We'd also reimagine songs, reworking 'It's Not Unusual' as a ballad, for example. The show was well received and ran for several months. At one time virtually every lamppost and derelict shopfront in the West End was covered with posters featuring a large black-and-white photo of my face. I know that for a fact because I stuck them there myself!

If a job was going to make me money then I would take it, regardless of whether I was qualified. One day my friend Walt, who worked as the manager of private members club Home House, called to ask if I knew any hair stylists who might be available at short notice. One of his guests was going to a ball that night and needed someone to do her hair.

'I can do that,' I said instantly.

Walt was dubious – understandably so, because he knew I was an actor.

'No, really!' I insisted. 'I've been styling and cutting hair my whole life.'

---

* I've since been on *Saturday Kitchen* on several occasions and have told James about the small part I once played in his career!

This wasn't entirely untrue. I'd certainly spent a lot of time in hairdressers over the years, because when I was a kid Mam would take me to the salon in Bargoed every week. While she was getting her roots fixed or extensions fitted, I would sit and watch the stylist as he worked. This guy was very cool – young and handsome with armfuls of tattoos; he clearly wasn't a local lad.* I must have spent hours watching as he cut hair, and would then put what I'd learned into practice on my dad.

Back to Walt: he was clearly out of options, because he agreed to give me the job. 'But I'm telling you, Luke, if you fuck this up I will never forgive you.'

I went to Boots and bought hairspray, hairpins and a copy of *Closer* magazine (to see how Cheryl Cole and Kylie were wearing their hair) and then got the bus to Home House. On the way there I kept telling myself this was simply another acting job. *You're just playing the role of a hairdresser today. You can do this.*

When I got to the woman's room she showed me the dress she was wearing to the ball.

'What do you think would work?' she asked, sitting in front of the mirror.

I swished her long, blonde hair around in a hairdresser-y way. 'Well, to make the most of that off-the-shoulder neckline, I think we should put your hair up.'

'Whatever you like, darling, I'm in your capable hands! Champagne?'

All those hours doing French plaits and chignons on Emma and Laurie when I was growing up came in handy. I curled the woman's hair, folded it into a plait – leaving some soft bits loose at the front – then hairsprayed the living shit out of it. Incredibly she loved it, and I

---

* On Millennium Eve I was at a rooftop party in Primrose Hill with ballet Simon and he introduced me to a Welsh friend of his, who he said was a hairdresser. I looked at this guy and said: 'Did you used to cut hair in Bargoed?' He nodded. Unbelievably it was the same man!

left a couple of hours later buzzed on champagne and with £90 in my pocket. Walt was so grateful he gave me free membership to Home House, though I never went because I couldn't afford the drinks!

. . .

Not long after Tim and I got back from travelling around Southeast Asia it started to become clear that the relationship wasn't working. We'd stopped talking, which was something we'd always done very well. That summer we went to Paris, which in hindsight is possibly the worst destination for a make-or-break holiday. Everyone we passed was holding hands, kissing or sharing an ice cream, but we weren't. With every step the city seemed to be telling us: *you guys are done*. In a way, Paris finished us off, because it held up a mirror to our relationship.

We were sitting by the Seine one afternoon when Tim said: 'It's over, isn't it?'

I felt the same, but he was the one who'd had the strength to say it. There were a lot of tears; we agreed it was good we'd got back together but that we'd now reached the end of the road. I was extremely upset. It had been such an important relationship for me: Tim had opened my eyes to the world, he'd introduced me to so many people, we'd travelled together and shared so much. I knew that losing him would leave a huge void in my life. That afternoon we walked back to the hotel arm-in-arm, knowing it was the right decision but horribly heavy with the pain of it – then predictably had the best sex of our entire relationship.

Two weeks after I got home a box arrived with my all stuff from Tim's flat. Not just my toothbrush and socks, but all the presents I'd given him, birthday cards, even the letters I'd written. I was shocked: it was as if he needed to purge every memory of me. When we broke up Tim had told me I'd been the first person he'd ever loved, but he was clearly far more hurt than I'd realised, so I resolved to give him some space even though we'd promised to stay in touch.

Tim and I didn't speak for the next ten years. I'd hear what he was up to from friends, but we never saw each other. Then, almost a decade to the day since our split, I bumped into him in East London, where we were unknowingly both living at the time. It was like no time at all had passed. We slowly became closer and ended up back in each other's lives – as friends this time. One day I asked him about the box.

'You know, it was brutal what you did,' I said. 'You didn't need to send all my letters and presents back. You didn't even put a note in the box.'

Tim's face was blank. 'What box?'

Eventually we found out that Tim's flatmate had sent it. He'd packed up all the stuff while Tim was at work, thinking he was protecting him, but we lost ten years because of that box.

Nowadays Tim and I are in each other's lives the whole time. We share a house in Ibiza and holiday together several times a year. People say 'there's never a dull moment with so-and-so', but in his case it is literally true. Everyone loves Tim: he's kind, loving, authentic and can spark up a conversation with anybody. His favourite question is: 'For a pound …?' We can be at a restaurant or at a funeral and he'll suddenly ask: 'For a pound, what's on the wall behind you?' You never see the money, of course, though I'd be a millionaire if he ever did pay up.

36

A few years ago I was invited to the Oliviers to present an award. I was waiting in the wings as the presenter introduced me: 'And now, please welcome West End theatre royalty – Luke Evans!'

And I was standing there thinking: *Guys, you have got this seriously wrong.* I was never even close to theatre royalty. I wasn't even a minor aristocrat. I was the deputy footman who'd get called in if the main footman was off sick. People love to spin this glittering tale about my glorious West End career that I left behind to make movies, but I'm afraid it's utter bollocks. The truth is that I was finding it so hard to make a living in theatre that I had decided to give the whole thing up.

By my mid-twenties I had begun to accept that my career wasn't working out the way I'd hoped. I'd assumed that I'd be working consistently in theatre or TV; even a role in a soap would have been nice. Not movies – God no! It wasn't even a conversation. That was a whole other world, one completely out of my reach, but I'd hoped at least to have a degree of stability by now. Yet here I was still living hand to mouth, unable to save because I needed the money to keep me going until the next theatre job came along. My idea of financial planning was flipping credit cards so I didn't make my debt any bigger than it already was. Also, I'd decided not to take another tour, because I hated staying in other people's houses, and that had eliminated a huge amount of potential work. As much as I still loved performing, I realised it couldn't give me the most important thing I needed from a career, which was security.

This was about twenty years ago and back then the lead in a West End show would earn about £1,500 a week, an understudy maybe half of that; good money, but only if it was regular and consistent, which theatre work for me most definitely was not. Your show might be a success, which meant you could renew your contract for another year, or it might close early; either way, whenever it ended you would be back to zero and have to start auditioning again. There were no guarantees you'd get another show next month – even next year – and in the meantime you'd have to find ways to earn money. You couldn't take the interesting jobs, because those were usually full-time and you had to be available to jump back into a West End show at a moment's notice, so it would need to be something menial and unqualified, and I didn't spend three years training at college to be a hotel waiter. I was constantly worrying about money and it wasn't a pleasant place to be. Who was going to look after my parents when they were older? I had no siblings, no family money; it was all going to be down to me. I clearly needed a change of direction.

Now I just had to work out what I was going to do with the rest of my life. I didn't have A levels or a degree, so I'd have to rely on someone believing I had skills you couldn't get from university. I needed an entry level role with a lot of potential for promotion; perhaps I could work my way up through the ranks to a well-paid job in the City or get a job in a restaurant with a view to eventually becoming manager? I wanted a career that gave me consistency, stability and scope for increasing my earnings, so I could plan and secure both mine and my parents' future.

While all this was going on, I got offered a part in a new musical, *Avenue Q*, as an understudy. After playing the alternate lead in a Cameron Mackintosh production this would be a definite step down, but I needed the money, and if I had to be an understudy at least it was in the original West End cast of a successful Broadway show. Also, I would have to learn puppeteering for the role, which was something I'd always wanted to try. I figured it would be a fun, low-pressure job, and the regular wage would mean I could afford to stay in my place on Charing Cross Road (though only if supplemented with occasional mystery shopping gigs).

Jim Henson's company came over from America to teach us how to bring the puppets to life. These furry guys were the show's real stars. We human actors would go on stage in plain grey jeans and T-shirts with the puppets on our arm, so our faces were visible to the audience while we did the character's voices and sang their songs. Think *Sesame Street*, but an X-rated adult version.

It was a fun show to perform and I loved being around the creative team, who were all American, and listening to their Broadway stories. At the time the show's writers were working on a new musical with Trey Parker and Matt Stone, the creators of *South Park*. It was called *The Book of Mormon* and would obviously go on to be another massive hit. The boys behind *Avenue Q* would later write the music for *Frozen* and many more. They were unbelievably talented.

As I was an understudy I only got to go on stage every couple of weeks or so, though I still had to be at the theatre every night. I shared a dressing room with the other understudies, Matt and Gabriel; Matt has since won an Olivier for his role in *Kinky Boots* and Gabriel is currently starring as Mrs Doubtfire in the West End production, so we haven't done badly considering we were all understudies! This was the year that Leona Lewis was in *The X Factor*. I was obsessed with her. Gabriel brought a TV to our dressing room so we could watch the show, which was a big mistake because we'd always miss our cues when Leona was on. She later came to see the show; an unbelievable moment for us super-fans.

. . .

Several months into my run in *Avenue Q* I was getting ready to go on stage for the evening performance when my mobile rang.

'Luke, it's Mam.'

I could tell something was wrong just from the tone of her voice.

'What's happened?' I asked instantly.

'I'm at the hospital with your dad. He couldn't lift his head when he got up this morning. He was having to crawl across the floor, because he couldn't stand up.'

Mam sounded terrified. I wanted to yell: *Why are you only telling me this now? Why didn't you phone me this morning?* I wanted to get straight on a train back home, but I was minutes away from going on stage. I could feel my heart thumping in my chest and took a breath, trying to quell my own rising panic. The last thing Mam needed right now was for me to go to pieces on her.

'Do the doctors know what's wrong with him?' I asked.

'No, but he's having tests right now.' There was a pause. 'Luke, I'm so scared. What if it's something serious. What if ...' She tailed off into sobs.

'He'll be fine, Mam. He's in the right place,' I said, with far more confidence than I was feeling. 'The doctors will find out what it is and then we'll deal with it, okay? I'll be on the first train home tomorrow.'

. . .

In the end, it took a week for them to work out what was wrong with Dad. At first the doctors thought it was labyrinthitis, an inner ear infection that causes vertigo, but they eventually scanned his neck and discovered the remnants of a burst blood clot very close to his spinal column. They calmed the worst of the symptoms with medication and sent him home in a wheelchair, but he was very fragile and the dizziness was debilitating. He couldn't stand up or bend down; for someone who had never been ill, it was terrifying. It shook him massively.

As the weeks went by and the vertigo persisted it became obvious that Dad wouldn't ever be able to return to work. While his condition would improve, the doctors said he would always suffer from dizziness, which would make it impossible to do a physical job like bricklaying. Overnight he had gone from a healthy, able-bodied man, who for the past twenty-nine years had built houses virtually single-handed, to being told he would never do his job again. He was only fifty-three.

I helped Dad get the benefits he was entitled to, but my parents still had a mortgage and without any other source of income it was looking likely they would lose the house. The Witnesses left the occasional hamper of bread and milk, but that wasn't going to pay the car's MOT or the gas bill. When I suggested Dad start drawing on his pension, he admitted he didn't have one. Apparently the elders told them there was no point paying into a pension or a worldly bank account: 'You won't need it, because Armageddon is coming!' My parents had some meagre savings and that was it.

I was so pissed off – with the elders, but also my parents.

'You know that elder who owns that shop down the road?' I said to them. 'Do you think he has a pension? Because I bet he does!'

As angry as I was, though, I could see I was making my parents feel even worse about what was a hopeless situation. In that moment, I realised I was the only one who could secure their future. I only had a few thousand pounds in savings, but I was young and healthy with hopefully many years of work ahead of me: I must be able to sort it out. I could take ten jobs if need be, I could keep going, but for my parents this was it.

While these conversations were going on, Mam called to tell me that the family next door were moving out. You'll remember the delightful neighbour, the man who we thought had shot our cat? His house had been put up for sale. After finishing the call with Mam, I phoned up the estate agent and secretly made some enquiries. I was thinking I might somehow be able to buy the house – paying the mortgage from my earnings – and then rent it out so that my parents could live off the income. I didn't tell them any of this, because I knew they'd have instantly put me off; they would have hated to be a burden. It was a good plan, but it failed at the first hurdle: the minimum deposit I could put down was £10,000 and I only had about half of that.

At the time, my flatmate was a friend of mine called Jamie. Sam had moved out and Jamie and his alphabetised DVD collection and pleasing cleanliness neurosis had moved in. We had met in Edinburgh while I was there with *Miss Saigon*. Jamie had been the boyfriend of a friend from London; he was tall and very handsome with a deep voice and seemed quite upper class to me. He was living in a gigantic house that he'd inherited from his godparents, both of whom he'd nursed through degenerative illnesses, which he'd sold before moving to London. Jamie offered to lend me the extra £5,000 I needed to pay the deposit. It certainly wouldn't be the last time that Jamie stepped in and solved my problem (in fact, as my assistant now and right-hand man, he's probably already done it several times this week).

I paid the deposit and arranged a survey, and when the sale had gone through I went to see my parents.

'The For Sale sign's gone,' Mam told me. 'I hope whoever's bought the place is nice.'

'Shall we go and have a look inside?' I asked.

'What do you mean?'

'I've got the keys.'

She frowned. 'Why on earth do you have the keys to the neighbour's house?'

'Because I've bought it.'

I can still remember the confusion on their faces. I kept having to repeat myself, as they were struggling to process what I was telling them. Initially, I think they were just shocked that I'd managed to pull it off: I couldn't even drive at this point, yet I'd dealt with the estate agent, got the money together, done the paperwork and bought a house right under their noses without them knowing anything about it. Mam was overwhelmed and Dad broke down in tears, but once it had sunk in they were straight down the street and through their new front door. Watching them walk around that house, excitedly discussing what alterations they might make, made every bit of effort and stress worthwhile. I felt very good about myself that day. I had done something that wasn't ever going to benefit me, but had fundamentally changed my parents' life.

Just as I planned, we rented out the house to give my parents a steady and reliable income, so they could buy groceries and pay their bills. My sole concern was to secure their future. Their religion might have tried to come between us, but as far as I was concerned my parents' beliefs were none of my business. As long as I had them in my life, and they were happy and healthy, that was all I cared about.

While I was visiting my parents, someone from the congregation reported them for associating with me. The elders came round to the house and were just about to start their usual lecture about the fact I was disfellowshipped and should therefore be ostracised when my Dad interrupted them.

'I know what you're going to say, but you can stop right now. When I got sick who put petrol in the car? Who paid for the electricity? Who paid for the food in the fridge? Was it you? No, it was our son. Even though you've tried to keep us away from him, has Luke ever told us to leave the church? No. He's moved as far as he possibly can from us, so he wouldn't bring reproach on the religion, and you're still trying to drag him back into this. Well, never again. Don't come to our house and tell us not to speak to our son, because if it wasn't for him we wouldn't even have this house.'

I couldn't believe it when Mam told me this story. She said she'd never seen him be so direct and articulate. Dad had always been a stickler for rules and very conscious of setting a good example in the neighbourhood, so to hear him speak so decisively to the elders, the revered shepherds of the flock, was astonishing. If I'd needed a demonstration of the depth of his love for me – well, this was it.

'This is going to stop,' Dad had told them – and from that point on it did. The elders got up and left, and they never mentioned me to my parents again.

37

While I was in *Taboo* George had introduced me to William Baker, Kylie Minogue's creative director, the man who put her in those famous gold hot pants for the 'Spinning Around' video. I was coming to the end of my run in *Avenue Q* when William got in touch to say that he was staging a contemporary remake of the musical *Rent* in the West End and wanted me to be involved. I'd always loved *Rent*, the money was good and I would be playing Roger, one of the leads, singing songs I could really get my teeth into.

The show was a modernised version of the original musical, renamed *Rent Remixed*, and the cast included Siobhán Donaghy of the Sugababes and Denise Van Outen, who would later be replaced by Jessie Wallace from *EastEnders*. We opened in October 2007 at the Duke of York's Theatre. With William at the helm, Kylie obviously came to see the show. She was just as lovely as you'd imagine and I was thrilled when she asked me to appear on *The Kylie Show*, a special she was filming for ITV. Here was this absolute icon, whose album was the first I'd ever bought, and she wanted me to sing with her on television! It was a proper pinch-me-moment. Sadly, we didn't end up singing together thanks to ITV format rules, but I played Kylie's love interest in her performance of 'Tears on My Pillow' in which she plays a cabaret singer in wartime Paris and I'm an American soldier. You can still watch it on YouTube. I shoot longing looks at her across the bar, then we end up dancing together. I have a still from the video, signed by Kylie – 'To lovely Luke, thank you, Kylie' – still hanging on my wall as a reminder of a very fun day.

While *Rent Remixed* wasn't terrible, the updated production didn't quite work. The original was a period piece, set in rundown New York during the AIDS crisis of the late eighties, and in this new version the gritty realism that was so integral to the show's spirit was lost. The reviews weren't great and the show closed early. I was twenty-seven, creeping ever closer to thirty, which was the age by which I'd decided I needed to be financially secure, and I knew it wasn't the calibre of show I wanted to be appearing in. It didn't help that my boyfriend at the time, a LAMDA-trained actor who was doing Shakespeare at the Old Vic, had made it clear to me that he didn't consider what I was doing to be 'proper' acting. I'd see all these cool opportunities he was getting and feel increasingly demoralised about the direction my career was headed. It was a sad decision to make, but I knew I was finally done with theatre (and also the boyfriend). To say I was feeling shit about myself is an understatement.

Then one afternoon I came into work and found a letter waiting for me at the stage door. I took it up to my dressing room and opened it.

Dear Luke, it began. *My name is Duncan Millership and I work at PFD.*

That instantly got my attention: PFD was one of the top talent agencies in London.

I represent Jessie Wallace, the letter went on, *and I was in last week to watch her first night. I wanted to let you know how impressed I was by your performance. I can see that you can really act.*[*]

Well, that stopped me in my tracks. It was the first time anyone had ever said they viewed me as an actor, which was an entirely different species to musical theatre performer. Duncan asked if I'd like to meet him at Soho House for a coffee a few days later. Flattered and intrigued, I accepted.

. . .

---

[*] Which I interpreted to mean act without singing.

Duncan was waiting for me at a corner table by the window. He was sharply dressed, quite slight, with a kind face. He was a fellow Welshman, it turned out. Once we'd ordered, he got straight to the point: he told me that he thought there could be opportunities for someone like me, and that he would love to represent me. I remember the moment so clearly. Here was a very successful agent, his finger on every pulse in the business, and he wanted to sign me. I was glad the room was so dimly lit, as I'm sure every single emotion was playing out across my face. I must have managed to stammer out my thanks, because Duncan said: 'Great, let's get things moving. Before we can do anything, though, you'll have to leave your current agent.'

This wasn't going to be a problem. I had parted company with Grantham Hazeldine a few years before and moved to another agent, but I hadn't been happy with her for some time. As we were walking out (maybe I was floating?) Duncan asked if my agent had put me up for the play they were casting at the Donmar.

'Oh no,' I said, 'the Donmar isn't even on our radar.'

For those who don't know, the Donmar Warehouse is a small independent theatre in Covent Garden, famed for the stellar calibre of directors, playwrights and actors who work there. Nicole Kidman had starred in a play there a few years before. It was definitely not somewhere for an all-singing, all-dancing show pony like me.

Duncan persisted, though. 'I can't put you up for it because I don't yet represent you, but tell your agent to get you in there. It's a play called *Small Change*, about two Welsh boys, and you're right in the casting bracket. It's exactly the sort of thing you should be doing.'

I phoned my agent as soon as Duncan left.

'Oh no, darling, I'm never going to be able to get you in there – it's the Donmar! Let's stick to what you do really well and we'll get you another job when this one finishes. Okay?'

Demoralised, I ended the call. Duncan had lit something inside me, though. Still standing outside Soho House where he'd left me moments earlier, I called his number and told him my agent couldn't get me an audition.

'Well, just write a letter to the casting director and drop it at the stage door,' said Duncan. 'Her name's Anne McNulty. They haven't confirmed anything, but I know they're finalising casting now.'

It felt like a massive long shot; still, what did I have to lose?

I went straight to a card shop on Neal Street, where I found a card with a ticking clock on the front (which felt like the perfect metaphor for my life) and wrote a letter to Anne McNulty. I told her that I was a 27-year-old Welsh actor, currently appearing in *Rent Remixed* down the road, and that I would love to meet her for a chat. I didn't mention that I knew about *Small Change*; I figured that if I could just get to meet her, I would be on her radar for future productions. I left the letter at the box office, as I couldn't find a stage door, and they promised to give it to her.

I wasn't hugely surprised when I didn't hear back from Anne. After all, this wasn't how things were done in the industry: introductions were made by agents, especially when dealing with the casting director of one of London's most prestigious theatres. You didn't drop off a letter in a mad punt on being seen. And perhaps it was for the best: I'd bought a copy of *Small Change* and the writing was so poetic and complex that I barely understood the first page.

Then a week after I dropped off the letter, my phone rang.

'Hello, is that Luke?' It was a woman's voice with a lovely Yorkshire accent.

'Yes?'

'Hello, lovely one, this is Anne McNulty. I'm so sorry it's taken me a while to get back to you, I've been stuck in auditions. Anyway, would you like to come in for that meeting? Ten o'clock tomorrow morning – okay?'

Anne was a delight. We talked about my career and I admitted to her I'd never done a play before. Aware that she was casting Welsh characters, I made sure to amp up my accent. As we were nearing the end of the conversation, she said: 'It's funny you got in touch, because we're currently casting a play and you're right in the age bracket.'

There was no point lying. 'Yes, I know about that.'

'I thought you might,' she replied with a wry smile.

Small Change was a four-hander about two Welsh boys and their mothers, following them through their lives from early childhood. The play hadn't been performed for a quarter of a century and the production was going to be directed by the writer, Peter Gill. In theatrical terms, it was a moment.

'We've seen 250 boys for the two roles and Peter doesn't even have a short list,' said Anne, 'but we've only got a couple more days of auditions, so let's get you in tomorrow to read one of the monologues for Peter.'

I was elated. Not only had I got to see Anne, I now had the opportunity to audition and there was a chance – a tiny one, but still a chance – that something might happen.

. . .

The next morning I went to the rehearsal room. Anne was there with the play's writer, Peter Gill, a small, distinguished white-haired man in his late sixties.

'Hello Luke,' he said, in a soft Welsh accent. 'So where are you from?'

'I'm from the Valleys. Aberbargoed.'

'Hmmm. Does the Taff run through there?'

'Well, the Rhymney runs through my village, but it ends up in the Taff.'

'Ah yes, I used to swim in the Taff as a boy …'

We talked for a while and then Peter and I read half a page together. I'd had no training for this sort of audition, where I was to be judged solely on my acting, but at least I'd learned the lines the previous night so was off book.

'Lovely,' said Peter, when we had finished. 'How old are you, Luke?'
'Twenty-seven.'
'Okay. Well, thank you very much.'

I looked at Anne and she smiled, nodding towards the door.

* * *

They called that night and asked me to come back the next day to read with another actor, then again later in the week, and then on the Friday, as I was walking through Covent Garden on the way to *Rent*, Anne phoned to tell me I'd got the part. I would be playing Vincent alongside Matt Ryan as my best friend Gerard, while our mothers would be played by *EastEnders*' Lindsey Coulson and Sue Johnston from *The Royle Family*.

I remember thinking it didn't even matter what happened after the play – I'd achieved something I never would have believed possible. Nobody else in my world had gone from musical theatre to such a serious, cerebral play.

I phoned my soon-to-be-ex-agent. 'You know that audition you said I couldn't get?'

'Which audition's that, darling?'

'The play at the Donmar.'

'Oh yes, of course. As I said, I'm afraid there's no point even trying to—'

'I got it,' I said. 'I sent a letter to the casting director at the Donmar, I auditioned and now I've got the role.'

We were done.

When I got to the theatre that evening I told everyone I'd got the part. They'd been excited I'd even had an audition – 'For a play! At the *Donmar*!!' – and now they were thrilled, hugging and congratulating me.

That night, when we sang the final song of the show, 'It's Only Love', it felt as if the entire cast was singing it to me. We were on stage facing each other and they were smiling at me, the audience briefly forgotten, as if they were saying: *You've done it!* I was choked with emotion. I'd decided I was finished in theatre and now out of the blue I had this incredible opportunity.

Still, I could have had no idea what was actually waiting for me around the corner.

38

We started rehearsing *Small Change* – we four actors and Peter – at a cosy room in Chelsea. Well, I say rehearsing, but for the first two weeks Peter did nothing but talk. Politics, society, class, Trotskyism, Marxism, Thatcherism: he would start on a subject, digress for a bit, then return to the original topic. It was a lovely time, chatting and drinking tea together, and Peter was a joy, but as the days went by we began to wonder if we were ever going to pick up the script. I was going home every night and learning my lines, because as confusing as the dialogue seemed on the page, at least then I'd be ready to take Peter's direction when the time came. Still, we were growing increasingly twitchy and one lunchtime after another nervous conversation Sue agreed to raise the issue that afternoon.

'I was just wondering, Peter, when are we going to open the script?'

'Oh, don't worry about that, my love. I've got it all planned.'

Next day: more talking. And the next. It wasn't until three weeks before opening night that Peter finally picked up the script.

From the start, I was a long way out of my comfort zone. *Small Change* is a challenging play. The timeline jumps all over the place: at one point you might be a six-year-old, staring at the sky, then a moment later you'll be a teenager going off to university. There's no explanation of any of this to the audience, so the only way to indicate the shifts in age and circumstance is through tone and body language. The set certainly didn't give anything away: all we had to work with was a raked red plinth with four dining chairs, a five-pound-note and a newspaper. When Mam later brought my grandmother to see the play, I warned her, 'Nana's not going to understand a single word of this'. Yet as complicated as Peter's writing was, my little working-class grandmother, who had spent her life making babies, smoking cigarettes and eating Mars bars in her front room, really got it. She wasn't overthinking it or trying to be clever, so she could anchor herself to parts of the story. That was the power of Peter's writing: it could move you without needing to spoon-feed you the plot.

During rehearsals, Peter spent a long time moving us around the stage like chess pieces. 'You go and stand over there,' he'd say. 'And maybe you go here? And you two sit on the edge of the plinth.'

We'd try that – and then he'd change it all around again.

In time, however, I came to understand his way of working. It was like he was weaving a tapestry: he would loosely tack the different threads onto the canvas, trying out different patterns, then standing back to see how it looked before deciding exactly how to stitch them in. We were encouraged to ask questions and make discoveries for ourselves. It was an organic process, unlike any way in which I'd worked before. Still, we trusted him implicitly: he was a theatrical maestro, and it wasn't the first time he'd directed the play.

As both director and writer, Peter was particularly concerned with the rhythm of the dialogue. We'd be rehearsing on stage and suddenly from the dark of the auditorium we'd hear the *snap-snap-snap* of his fingers, which meant we needed to pick up the pace. He would run a metronome at different speeds to ensure we were at the right tempo. He was very firm about this, which was fine with me: I'd do it any way he wanted. I'd just been in a musical with Kat Slater, now all of a sudden I'm in this beautiful four-hander at the Donmar!

Imposter syndrome had kicked in the second I set foot in the room with Anne McNulty for that first meeting. I can't exaggerate what a giant leap it was for a musical theatre performer to get a job like this. As far as Anne and Peter were concerned, though, I was an actor. They didn't know anything about me. I had to remind myself constantly that I had a right to be there. I dealt with my anxieties in my usual way: by observing and adapting as we went along. I can't have done too badly at this, because my amazing co-star Matt Ryan, who was a classically trained actor, was shocked when I admitted that this was my first-ever play.

* * *

In April 2008 *Small Change* opened for a three-month run at the Donmar. The reviewers loved it. I was nominated for Outstanding Newcomer at the Evening Standard Theatre Awards, which was ironic as I'd been doing theatre for eight years by this point. It felt like a new beginning, and needless to say my plans to leave the profession were put on hold.

Duncan, who was now my agent, immediately started bringing in casting directors to see my performance. He wanted to use the play to introduce me to as many people as possible. Nobody knew who I was, but it didn't take two seconds to say yes to a free ticket for the Donmar, as people knew they'd be in for some seriously good theatre. Duncan kept talking about bigger and bigger things, even movies, which still felt like an entirely different galaxy to where I was currently. Whether it happened or not, I was just happy to finally have somebody really fighting my corner. Duncan had seen something in me that no one else had and it was now his job to introduce the world to Luke Evans.

The first casting director I met was a woman called Lucy Bevan, who came to see the play and took me out for a drink after the show. She was very complimentary about my performance, asking why I'd begun my career so late; when I told her I'd been working in musicals since the age of twenty she was clearly surprised. At the time, Lucy was casting for a movie called *Dorian Gray*. I didn't end up getting a part, but she sent my tape to Hollywood, where it found its way onto the desk of some agents. Duncan was obviously responsible for my work in the UK, but if I was to break into movies I would need an American agent who would work with Duncan as a team and take a collective percentage.

Within weeks, agents from William Morris and CAA (Creative Artists Agency), two of the top agencies in Los Angeles, flew over to see the play. I'd never set foot in The Ivy restaurant, but on one day I had lunch there with the CAA scout and was back again for dinner with George Freeman of William Morris and a manager called Lena Rocklin.[*] I think I probably had the Shepherd's pie, twice. 'Welcome back, sir,' the waiters said smoothly, giving nothing away, as I handed them my coat for the second time in a matter of hours.

The agents were passionate and enthusiastic about the play and my performance. I was nervous, so just listened to them talk – and Americans can really talk. I'd never had this kind of attention before; nobody had ever been excited about me. My mam's voice echoed in my head: *If it feels too good to be true, that's probably because it is …* But I reminded myself to just enjoy the moment, regardless of what came next.

The following day Duncan called. 'You've got a decision to make, Luke, because CAA and William Morris both want to sign you.'

It was madness. I had two of the top agencies in Hollywood fighting over me. I decided to go with William Morris, partly because of the package they were offering – if I signed with them I would also get Lena as my manager – but also because I remembered Charlotte signing the iconic William Morris book, which contains the signatures of all the agency's famous clients, including Marilyn Monroe and Charlie Chaplin, when I was with her in New York.

CAA was not happy.[†] The guy they'd sent over to see me had clearly been told to come back with a firm agreement that I would sign with them, and they pushed hard to make me change my mind.

---

[*] This was the OG Ivy in Covent Garden, before it was turned into a chain.
[†] I later moved to CAA and am with them today, so it worked out in the end.

Things had been moving so fast for the past few months I'd been living in a state of near-constant disbelief, but this was almost too much to take in. I was exactly the same person I'd always been, but it was as if Duncan had shone this light on me or pulled back a curtain and all of a sudden the industry was like: 'Ooh, what's that? We've not seen one like that before! I want it! No, it's mine! Give it to me now!'

I didn't know how it had happened, but some magical combination of luck, timing and fate seemed to have put me on a new and undreamed-of path. In a matter of weeks I had gone from deciding to leave acting for good, to signing with the biggest talent agency in the world.

ACT THREE

39

Once I'd signed with William Morris, it was as if someone hit the fast-forward button on my life. After years of scrabbling around for jobs it suddenly felt like my career had momentum. Shortly after *Small Change* finished, I was on a flight to Los Angeles to screen test for a movie called *Warrior*.

It was the first time I'd got on a plane and turned left. You wouldn't believe how many photos I took on that flight; I remember thinking that even if the trip was a total disaster, at least I'd got to travel business class once. Tom Hardy, my potential co-star in the movie, was in the row behind me, but I didn't think I should introduce myself. Tom was an established actor, having already appeared in a number of movies and the television series of *Wuthering Heights*, whereas I was this little Welsh musical theatre dude who happened to be on the flight with the hope of landing a role opposite him. I felt ridiculously out of my depth.

We fleetingly said hello at the airport, then were picked up in separate cars and whisked to our hotel on Sunset Boulevard. I remember looking out of my hotel room window and seeing the iconic billboards advertising the latest blockbusters. It brought home the reality of what was happening to me: I was in Hollywood, about to audition for a movie. It was madness. *Maybe one day,* I thought, *with hard work and a lot of luck, it would be my face splashed over those billboards.*

Tom and I spent our first day hanging out at the home of the movie's director, Gavin O'Connor. He lived in Malibu, which as far as I was concerned was a drink, not an actual place. We spent the day drinking beer, talking about our lives and watching cage fighting on TV, because the movie was about two brothers who end up competing against each other in an MMA (mixed martial arts) tournament. It was very chilled – just guys hanging out together – but I was very conscious of having to play a role that day: not just in terms of the movie, but in that room as Luke Evans. The part I was up for was seriously butch, so I needed them to be able to see me as that character. I knew I looked the part physically, at least: I was no longer that skinny boy with the too-big head and patchy stubble from *La Cava*. My transformation began when I was dating Tim, who introduced me to the YMCA gym on Tottenham Court Road. As training became part of my routine, I started taking protein and being careful about what I was eating, and by the time I was in *Miss Saigon*, where I needed to be convincing as a US Marine, I looked like a man. The gym has been part of my life ever since.

As Tom and I would be the ones in the ring for the movie, we needed to feel the physical reality of being punched and kicked, so the following day we had a Krav Maga session. MMA is a violent mixture of combat sports from around the world, without the protection of gloves or a headguard, and Krav Maga is basically a slightly more polite version of that. It's the Israeli army's go-to fighting technique and is often used in movie fight scenes for close-quarters combat.

Our excitement about the session didn't last long. The first exercise involved one of us standing in a fighting stance while the other person repeatedly kicked your front leg as hard as they could, until you couldn't take the pain any more, at which point you'd swap legs. We were both battered by the end of it. On the flight home a couple of days later I woke up during the night needing a pee and was in so much agony I couldn't move my legs. I looked under the blanket and my thighs were black with bruising. Under the circumstances, I decided I could hold my pee for a bit longer.

On our last day together, Tom and I read through some of the script. When a movie is being cast the potential lead actors will usually have a chemistry test to see whether there's a rapport between them. These can be awkward if it's a love story, as they'll usually choose a scene that's particularly emotionally charged: you'll have only just met someone and all of a sudden you have to go from swapping niceties about the weather to convincingly falling in love with each other. They want to see if there's a spark – a raw glimmer of something special – because if the magic's there in a sterile rehearsal room when you're strangers, imagine the potential after being brought to life by direction, location, make-up and costume.

At the end of the day, the movie's casting director, Randi Hiller, drove me back to the hotel. I was going home the following morning and while the trip had gone well, I sensed – correctly, as it turned out – that the role wasn't mine. It had been the most incredible experience, though, one that I thought would never happen for me, and I told Randi as much and thanked her for giving me a chance. It pays to be polite in this business: a few years later Randi went to work at Disney and would go on to suggest me for the role of Gaston in *Beauty and the Beast*.

I got home and was plunged straight into more meetings, auditions and screen tests. Meanwhile, I was cast in another play at the Donmar, a revival of a musical called *Piaf* about the life of the legendary French singer. Although Duncan and the team were lining me up for movies, everyone thought I should do the play. I hadn't had any other firm job offers yet, it was only a three-month run and it was directed by Jamie Lloyd, who until recently had been the right-hand man of the Donmar's artistic director, Michael Grandage. As a director Jamie is brave and clever, unafraid of pushing boundaries, and what he created in *Piaf* was extraordinary. We had a standing ovation every night and after our run at the Donmar we transferred to the Vaudeville Theatre in the West End for another three months.

While I was in *Piaf* my agents told me that after the play I would need to go out to Los Angeles to do the rounds of the studios, casting agents and producers. They reckoned I would have to be there for about three months, as there was a lot of work to do. I might have been an actor for ten years, but Hollywood had no fucking clue who I was. My agents were going to set up the meetings, but I would need to finance the trip myself – and because LA is not a cheap town and the Donmar earned you more in prestige than money, I urgently needed to find another job. My friend Alex from the Chapel Bar came to the rescue, employing me as his PA. For the next few months I would get to Angel at 9am, work in the restaurant until 5pm and then go to the theatre for *Piaf* in the evening.

While I managed to save up a few thousand pounds, I knew a hotel room would burn through that in weeks, so I got in touch with a stylist friend, David Thomas, who was now living in Los Angeles and had a hugely successful career working with everyone from Britney to the Backstreet Boys. I'd performed at his birthday party in London a few years previously (this was during the period I was doing the 'Up Close and Personal' gigs) and he'd told me that if I ever needed a place to stay in Los Angeles I should give him a call. He sounded pleased to hear from me. 'Stay as long as you like,' he said, even offering to arrange my flight.

There was one other matter that needed taking care of before I headed to the West Coast: at the grand old age of twenty-eight, I finally needed to learn to drive. I wouldn't be able to afford taxis and it's true that nobody ever goes anywhere on foot in Los Angeles. While I was there for *Warrior* I once walked from my hotel to the nearest Starbucks and I didn't pass a single pedestrian. Everyone else was grabbing their coffees then getting straight back in their shiny cars and driving off. So I found a lovely Welsh driving instructor called Cliff in London, booked an intensive ten-lesson course and passed my test first time.

The day before I flew to Los Angeles I had a screen test for the role of Apollo in a remake of the classic movie *Clash of the Titans*. When you're going to auditions you want people to be able to see you as the character, but it's tricky to give off a Greek god vibe without looking like you've turned up in fancy dress, so in situations like this I would ask myself: what would Brad Pitt wear? The answer was a decent pair of boots, good jeans and a nice T-shirt, maybe a denim shirt. It's a simple shortcut to looking as good as you can without appearing like you've made too much of an effort.

The screen test was at an office on Old Compton Street. I went into a small, nondescript room where a camera had been set up and they filmed me reading a scene with the casting director. I was there for ten minutes max, met up with my friends for a goodbye lunch at Café Boheme in Soho and then went home to finish packing my bags for Hollywood.

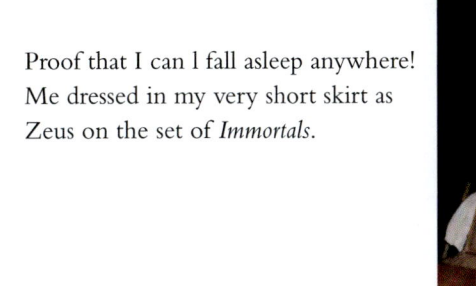

Proof that I can l fall asleep anywhere! Me dressed in my very short skirt as Zeus on the set of *Immortals*.

Me with my good friend Henry Cavill, both of us looking fresh and young. Those were the days!

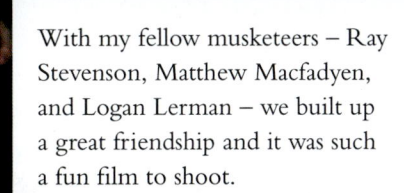

With my fellow musketeers – Ray Stevenson, Matthew Macfadyen, and Logan Lerman – we built up a great friendship and it was such a fun film to shoot.

In New Zealand on set with some of the actors from *The Hobbit*.

My dad being made up as an extra in *The Hobbit*. I think in this moment he was questioning his decision, but he ended up loving it!

At San Diego Comic-Con, with the wonderful Orlando Bloom and Lee Pace.

Me and Dean in South Korea on the *Fast & Furious 6* press tour, with our entourage of security. Dean is still in touch with at least one of them.

On the set of *Dracula Untold* having a camera fitted to a harness across my chest.

With Dean and Gransha on the set of *Dracula Untold*. I was so proud to have them there that day.

Me and Gary Oldman realising we'd both played Dracula.

With my parents at Shepperton Studios when they visited me on set with their dog.

This picture was taken seconds after Celine entered the room, exclaiming 'Gaston!!' at me.

My friends Olly and Lorna. They're married to each other and their kids are my godchildren.

Having all my friends and family at a dinner table is my favourite thing in the world.

Me and Tim on holiday on the Galapagos Islands.

My singing teacher and friend, Louise Ryan.

My manager, Duncan Millership, who helped change the course of my career.

At the Emmys with my co-stars from *Alienist*, Dakota Fanning and Daniel Brühl.

Onstage at the Royal Albert Hall for Queen Elizabeth II's 92nd birthday. It was an honour to perform alongside the likes of Kylie, Tom Jones, Shawn Mendes, Craig David and Anne-Marie.

At the Royal Variety Performance at the Palladium in 2019. I opened the show with the fanfare trumpeters of the Band of the Irish Guards. I also performed my single 'Love Is a Battlefield'.

In Portofino with Jennifer Anniston and Adam Sandler sitting in my character's Rolls Royce between takes filming *Murder Mystery* – what a job that was!

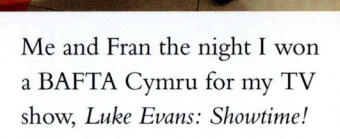

Me and Fran the night I won a BAFTA Cymru for my TV show, *Luke Evans: Showtime!*

Me and Fran on one of our travels, on top of one of the largest sand dunes in Namibia.

40

The schedule for my first day of meetings in Los Angeles went something like this:

9am	Warner Brothers
10am	Universal Studios Lot – meeting with producer
11am	film self-tape
1pm	lunch with independent producer/director
3pm	NBC – general meeting
4pm	meeting with casting director
5pm	screen test

And I had three months of this to look forward to. Not that I minded in the least; I was getting to sit down with people who up until a few weeks ago wouldn't have spoken to me, unless it was to ask for the bill. The first challenge, however, was trying to manoeuvre David's giant black Range Rover out of his driveway in West Hollywood. He had offered to lend me his car, but I hadn't driven since passing my test a few months earlier (and never on the right-hand side of the road) and on that first day my hands were so sweaty with fear they were slipping off the steering wheel.

I was only three weeks into my Los Angeles trip when Duncan called with unbelievable news: I'd been offered the role of Apollo in *Clash of the Titans*. I remember ending the call and standing frozen to the spot for what felt like minutes, just staring at the wall, as my mind tried to make sense of what I'd heard. My first ever movie role, and it was in Warner Brothers' colossal remake of one of the world's most famous fantasy films! Once I'd got over my initial euphoria, my overriding thought was: *Why me?* Everyone in my peer group had gone up for that movie; why did I get the role? For the first years of my movie career I was dogged by this constant niggle that I was going to be found out. *I'm so sorry,* someone would say, *but we've made a terrible mistake and you'll have to leave.* It was a struggle to convince myself that if I was getting a particular role — especially above an actor whose ability and talent I admired — then I genuinely deserved to be there. It's a work in progress, even today.

Now that I had an actual job offer, I would have to cut short my trip and return to London — though at least for my final week of meetings William Morris would be able to brief people that Luke had just got the role of Apollo in *Clash of the Titans*. In a town that dealt in reputations, I suddenly had currency.

I landed in London and went straight to an audition for *Sex & Drugs & Rock & Roll*, a biopic of the Blockheads singer Ian Dury, and that same afternoon I had another audition for a movie called *Tamara Drewe*, based on the cartoon strip by Posy Simmonds. The following morning, battling jet lag, I auditioned for an action thriller called *Blitz*.

I ended up getting every single one of them. Within the space of a week, I had gone from being a complete unknown to landing four movies. It happened so fast I was struggling to make sense of it, but speaking to my team — Duncan in London and WME in Los Angeles — I got the impression that this was all part of their plan for me. They were obviously excited that it was happening so quickly, but they didn't seem especially surprised. They clearly had far more confidence in me than I had, because I hadn't been prepared for any of it. Over the course of that week Duncan kept calling me up, telling me I'd got each job — and then he would tell me how much it would pay, and the sums he was mentioning blew my mind. The truth is that at this point I was probably thinking about the money before anything else. I realised that even if these were the only four movies I ever got, the money could change my life. It was tiny compared to what you can potentially earn in movies but for me it was a way to secure my future. Even though I wasn't the lead actor in these films, they were good roles in movies with a lot of potential (no one ever knows if a movie will work until it's out).

As much as I was excited about my new career, I was also terrified. I can't overemphasise how little I knew about working in movies. I had no idea about basic stuff like what hours I'd be working, how I would get to the studio or who I should report to when I did. Ridiculous as it sounds, it didn't even occur to me that I was going to be standing in the room with people I'd been watching on screen for years. Things were happening so fast I didn't process any of it until the first day I set foot on set. I remember having to rely heavily on Duncan in those early days.

'So what's going to happen tomorrow?' I'd ask him.

'Well, you're going to be picked up at 9am for a body cast.'

A long pause. 'What's a body cast?'

. . .

While I was waiting to start work on *Clash of the Titans*, my American agent George Freeman persuaded Ridley Scott, who was another of his clients, to give me a small role in *Robin Hood*, which he was currently filming in the UK with Russell Crowe. On my first day on set, I found somewhere to stand where I wouldn't be in the way and took in every bit of this magical new world: the hundreds of people milling about, the labyrinth of cables, lights and cameras, the hiss of fog machines and the soft thud of the horses' hooves. Russell wasn't there that day, but one of the other actors told me that he often arrived by helicopter. It was thrilling.

I was playing one of the Sheriff of Nottingham's henchmen and had a single line of dialogue. I had to stride into the room where the Sheriff, played by Matthew Macfadyen, was sitting at a desk, and say: 'A man – won't say his name. Demands an audience with the Sheriff.'

Just before we filmed the scene, Ridley took me to one side.

'You're George's boy, right?'

I could only nod. *Oscar-winning director Ridley Scott was talking to me!*

'And you're Welsh?'

This time I managed a few words. 'Yes, I am.'

'Okay. Give me the line?'

The line. What was the line? My mind was a blank; in that moment, I don't think I could have even told you my name. The seconds stretched on agonisingly.

'I'm so sorry, Ridley,' I said eventually. 'I can't remember the line.'

He looked at me for a moment; I could only imagine what was going through his head. 'Just do it in your own accent,' he said, and walked off.

I dropped my head in my hands. *Luke, you absolute fucking idiot.*

Unsurprisingly, I wasn't given any more dialogue, but as they often needed one of the Sheriff's henchman to appear in the background, I kept being called back to set. There is a lot of hanging around when you're making a movie. They say the camera rolls for an average of two hours in every twelve, as it takes time to set up the equipment, make sure the lighting is right and aeroplanes aren't flying overhead messing up the sound. So they'd book me for an extra week at a time, though I'd often only end up working for a day of that. Not that I would have dreamed of complaining. People often say movie sets are boring. Oh my God, are you kidding me? I was getting to hang out in this fascinating environment, learning new skills and being paid well for the privilege.

I had weeks of training to prepare me for the brief seconds I appeared onscreen on horseback. Until this point my only experience with horses was pony trekking in Aberbargoed. There wasn't much skill involved in this: you'd trudge along for an hour, then the moment it was time to turn round these stumpy little ponies would gallop back to the stables at full pelt, while you desperately tried to cling on. To prepare for *Robin Hood*, I was sent for riding lessons with Steve Dent, the UK's leading horse trainer for film. It was a gloriously hot summer. I'd go up to his stables in Hertfordshire early in the morning and Steve's daughter Sam and I would go galloping over the fields together. I couldn't believe this was actually considered work.

For one scene in *Robin Hood*, Matthew and I had to ride our horses through an archway to meet with Cate Blanchett, who played Marion. She was a huge star even then, instantly familiar to me from *The Lord of the Rings*. In this particular scene she was hoeing a field, but even in a plain dress with mud on her feet Cate carried herself with such poise you felt as if you were in the presence of someone very special. While we were waiting between takes, Cate looked up at me on my horse, smiled and said hello. I couldn't believe I was that close to a real Hollywood movie star, because I felt like I was only there to fill a saddle on a horse. It was one of many moments I've had in my life when I've stepped outside myself, looked back and thought: *Well, this is bloody mental.*

As my contract kept being extended, I ended up being paid more than double my original fee. That first movie pay cheque for *Robin Hood* was more than my dad earned in an entire year. I suppose many people would have blown at least some of that money on something frivolous, but the first thing I did was pay Jamie back the money he'd loaned me to buy the house and then used the rest to clear my debts and pay off my parents' mortgage. While I had another four movie pay cheques coming later that year, what if the bubble then burst? I knew I needed to use whatever money I earned to secure my future before I even thought about splurging on a flash car or holidays. Success happening later in life was 100 per cent the best thing that could have happened to me. I knew what it was like to not have enough money to buy bacon for a sandwich and I was determined never to go back there.

41

I was standing in a chilly room in Shepperton Studios wearing only my pants having nappy cream briskly rubbed all over me. I was being fitted for Apollo's suit of gold armour for *Clash of the Titans*; the nappy cream was to stop my chest hair from being ripped out after they'd covered me foot-to-neck in gloop that would harden to make the full-body cast that the armour would be based on, created by the incomparable Welsh costume designer Lindy Hemming. I was then fitted with hair extensions by legendary hair and make-up artist Jenny Shircore. The extensions would be twisted into a tousled knot for the movie, but as they were put in weeks before we started shooting I had to live with bum-length hair for some time. I became quite adept at styling a messy bun.

I first met the rest of the cast at the table read, which is a structured read-through of the script with all the actors who have speaking parts. This was a big movie, being made by the crème de la crème of British film production. The cast was equally stellar and included Liam Neeson, Ralph Fiennes and Mads Mikkelsen. I didn't have many lines, so I spent most of that day observing these legendary artists at work, picking up hints on how to be a movie actor (because I still had no idea). Gemma Arterton, who I would soon be working with on *Tamara Drewe*, came up to say hello. 'I hear you're going to be my leading man?' she said. It was pretty surreal, because Gemma had just played a Bond girl.

On my first day of filming I arrived at Shepperton early in the morning and went straight to hair and make-up (I'd come to realise that you spent more time with these guys than anyone else on set) and then went to wait in my trailer. The hours slowly ticked by. It was summer, the armour – though magnificent and very gold – wasn't exactly lounge-wear, and my trailer was so cramped there was only space for a small chair and toilet. As I wasn't one of the big names on the movie I'd been given a 'four-banger', which is a quarter of a whole trailer. You can also get a double-banger.* After a while, someone appeared to ask what I wanted for lunch. You never go hungry on movies, and because this was a big studio production the food was particularly plentiful: piles of chocolates, fruits, sandwiches, health bars – there was always something on hand to eat.

Finally, sometime around mid-afternoon, I was called to set. Mount Olympus had been built on a sound stage with thrones for all the gods and a staircase up to Zeus' throne, which is where Liam Neeson sat. In this particular scene, Hades, played by Ralph Fiennes, strides into the middle of the set and I, as the petulant son of Zeus, have to interject during his conversation with the other gods. I'd never been taught the art of film acting, so I had to observe and then copy what everyone else was doing. And my first lesson that day? You don't have to speak louder than usual. In theatre I'd been used to projecting my voice so audiences could hear me in the gods, but these gods were speaking so quietly I couldn't hear a word they were saying and I realised that they must all be wearing mics. *Ah, so the volume and intensity must be taken care of in post-production*, I thought. I also noticed how small Liam and Ralph's gestures could be. When I watched their performances back on screen, I understood how the tiniest of movements – a subtle raise of the eyebrows or the slightest curl of the lip, actions that might almost go unnoticed by the viewer – could impact a scene in a massive way. From that first day on set, I began to learn the art of movie acting just by watching and absorbing other people's techniques.

---

* In *Robin Hood*, Russell Crowe had four trailers that were arranged in a square – known on set, unsurprisingly, as Russell Square.

As it was a struggle to sit in full-body armour there were six-foot leaning boards around set for the actors to relax against during breaks in filming. On my second day I found myself on a board next to Liam Neeson. Out of all the cast I was the most nervous around him, not only because of his renown as an actor, but also because this was his first movie since his wife, Natasha Richardson, had tragically died in a skiing accident, and we were all very aware of that. I would have been too nervous to start a conversation, but Liam turned to me and said: 'So, where are you from, Luke?' We had a really easy chat, as if we were just an Irishman and a Welshman enjoying a drink down the pub, rather than trussed up in armour and hair extensions on a movie set.

While we were filming *Clash of the Titans*, Emma Thompson was working on *Nanny McPhee* in the studio next door. Emma, who is one of the nicest humans I've met in this industry, was very close to Liam and Natasha, and one day she turned up on our set in full Nanny McPhee garb – complete with prosthetic nose, wart and teeth – strode across Mount Olympus and sat on Zeus's lap.

'Have you been a good boy today?' she asked Liam, in her character's voice.

Watching this unfold, I could only marvel at how magical this industry is. We were creating these two completely different worlds and they had collided in the most crazy, wonderful way, just a studio apart.

* * *

As the film was largely shot at Shepperton, it meant I could sleep in my own bed every night, which was a luxury I'd soon have to forgo as work increasingly took me away from home. At the time I was living with my boyfriend Lee, a maths teacher from Middlesborough. A friend had brought him to see me in *Small Change* and I'd taken an instant liking to this stocky, handsome Northerner. I'm far happier being in a relationship because I like to have someone to share my experiences and adventures with, and Lee was just as excited as I was as my life changed from that of a jobbing theatre actor to become a whirl of Hollywood agents, screen tests and film sets. With all the crazy things that were going on, I loved having someone to come home to and say: 'You'll never guess what happened to me today …'

Lee and I moved to an apartment in Shoreditch and bought a tank of tropical fish, which I became obsessed with. I would spend hours tending to the aquatic plants and sorting out the rocks, grass, pumps and bubbles: it was the canaries and finches of my youth all over again, but this time with fins rather than feathers. We were very happy in that flat. Lee was training to be a psychologist, and I would usually come home to find him studying at the kitchen table. Our friends got on brilliantly and we all spent New Year's together that year at a big house in Northumberland. I didn't realise it at the time, but these would be my final few months of 'normality' before my movie career took off and my life was changed forever.

42

I filmed five movies in 2009 and then another four in 2010. I knew very little about the industry when I started out. I'd often go to the Odeon with Mam, but I certainly wasn't a film buff. I was your average working-class person who went to the pictures to be entertained by the spectacle of *Titanic* or *Schindler's List*. I had no idea about the history of film, the evolution of cinema, the different methods of acting. My world was musical theatre: Michael Ball, Elaine Paige, Patti LuPone. You could have mentioned Orson Welles to me and I wouldn't have had a clue. So when my movie career started it was a very steep learning curve. People I was now working with in the industry might mention a certain actor's performance and I wouldn't know what they were talking about. 'Oh yes, extraordinary,' I'd mutter, praying they wouldn't ask any further questions. I knew I needed to educate myself, so in my spare time (the little there was of it) I worked my way through the list of the top fifty movies of all time, studying all the iconic performances from James Dean to Meryl Streep. It was a crash course in the world of film and by the end of it I at least felt I could hold my own in a conversation when I was at work.

Marlon Brando had a particularly significant effect on me because of his pioneering naturalistic style of acting. I remember being stunned by his performance as Stanley Kowalski in *A Streetcar Named Desire*: the way he tugged at his shirt or messed with his hair in the middle of a scene. Little unconscious gestures all of us do that instantly made the character come alive. No other actor was doing that at the time, it was revolutionary. I saw a man so at ease with his physicality that he could confidently break the rules, and his naturalistic technique has been an inspiration throughout my career. Audiences immediately connect with an actor when they forget they're watching a performance and just see a real human being, someone who has to pause to think about the next word, take a breath or scratch their face. Certain actors are brilliant at this, including Brad Pitt, Leonardo DiCaprio and Nicole Kidman, who I was lucky enough to work with on *Nine Perfect Strangers*. When we were filming, Nicole never did the same take twice; the words were obviously the same, but every time she would subtly bring different colours to her performance. It was extraordinary to watch.

Of course, Brando had an incredible acting teacher, Stella Adler, but as I didn't have anyone to guide me these movies became my source of knowledge and inspiration. I watched these great performances, observed what the actors did and tried to pull out elements I could use in my own career. To this day I often pick up ideas for my own performances by watching other actors, especially the older ones. Their experience and knowledge has been the best masterclass I could have hoped for.

After *Clash of the Titans*, I had a small role in *Sex & Drugs & Rock & Roll* with Andy Serkis, then a slightly bigger role in the action thriller *Blitz*, in which I played a detective alongside Jason Statham and Paddy Considine. My character drove a Land Rover Discovery and when I told the guy who was looking after the cars on set how much I enjoyed driving it, he offered to lend me one for a month to use at home. Days later, a beautiful, brand new Discovery was delivered to our flat in Shoreditch. It stood out like a very expensive sore thumb on our street. Lee and I made the most of it for a few days, until one morning I came out to find a huge dent right in the middle of the bonnet. The car people were very understanding, but that was the end of the free car.

My last scene on *Blitz* was a night shoot, after which a car from the *Tamara Drewe* production team picked me up from the London set and drove me to Bridport in Dorset. The following morning I had my hair and costume fitting and the day after that we started filming. That was how quickly I had to transition from gritty CID detective to a country bumpkin handyman in an idyllic Dorset village.

The *Tamara Drewe* shoot was incredibly fun and enjoyable. I had a great role – my first romantic lead – and was working with a glorious bunch of actors and the legendary director Stephen Frears, whose film about a gay relationship, *My Beautiful Laundrette*, I'd watched when I was a teenager late one night on the little black-and-white TV in my bedroom with the sound turned right down. It had deeply moved me. I had met Stephen at my screen test, albeit very briefly. I'd just finished reading a scene with the casting director when he walked in.

'Can he act?' he asked the casting director.

She replied that yes, I could act.

'Great,' said Stephen. 'See you in Dorset, then!'

And off he went.

As Stephen was of a certain age he liked things to be comfortable, so we were staying in a beautiful hotel amidst the pretty villages and rolling fields of the Dorset countryside. I learned how to make hazel fences for the role and spent much of filming digging holes and planting vegetables, which was a lovely change of pace after the frenzy of the previous few months. On my days off Gemma lent me her convertible Mini and I would put the hood down and drive through the winding lanes to the Jurassic coast for a swim. It was the perfect way to finish the year.

Tamara Drewe was also my first experience of a West End premiere – well, at least the first where I was appearing in the movie. Back when I was a theatre actor I had a part-time job as a waiter with a catering company who used to serve canapés and drinks at all the premieres. I still have a scar on my arm from where a hot serving tray lid fell and split the skin.

I was given a stylist and groomer to help me get ready for the red carpet. Now this was definitely movie star territory: a rail of gorgeous clothes to choose from, and I could keep the outfit I wore to the premiere. It's one of the perks of this business: if a designer lends you something to wear for a press junket, fashion show or premiere they'll almost always let you take it home. Thanks to these stylists and designers, I now have some incredibly beautiful suits in my wardrobe.

For the premiere Leicester Square had been transformed into the Dorset countryside, the red carpet winding over a fake meadow dotted with hay bales and plastic cows. I pulled up in a car to see crowds of fans held back by barriers and huge screens set up around the square to broadcast the action. Taking a breath to steady my nerves, I got out of the car and was met by my publicist, who steered me towards the pen of press photographers. There must have been at least fifty of them, stacked several deep on ladders, all shouting my name. The camera flashes started firing before I'd even managed to get into the pose that I'd practised in the mirror: one hand in my pocket because it felt the most natural, though I'm sure I looked anything but relaxed. The noise and chaos was thrilling. These days I know exactly what to do in front of a camera, but back then I didn't have a clue.

After the photographers, I was herded onto the press pen, walking down the line of journalists from ITN, *This Morning*, newspapers and magazines. I already had a few movies in the bank by this stage, so they were asking me about *Clash of the Titans* and *Blitz*. 'So tell us about this movie you've just done with Jason Statham?'

After watching the movie, we all got picked up and shipped to Home House for the party. It was a lovely full-circle moment for me: the last time I was there was as a fake hairdresser, trying to scrape together enough money to stay in my flat, and now I was back as a bona fide movie actor!

I brought all my friends and family to the *Tamara Drewe* premiere, including Lee and my parents, and I walked the red carpet with my friend Holly, primarily because she was the most glamorous person I knew. Later that night Holly went to the bathroom at the after-party and got talking to another woman who was washing her hands.

'So you're here with Luke Evans?' she asked.

Holly said yes, and told her that we were very old friends.

She thought nothing more of it, until a week later when an article appeared in the *Daily Mail* stating that Holly and I were dating. It turns out the woman she had been chatting to in the bathroom was the newspaper's gossip columnist.

Holly was mortified. 'I didn't say we were boyfriend and girlfriend, I promise!'

It didn't bother me at all; I'd never been tabloid gossip fodder before, so I just thought it was funny. Perhaps I would have handled things differently if I knew what the impact of that one small article would go on to be.

· · ·

Until Hollywood came knocking, I'd been living as a gay man for well over ten years. My family, friends and colleagues knew who I was, so my sexuality wasn't something I ever had to think about, but when I started working in movies it suddenly became an issue again because at that time you just didn't get openly gay actors playing straight romantic leads. My sexuality became a 'thing' to be handled and strategised, rather than simply being just another aspect of my identity, like having green eyes or being Welsh. Working in this industry can be tough, but in the fifteen years I've been in movies it has been the struggle to balance my desire to live an authentic life with the commercial pressures and often old-fashioned attitudes of Hollywood that has been by far the biggest challenge.

Duncan was aware I was gay when he took me on as a client, but nobody else in my new team knew. If any of them had asked me, I would have been honest, but the subject never came up; we were too busy talking about work. Or maybe they'd already guessed? My career was rapidly taking off, so my personal life wasn't an issue. I'd told Duncan that there were articles out there in which I talked about being gay, but he assured me that we'd know when we needed to make a point of talking about my sexuality and in the meantime it would be a distraction to have it at the forefront of the conversation. I didn't owe anyone an explanation. People were casting me in these straight, macho roles and the fact they believed in me as those characters was all that mattered. I totally got it. It was a business decision: we needed to keep people's eyes on the right thing, which was my talent, my roles, my movies.

Nevertheless, it was playing on my mind that if the truth was made public – or if, God forbid, someone sold a story about me – then this amazing new career I'd never thought possible could be snatched away simply because of who I was. It was the same feeling I'd had before coming out to my parents: that I could lose everything because of something I had no control over and was actually very proud of. All of a sudden there was a shame attached to being gay again. At the age of thirty, after everything I'd gone through to be true to myself, I decided not to talk about this key aspect of my identity. I wasn't at all comfortable with this, but at the time I believed it was the only way I'd be able to build a career in an industry that historically hadn't been welcoming to gay people. My team were positioning me very strategically: as the heartthrob, the romantic lead, the action hero. Could I achieve all that as an openly gay man? I had no idea. There was no one else in the industry I could look at and think: *Ah, so that's how that particular gay actor navigated this.*

Lee only visited me once while I was filming *Tamara Drewe*, primarily because we couldn't be open about our relationship. It was an uncomfortable time for both of us. I had to introduce him as my 'friend' to other people in the business, though I did end up telling Gemma about who he was. Our bedrooms were next to each other in our hotel and when I confessed that Lee was actually my boyfriend she said with a smile: 'Honey, I'm in the room next door – *I know!*' It was such a relief to be able to be open with her and know that she had my back regardless, because she knew how the industry worked and the pressure I was under. The big American studios were still very much of the 'a man is a man' mindset.

When that picture of me and Holly appeared in the newspaper after the *Tamara Drewe* premiere, I told the rest of my management team that I was gay. My publicists told me not to worry, that they would make sure I wasn't ever put in any position where I was made to feel uncomfortable. They would not respond to gossip. I knew that it would come out eventually (and I knew I would never deny it once it did) but I hoped that if I got a good body of work behind me then the fact I was gay might not change anything.

43

While I was finishing work on a movie about gambling called *Flutter*, in Newcastle, I was offered the role of Zeus in *Immortals*, another Greek god sandals-and-swords epic. This was the first movie where I didn't have to audition, which felt like a real milestone, and it was another big studio production. My career was definitely heading in the right direction. The only problem was that I'd spent the past few months eating pies and pasties on *Flutter* and drinking pints with the cast, and now I was going to have to be convincing as the king of the gods, wearing little more than a loincloth, alongside Henry Cavill, a man so famously buff he would be cast as Superman the following year.

The *Immortals* director, Tarsem Singh, told me I needed to get to Montreal as soon as possible, because the rest of the team had been in training for months and I only had seven weeks before filming started to catch up. It wasn't that I was particularly out of shape. You can see my natural body in *Tamara Drewe*: I look like an averagely fit man in his early thirties. My goal in training had never been to get super-ripped, because I hadn't thought I'd be going up for those sort of roles, but now my body was going to be under the spotlight in a way it had never been before – and for the first time in my life I had an actual belly, thanks to all the Greggs sausage rolls in Newcastle. I knew this was going to be a challenge.

On my first day in snowy Montreal I turned up at this warehouse to find a boot camp of stuntmen, trainers and actors, and as soon as they took their tops off I realised that I'd said yes to the wrong job. Henry was in insane shape. There was no way I could get even close to his physique within seven weeks.

Holy shit, I thought, feeling a bit sick. *What have I done?*

That night I called my manager, Lena Rocklin.* 'You've got to get me out of this job,' I told her. 'It's a huge mistake. I can't be topless onscreen next to Henry Cavill. I'll look ridiculous.'

Lena had little sympathy. 'You can't quit,' she said flatly. 'Just throw yourself into it.'

The message was loud and clear: *Pull yourself together.* So I did.

I trained six days a week and stuck to a painfully strict low-calorie diet. One of the trainers would come to my apartment at 7am every morning and we'd run up and down the twenty-six flights of stairs in my building before a meagre breakfast of salmon, two boiled eggs and one slice of bread, then we'd go to the warehouse to start work. We'd spend all day every day practising stunts, lifting weights and training. There was a lot of camaraderie among the team, which included stuntmen from all over the world, and they were so inspiring it was easy to be disciplined. I was healthier than I had ever been in my life. We each had a huge flask with our name on it that you'd fill with three green tea bags and have to drink the lot before lunch. After a short break for food – a small amount of chicken, rice and salad – we'd resume training, then at some point we would all have to lie down on the crash mats and take a nap, which was easy for me because my superpower is that I can sleep anywhere.

I dropped thirty pounds in seven weeks and by the time we started filming I was lean, shredded, waxed and ready for my costume: a gold lamé miniskirt, cape and a crown of gold leaves. I should have been feeling supremely confident; instead, I was panicking about the amount of skin I would have to show.

I had suffered with psoriasis since my second year in college. I'd gone on holiday with Charlotte and Maria Church to Agadir in Morocco and

---

* For those who don't know, agents do the fee-negotiating and deal-thrashing, whereas managers work with you on a more personal level. They're the ones you call when you've eaten all the pies and are suffering from loincloth anxiety.

had felt a bit out of sorts on the flight, but by the time we arrived at the resort I had developed the worst sore throat I'd ever had. I should have taken some time to recover, but Maria is a force of nature and I was there as her wingman, so after Charlotte had gone to bed each night we would stay up together smoking and drinking until the early hours. I got sicker and sicker; I even took a photo of my throat to remind myself just how bad it got. Then two days after getting back to the UK I was horrified to see little red spots appearing all over my body. I was eventually diagnosed with guttate psoriasis, which – as in my case – can be often triggered by a serious streptococcal infection, and once you have it there's no cure.

As you can imagine, having to be semi-naked in college every day while covered in scaly red blotches was traumatic. The rash was impossible to cover up and stressing about it made it worse. I tried every treatment out there, but the only one that worked for me was UVB rays. I would go to a clinic in Harley Street every three days and stand in front of a UVB tube, starting for just three seconds and then building it up by another three seconds with each session. The moment it started to improve, so did my mood, and that combined with the treatment made it go away.

From then on the psoriasis would flare up again whenever I was stressed or under pressure. It's not a pleasant thing to suffer from when you're in an industry where your appearance is picked apart. I had a bad flare-up while filming *Immortals,* leaving me with marks all over my skin that needed to be carefully concealed. I have so much respect for make-up artists: those guys would get down on their hands and knees every day and painstakingly dab foundation all over the rash, because they knew how self-conscious I was about it. They're like nurses in a way – nothing fazes them.

* * *

Henry and I became great pals during filming. We were allowed one cheat night a week when the pair of us would go out for steak and beer. Over dinner one night he asked if I had a girlfriend; if it had been anyone else on the shoot I would have kept things vague, but Henry was such a nice guy that I told him I was gay.

He just took it in his stride. 'Oh, fantastic! I used to work on the door of a gay club in West Hollywood.'

I told him that I didn't want anyone else to know. As I was playing such a macho role I needed the other guys to respect me, and if there was just one homophobic person on the team it could have become an issue. This was a big movie for me and I didn't want any of that drama getting in the way of doing my job. I looked the part and could do the role – that was why I was there. Nothing else was relevant.

The way Henry treated me didn't change at all after he found out I was gay, but that's not always been the case. Early in my career, when I was getting these very masculine roles and my sexuality wasn't common knowledge, I would sometimes get this sense of competitiveness from straight actors I was working with. I was often very comfortable with the leading actress, and some men would clearly see this as a threat. Like gorillas jostling to be alpha male, they needed to be number one on set: the strongest, most powerful and most liked by the females. It was a real eye-opener for me, because all my straight friends knew I was gay so I'd never felt that tension from other men before.

I was once at a party in Cannes and was chatting to a famously handsome Hollywood leading man. I was excited to meet him, but I quickly got the impression that he didn't want to be talking to me: he kept looking over his shoulder, barely listening to what I was saying. Yet the moment he discovered I was gay, his whole attitude transformed. 'Oh, thank fuck for that,' he said, smiling for the first time, 'I haven't got any competition this evening!' And I realised that despite all his success, the blockbuster movies and adoring fans, he still felt so threatened that he needed to make sure he had the roomful of women all to himself. This industry can make people so insecure.

* * *

Clash of the Titans was the first film of mine that I went to watch at the cinema with the rest of the public during filming of *Immortals* in Montreal. Ironically I was watching myself on screen as Apollo, while I was playing the role of Zeus! I'd never dream of going to one of my own movies now: I learned my lesson after being recognised at a screening of *Fast & Furious 6* at my local cinema in Hackney. Towards the end of the movie people on my row and the one in front started to turn their heads and nudge each other – 'Hold on, I think that guy's Owen Shaw!' – so I made a swift exit just before the credits. Back then, however, it was all new and exciting. I will never forget sitting in the dark and watching the opening credits appear, with the iconic Universal globe revolving on the screen. I remember thinking: *How many movies have I watched in my life and seen that introduction? And now it's coming before* my *project*. It was a huge, bizarre sensation; I still get it today. It brought home the gravity and weight of what I was now a part of.

44

After we wrapped in Canada, I flew straight to Munich to start training for my next movie, *The Three Musketeers*. My first thought on reading the script was: *Well, at least I won't have a problem with the horses.* After all the training for *Robin Hood* I knew I'd be well away. Fencing, however, was new to me, and I would be doing a lot of it during the movie, sometimes with a blade in each hand. We spent weeks training with a former Olympic gold medallist, a German called Imke Duplitzer, who taught us the art of épée. It's a very stylised, graceful technique: your stance, posture and flair are all important and it looks more like a dance than a free-for-all fight.

Because my character, Aramis, was a priest, my sword was in the shape of the cross. Over the years I've kept every one of the swords I've had made for me and had them all mounted in the entrance hall to my old house, but initially I didn't think to hang onto the one from *The Three Musketeers*. By the time I'd built up a collection, including blades from *The Hobbit* and *Dracula Untold*, it was bothering me that I didn't have that first sword, so my assistant Jamie managed to track it down and I bought it for £700. It was worth every penny: I'm always in awe of the craftsmanship involved in making these things for movies. My sword for *Dracula Untold* was particularly impressive, the hilt engraved with a dragon (as I was known as the son of the dragon) and set with a red stone. At the end of the movie, the production company gifted it to me with a message engraved on the blade: *Luke, looking forward to going to battle together for many movies to come. Love, your Universal family.* It felt like a fair exchange for all the pain, blood and injuries I got during filming!

I also have a collection of the rings worn by my characters, including John's from *The Alienist* and the military ring I wore to play a naval officer in *Midway*. So much of the work that goes into props is never even seen by the audience. I was part of the design process for Gaston's ring in *Beauty and the Beast*, suggesting that it have a stag's head engraved onto it because of the character's well-known fondness for antlers. Dracula's ring is a particularly beautiful piece: handmade from solid silver with a ruby, complete with dents and chinks to give it more of an antiquated feel, and I often wear it.

The Three Musketeers was a very fun shoot, largely thanks to my co-stars. My fellow musketeers were played by Matthew Macfadyen, who I'd already worked with on *Robin Hood*, and the wonderful bear-like man that was Ray Stevenson. We built up a very close friendship, drinking whisky on Friday nights and going out for dinners: three British boys just hanging out together. James Corden was also in the movie and he was a delight, making me laugh during every scene we had together. One night in Berlin the pair of us sang Take That songs to the crowd in our hotel bar. My friend's wife was so drunk that she took off her bra, threw it at James and it hit him right in the chops during 'A Million Love Songs'. We don't see each other very often, as is the way in this business, but it's like no time has passed when we do.

I've formed some really close friendships on movies, but they're very hard to maintain in this industry because you're always being pulled in different directions – and not just to different cities, to entirely separate continents. Besides, any new friends I make now are just a bonus. I was thirty years old when I started working in movies and already had an established group of friends; I certainly wasn't looking to change my whole social circle – which a lot of actors do, by the way. They move to Los Angeles and start afresh, finding Hollywood friends. That's not my thing at all. I already had my gang and I wasn't gonna give them up.

・・・

The first years of my movie career were so intense and fast-paced that I was away from home for months at a time. From Germany, I went straight to Budapest to start work on a Gothic thriller called *The Raven*.

I was playing a detective opposite John Cusack as the writer Edgar Allan Poe, and the cast was full of amazing actors, including Brendan Gleeson, Alice Eve and Oliver Jackson-Cohen. It was a fantastic story and I was playing the lead opposite John. I would go back to Budapest ten years later to film two seasons of *The Alienist* and would find it a beautiful city, but back then it was a dark place, both literally and figuratively. We filmed part of *The Raven* in Serbia, where there were packs of stray dogs outside the studio, and these poor things would always hang around my trailer waiting for food. Being a hopeless animal lover, I would give them everything I had – though that wasn't usually much of a loss: gristly sausages and boiled potatoes.

It didn't help that we were filming during winter, so were dealing with freezing temperatures, snow and biting winds. My agent came to visit me during the shoot and we didn't leave the hotel during my time off because it was so cold. As it was a Gothic thriller, we had something like seven weeks of night shoots. You'd wake as the sun was going down, leave for work in the driving rain, film all night and then get back to your hotel as the sun was coming up and have to go to bed. It was pretty grim.

With all their money, you might wonder why production companies would choose to shoot a movie someplace like this? Well, for one, Budapest is a fantastic location for period movies such as *The Raven* and a later project of mine, *The Alienist*. The city had a golden age at the turn of the twentieth century, around the same time as New York, and the well-preserved buildings and cobbled streets offer a convincing stand-in for period America. More importantly, Hungary offers huge tax incentives for movie and TV productions that are made there.

⋯

My first movies had been filmed in the UK, but once I started working abroad it became much harder for Lee to visit. He came out once, while I was in Montreal for *Immortals* during the six-week school holidays, and it was a disaster. He wanted to explore eastern Canada, but I couldn't join him because I was always working. He was stuck in a hotel room alone for most of the time and ended up cutting his visit short and going home, which was very sad for both of us. I was on this amazing adventure, earning unimaginable money, but I couldn't give my partner the one thing he wanted, which was my time.

Lee didn't come out to see me while I was in Germany or Budapest; it was becoming obvious that what was happening to me was going to pull us apart. It wasn't what he'd signed up for and we split after *The Raven*. We both knew it had run its course, so in the end it was a mutual decision, but it was still painful. We managed to stay friends, though, which I'm so grateful for. Blame can always be planted for choices you make in a relationship, but with time you can hopefully look back, understand you were both trying your best and appreciate what you brought to each other's lives.

A couple of years later, while filming *Dracula Untold* in Northern Ireland, I dated a handsome riot policeman called Ryan and he ended up moving to London with me. After we broke up, a friend forwarded me a photo they'd found on social media: it was a picture of Lee and Ryan together. They had become friends through their connection to me! They came to my fortieth birthday party a few years ago, both wearing skull masks and matching T-shirts with a picture of a tombstone that read GHOSTS OF BOYFRIENDS PAST and the years we had dated. I was pissing myself: 'Oh my God, it's the first wives club!'

Although I've not kept in touch with all my exes, it's been important to me to stay close to those I've had more meaningful, longer-term relationships with, especially the partners I've been with during significant times of my life, such as Lee. If you've been together a long time and have got on well for most of it, I think it's sad to then cut that person out of your life, because even if that relationship didn't turn out to be the whole book, it was still a very important chapter.

45

I hate watching horror movies. Thrillers are fine, but evil spirits, witchcraft and torture? No thank you – I won't allow that sort of thing in my brain. I'm sure it's a residual effect of being a Jehovah's Witness. Filming a role in a horror movie, though – well, that's a completely different matter. While I've done some extremely gory things in my career, at the time it felt more like we were making a slapstick comedy.

The Raven had some dark and disturbing scenes, but my next movie was a straight-up gore-fest called *No One Lives*. Although it was a smaller indie movie I was keen to do it, primarily because it would be the first movie that I'd filmed on American soil.

At this point in my career I was very much steered by my agents when it came to the projects I chose. My team wanted me to be in the biggest movies that would be seen by the most people, because that's how you gain a profile in this industry. The bigger the films you're in, the more doors will be opened for you around the world.

We shot *No One Lives* near Abita Springs in Louisiana, though most of the scenes were filmed outside town in the middle of Bumfuck, Nowhere. I didn't have much in common with the rest of the cast, who were all twenty-something Americans and/or wrestlers (the movie was financed by World Wrestling Entertainment) and so I did a lot of solo sightseeing during my time off. I'd finish my scene in the early hours, drive to New Orleans over the famous Lake Pontchartrain Causeway Bridge, arrive at my hotel at 4am and sleep until 10am, then get a coffee and pastry and wander the streets. Whenever I have a day off while I'm on location I will always make sure I get out and explore my surroundings, even if I'm exhausted and just want to sleep. I've been lucky enough to travel to some amazing places for my career, but if I just went from the hotel to the set and back again then I might as well have stayed in the UK. I want to see that famous waterfall and taste that iconic local dish, so I feel as if I'm having a break from work. I think that's why people look at my Instagram and think I'm always on holiday, because I only ever post the interesting bits between my long weeks on set.

I played my first bad guy in *No One Lives*, a psychopathic murderer who is kidnapped by a criminal gang and then kills them off, one at a time, in imaginatively brutal fashion. As I mentioned earlier, things that can look horrific on screen are usually very funny to film. There's one scene in particular from this movie that sticks in my mind. I have just killed this gigantic guy (played by a wrestler) and his gang find the body and put it in an outhouse under a tarpaulin. The camera rolls in slowly and then all of a sudden the tarp starts to shake, the dead man sits up, his face and shoulders slide off and I appear from inside the body, covered in blood and butt naked. The idea is that I've split the corpse up the back and hidden inside – the character, you'll understand, is a pretty disturbed individual. As horrific as this appears on screen, after I'd clambered out of the body and they shouted 'cut', everyone on set burst out laughing. I did look ridiculous: slipping around on the blood-covered floor in a flesh-coloured thong, covered head-to-foot in syrupy movie blood, having just emerged from a corpse. There was so much fake blood involved, it stained the dry skin around my thumbs and my hands looked as if they had been dipped in red paint for the rest of the shoot. The silicone cast of this guy's body was freakishly realistic – it had been meticulously painted with his features, from his eyelashes to his tattoos, and moved and fell with the same weight and texture of flesh – but once you've handled it (and climbed inside it) it's just another prop.

The next scene in the movie is me emerging from a lake, having washed off the dead man's blood. I've rarely been put in a position during a movie where I've been asked to do something I've been uncomfortable about, but filming that scene was one of those occasions.

We were shooting in a swamp near Abita Springs. It was night time, though I'd never experienced heat and humidity like it. The lake in which we were filming was perfectly flat, an eerie mist rolling across the water from a smoke machine, and the surrounding forest illuminated by the vast movie lights. I'd noticed there were more people on set than usual, but didn't think much of it.

Before we got started, the director talked me through the scene: I had to submerge myself in the water and then slowly rise up and walk out of the lake. It sounded straightforward.

'There are just a couple of things I need to tell you first,' said the director. 'Nothing to worry about, but the lake is infested with water moccasins.'

'What are they?'

'They're large and aggressive water snakes that have a poisonous bite, but they swim on the surface, so we'll have firefighters wearing infrared goggles who'll be watching the water. If they see any ripples approaching you, they'll just hose the water and that'll scare them off.'

'Okay …'

'Also, we'll need to take a few extra precautions because there are very small creatures in the water that can get into any openings on your body.'

'Precautions?' I asked.

'Yes. Just to be careful, you understand. So we'll have three condoms on your penis, Vaseline rubbed over your anus and then we'll put you in rubber underwear so you're fully protected. Oh, and a pair of rubber water shoes, because the lake's full of leaves and God knows what's lurking under there!'

He laughed. I didn't.

'One last thing,' said the director. 'The lake's stagnant, so do not open your eyes underwater and under no circumstance get any of the liquid in your mouth. Okay?'

I stared at him for a moment. 'Is this really the best lake you could find?'

'It's the only one in the vicinity we could use, but if you stick to the rules I'm sure you'll be fine.'

It seemed like madness, but everyone was waiting and ready to go so I didn't feel I had a choice. I took one last look at all the paramedics and firemen gathered on the shore, then walked into the water, took a breath and went under. There was a speaker under the water so when I heard 'action' I slowly rose up, opened my eyes and the second they yelled 'cut' a jet of water from the hose instantly blasted me in the face to wash off the stagnant water.

Coincidentally, I found myself in a very similar position while filming a series in Colombia, though this time the lake they wanted me to go into was full of alligator-like caimans and had seven times the safe level of E.coli bacteria. Perhaps I would have gone through with it if I'd still been young and hungry, but this time I told them absolutely fucking not!

46

Before I got *No One Lives*, I'd gone for an audition with Amy Hubbard, the casting director for Peter Jackson's *The Hobbit* trilogy (who was also the casting director for the *Lord of the Rings* trilogy). I was put on camera reading a scene in which I played a character called Bard the Bowman, though I knew nothing more about the role or project. The months went by, but I heard nothing back. Occasionally I'd mention it to my agent – 'what happened with that Peter Jackson project?' – but the feeling was it hadn't gone my way, so we moved on.

Then eighteen months later, the day before I was leaving for New Orleans to start work on *No One Lives,* I got a call. Peter Jackson had now seen the audition tape I'd done with Amy Hubbard and wanted me to fly to New Zealand to do a screen test for *The Hobbit* as soon as possible.

I couldn't believe it. I had literally just zipped up my suitcase ready for my flight the next day.

'What do we do?' I asked my team. 'How can we make this work?'

To my immense disappointment, the answer was: we can't. I wouldn't be able to fit in even a quick trip to New Zealand as I was going straight into costume fittings in Louisiana, and it would be hugely unprofessional to pull out of *No One Lives* at this stage, plus there were no guarantees I'd even get the role on *The Hobbit*. I had no choice: I would have to let it go. This humungous opportunity had been dangled in front of me, only for it to be snatched away again.

I was still upset when I boarded the plane to New Orleans the next day, though I comforted myself with the fact that at least I had a job to go to and that it was my first movie I would film in America. (Even if it wasn't a once-in-a-lifetime Peter Jackson project that would probably be one of the movies of the decade and boost my career to an entirely new level. God, I was so gutted.) When I turned my phone back on ten hours later, however, I was met with an avalanche of messages. While I was in the air my team had told Peter's people that I couldn't make it to New Zealand for the screen test, so Peter had decided, on the strength of that one audition tape from eighteen months ago, that he would give me the job.

It was an awesome moment. During those early years of my career the roles kept getting bigger and bigger and I honestly couldn't understand how or why it was happening. With every offer, I would think: *Is this going to be it? Will this be the moment when it starts to plateau?* Thinking back to how this all felt, the word that comes to mind is 'unbelievable'. It was one incredible, unexpected moment after another – and it was happening so fast I didn't have any time to process any of it. There was no chance to sit down and chat things over with friends or family; I was working so hard and was barely ever home, so we were constantly playing catch-up. I remember calling my parents from New Orleans to tell them and they were totally perplexed. 'What's *The Hobbit*? Who's Peter Jackson? Where is New Zealand, exactly? You're going to be there for *a year*!?' I was proud of myself, but it was too much to take in, for all of us. And I hadn't read the book, so beyond what was in the press about the film (which had already been in production for four months by this point), I really had very little idea what to expect.

During my first week on *No One Lives*, the cast and crew all knew that I'd been cast as Bard the Bowman and seeing their reaction really brought home to me how enormously exciting this was. One day we were filming out in the sticks and this huge American supermarket cake arrived on set with CONGRATULATIONS LUKE picked out in swirly lettering across the frosting. The producers of *No One Lives* would have been well aware that because I was going to be in *The Hobbit* their movie would get a big kick up the bum and be seen by a far bigger audience, so it worked out well for all of us. As I cut the cake, covered in fake blood, I yet again marvelled at the extraordinary direction my life had taken.

My final scene on *No One Lives* was a night shoot; the next morning I would be getting on a plane to New Zealand where I would be living for the next eight months out of the same single suitcase I'd brought with me to America. The scene involved me driving a car through a forest, though in reality the car was being pulled on the back of a trailer. The camera started rolling, I was pretending to drive, then all of a sudden an enormous insect flew in through the window. Honestly, this thing was the size of a small bird. It buzzed around furiously, hit my face and then bit me on the leg. I yelped and jumped out of the car onto the trailer to escape whatever the hell it was. The bite wasn't too painful to start with, but by the time I arrived in New Zealand the following day, many hours and three flights later, I was in serious pain. I went to the bathroom at the airport, dropped my trousers and found a huge black lump on my leg. *Oh fuck.* They took me straight from the airport to Wellington Hospital for treatment, but the doctors never worked out what that bloodthirsty hell-bat actually was. I suppose it was a fitting conclusion to a crazy shoot. Still, at least the medication worked, and the next day, drugged and jet-lagged, I was at Peter Jackson's house for dinner to meet the rest of the cast. I walked into the room to see Legolas, Gandalf – all these instantly recognisable faces from *The Lord of the Rings*. Everyone was incredibly welcoming, but part of me thought I might be hallucinating.

Peter and his wife, Fran, work on movies as a team and live in a huge house in Miramar, a Wellington suburb known as the movie capital of New Zealand. Their screenwriter, Philippa Boyens, lives in the house next to them, and during the shoot the actors stayed in many of the other neighbouring houses: Gandalf down one end, Kili the dwarf at the other and Bard the Bowman in the middle. I was given the house that the movie's original director, Guillermo del Toro, had been living in before he was replaced by Peter. Peter originally hadn't wanted to take the helm of another gigantic project, but I think he's very aware of his legacy so he stepped in and took full control.

It was an idyllic place to live. Our houses were right on the sea, while behind us was a hillside thick with palms and jungle plants. One night I was woken by the whole house shaking, its wooden structure creaking and groaning so much it sounded like a boat on rough seas. It was the first time I'd ever been in an earthquake and I pelted out of the house in my underwear as quickly as I could; we'd already been warned that if there was a tsunami alert we'd have to get to high ground, and this felt like a big one. When I got onto the street, the telegraph wires rocking overhead, I expected to find the whole neighbourhood outside, but there was nobody there. *They'll come out in a minute and tell me what to do*, I thought, trying not to panic. Then suddenly, as quickly as it had started, everything fell still again. The only sounds were the lapping of the waves and the hum of insects. It appeared that what I had thought was a terrifying earthquake was actually only a minor tremor and clearly such an everyday occurrence that nobody else had bothered getting up. I sloped sheepishly back to bed, comforted by the fact that at least nobody had seen me quivering in the street in only my grits.*

On my days off I'd go fishing off the beach in front of our houses with Evangeline Lilly's partner, Norm, a lovely Hawaiian guy who set me up with all the equipment and taught me how to catch kahawai, a fish whose name means 'strong in the water' (fittingly named, as it turned out). It's lucky kahawai were delicious because I caught *a lot* of them during my time in New Zealand. You could eat them as ceviche, batter them, steam them or – my favourite – smoke them over manuka wood chips. One afternoon I went for a drive and climbed down a cliff to a

---

* In my family, 'grits' means pants. (And for any Americans reading this, 'pants' means underwear.)

little bay where I went fishing on my own, just me and this old Māori woman standing a little way up the beach. It was really windy that day, with these huge waves rolling in, and we were both catching so many fish. As Norm had taught me, I cut off the tails and stuck them upright in the sand to drain off a stress hormone that affects the taste and soon I was surrounded by a forest of fish heads poking up out of the beach. I looked back at the steep, rocky climb back to my car. I hadn't thought to bring a bucket, as I had no idea I'd catch so many fish, and I was trying to figure out how I was going to get them all home, when the old lady came over. 'Come with me,' she said, beckoning me to follow. She led me to the thicket of plants at the back of the beach, so gigantic and lush they looked prehistoric, then went up to a shrub that was like grass on steroids. Clutching a knife, she slit one of the leaves into three strands, clenched them between her teeth and then swiftly plaited them into a rope. We went back to my fish, my new friend expertly threaded this rope through the gills and then handed the lot to me with a grin. It was such a beautiful moment. Once I got back to Marine Parade I went from house to house giving every neighbour a fish for their dinner.

As we were all neighbours, we would often meet at each other's house for dinner. I remember sitting in the sand dunes outside my house with my agent, Ruth, who had come to visit. It was a beautifully clear night and we were having a last glass of wine, looking up at the stars, when we heard a shuffling noise nearby. It was usually completely dead at that time of night, so we looked round and saw a figure meandering towards us. They took a few wobbly steps, lurched to the side and then took a couple of long, deliberate strides to correct their course.

'Oh my God, that's Ian,' I whispered to Ruth, as he approached. 'Should we say hello?'

Ian had clearly spent a little too long at Philippa's (who was always extremely generous with the wine) and was now making his way home. We watched as he stumbled, steadied himself and then shuffled on.

'I'm not sure he'd be up for a conversation right now,' said Ruth.

Being around Sir Ian McKellen was an absolute joy. I clearly remember the first scene I shot with him. We were filming the arrival of the Elvish army in Dale, the ancestral home of Bard the Bowman's people, which had been destroyed by the dragon a hundred years before. In the scene, which is our characters' first meeting, Ian swings round to face me and says something like: 'Whose voice was that?' Even though I knew him well by this point, being suddenly face to face with him in the famous long beard, grey wizard's hat with a familiar furrowed brow, it took every ounce of my self-control to stay in character and not shriek: 'Ohmigod! It's Gandalf!'

I spent as much time with Ian as I could. We would go for long walks on Sundays when he'd talk about growing up in Lancashire with his sister, his life and incredible career – the jobs he'd done and people he'd worked with over the years. He walked so fast that it would be a struggle to keep up while still having enough breath for the dozens of questions I wanted to ask him. I think he was proud that I wasn't hiding my sexuality from the rest of the cast and also the fact that I was a gay man playing these macho, action roles. We would have such a laugh, Ian gently poking fun at me: 'Ooh, look at you, you're going to be a big, butch star!' He was joyous to be around and I loved spending time with him.

The crew who made *The Lord of the Rings* trilogy was now working on *The Hobbit* – and, in case you didn't know, Kiwis are the loveliest people on the planet. We were filming at Peter's Stone Street Studios, a former paint factory, where you could still see Bilbo Baggins's house, and all the monsters, armour and weapons were designed by the same special effects company, Wētā Workshop. Everywhere you looked, you came face to face with movie history. Although I had watched *The Lord of the Rings* when it first came out, I admit I wasn't a diehard fan like many of my friends. Nevertheless, I immediately began to warm to

Tolkien's world and understand the importance of the institution I was now joining and the privilege it was to be part of this legendary world.

When I first arrived, Peter described Bard to me as the Aragorn of *The Hobbit*, in other words the human character whose journey would be the crux of what the audience would relate to and follow. People could relate to him because he was an everyman, struggling to put food on the table and protect his kids. Then, all of a sudden, he has to step up and become a leader. I obviously needed to look convincing with a longbow and arrow for the role, so I spent much of my first weeks in New Zealand in training. My precision is pretty good, a skill I inherited from my dad, who's always played snooker and darts. It was more of a challenge jumping over obstacles while holding this two-metre bow than it was to actually fire the arrow and hit the target. Ironically, I rarely shot a single real arrow in the films – what you see on screen are all CGI arrows. We tried to make it work in rehearsal with the real thing, but the arrows were too long (and my arms too short) to be able to pull them out of the quiver and fire them as quickly and smoothly as necessary.

The fact that I was a Welshman playing a character famed for his longbow was particularly appropriate because I learned during the shoot that it had been Welsh longbow archers who had helped Henry V win the Battle of Agincourt. Peter and Fran wanted me to use my natural accent for the role of Bard, which meant that everyone in Lake-town ended up being Welsh as well. It was lovely to bring a bit of my home country to this world, especially because one of the languages Tolkien had based Elvish on was Welsh. As I prepared for my first day on set, I was very conscious of the weight of responsibility for bringing this famous character to life.

47

The first scene I filmed on *The Hobbit* was when Bard runs over the rooftops pursuing Smaug the dragon. They had built the whole of Lake-town on the largest sound stage in the Southern Hemisphere. Can you imagine the complexity involved in not only constructing an entire town, but one floating on a lake? The whole of this humungous studio had been filled with waist-high water. It was astonishing – even more so when you consider that they had to rebuild Lake-town four times during the course of the shoot. As a result of scheduling issues they had to take down the original set, de-flood the studio and build Smaug's lair in its place, then rebuild the town and flood it again for the next scenes. Lake-town burns down in the movie, which obviously couldn't be done inside a studio, so they rebuilt the whole thing again in the studio's car park. They constructed a concrete wall around the perimeter, lined it with a membrane and filled it with water. I'd be on my barge filming a scene and would pass the girls in the production office, giving them a wave as I drifted by. The night they blew up that set the whole sky was aglow; you could even see the flames from our houses, which were over the hill. I honestly have no idea how Peter got away with it, because the studio is right in the middle of a residential area in the Wellington suburbs.

Back to my first day on set. For the scene, they had built the Lake-town skyline in another studio: on the same scale as the original, but just the rooftops. If you haven't seen the movie, I run and jump between buildings, firing off arrows, while the dragon flies around breathing fire. It's an extremely physical scene. That morning, the stuntmen warned me that Peter would probably keep pushing me until I couldn't go any further, so I should say when I'd had enough. Rather than worry me, this just fired me up. Remember, I was coming to this off the back of a lot of very physical roles, so I was well prepared. Besides, I was going to be connected by cables to a track on the ceiling and stuntmen would be on hand to help pull me up after I jumped the gaps. I reckoned all bases had been covered.

The one thing I hadn't considered, however, was the fake ice covering the roofs. As I was holding my bow I only had one free hand, so every time I slid down a roof, my knuckles were getting scraped raw on the lumps of rutted plastic that were designed to look like ice and by the time Peter announced a break, I had no skin left on my knuckles.

The stuntmen huddled around me. 'Dude, you've done this like twenty times, it'll be fine if you don't want to do it again.'

'Does Peter want me to go again?' I asked.

'Yeah, probably.'

'Then we'll go again.'

They sprayed something on my knuckles to freeze the skin and stop the bleeding. We did another take – and another. By the time we had finished filming my hands were so sore I couldn't move them for days afterwards.

There was another point during this same sequence where I jump across a gap, swing from a chimney stack and then dangle from a roof, while flames shoot up around me as if the dragon had just set the house ablaze and fire was blowing up the alleyway. And these were real flames, by the way, not CGI. My clothes were fireproofed and they put special gel in my hair, but I lost a lot of eyelashes that day.

'That's great, Luke,' said Peter, after the first take. 'I've just got a couple of notes. When we do it again, can you make sure you swing out like you did that time?'

I was nodding, but inside I was thinking: *I swung out because I was desperately trying not to fall, I had zero control over what my body was doing, but okay …*

Peter went on: 'And next time can you not blink when the flames go past your eyes?'

I looked at him and then at everyone around him, who all knew him very well, and my facial expression must have been like – is this guy serious? – because they were all nodding. So I did it again and somehow I managed to swing out as Peter wanted and keep my eyes open when the fire shot up. I knew it would be difficult, but if I'd thought it was beyond my capabilities then I'd have asked for a stuntman to step in.

I always prefer to do stunts myself if possible. On a practical level, if an actor is able to do the stunt it makes things easier for everyone: the cameras can just roll and capture everything, while the stuntman doesn't have to twist himself into awkward positions to hide his face. I also feel that it's part of my responsibility as an actor to embody every bit of a character's experience, not just the words and emotions but the physical aspects of the role. Then there's the fact that stunts can be a lot of fun. In *Beauty and the Beast* I had to jump from a 30-foot ledge on a cable that allowed me to free fall for three seconds before it slowed down, so I could land in a cool pose. It was insane. I loved that I was getting to learn a new skill and try something so unusual; why would I pass such an exciting opportunity onto someone else?

Stunts *are* dangerous, though: there's no getting away from it. There's never been a day I've been filming a stunt that I haven't come home with bruises or cuts. Stunt coordinators are sticklers for safety and you rehearse endlessly and stick to the rules, but even so it will never be risk-free. I've worked on films where people have been seriously injured; I've nearly lost an eye twice now. For me, however, the benefits of tackling these physical challenges outweigh the risks (and I admit to finding the element of danger quite exciting) but if insurance won't cover me for a certain stunt, or I just don't feel I can do it, then I'm very happy to let one of the well-trained professionals step in and take my place.

Because many of my scenes were with non-human creatures, much of the time I was acting opposite something that wasn't there, so your imagination becomes your most valuable tool. The scene on the Laketown rooftops was shot in front of a green screen to allow Smaug to be added in post-production, so during filming I was chasing a big green ball on top of a giant telescopic pole, around a green room, with people in green onesies scurrying around the studio. It's challenging, because all the time you're wondering whether your reaction is too big, whether your eyeline is at the right level and what the finished scene will actually look like. I remember asking Peter if he had a picture of the dragon to help me visualise it. 'Nope,' he said. 'But it's really big.'

When it came to my scenes with the dwarves, I was usually working with stand-in actors, who were little people wearing the characters' costumes, rather than the main actors themselves. The actors who played the dwarves – Jimmy Nesbitt, Aidan Turner and the rest – had all been scanned in 3D and then their faces and hands scaled down to make silicone prosthetics to fit the little people. Whenever there was a wide shot, such as when I'm leading the dwarves onto my barge, it's the little people you see on screen, while the main actors would be off to the side speaking the lines through a microphone. It was very confusing to film because the stand-in actors weren't the ones talking, which made it difficult to remember exactly which one of them I was meant to be speaking to.

The most technically challenging scene I was involved in was when the dwarves are sitting around my dining table at my house in Laketown. To film this, Peter used a motion control system, which is rarely used because it's so complicated. Two versions of my dining room had been built in different studios. In one, everything was life-sized and green, including the chairs, table and everything on it, and this is where I filmed my part of the scene. As I was on my own, there was a picture of each of the dwarves on all the chairs with little bulbs on top that lit up to show who was speaking. Meanwhile, the actors playing the dwarves were on the other set, in which everything had been built a third larger than life-sized so that the actors all appeared smaller. In my place at the top of their table there was a guy called (no joke) Tall Paul, a gigantic ex-policeman actor, who was dressed in a wig and clothes to look like me and stood on a platform so he seemed even bigger next to the dwarves. When I put a spoon down on the table in my studio, Tall Paul would put a giant-sized spoon down in the other room. The master camera was filming the dwarves, while the computerised camera was on me, then Peter had a screen in his tent where they could merge the feeds together to make it look like we were all in the same room. It's at times like this that you realise why movies are so expensive and time-consuming to make.

We would rehearse the scene together in one room, then I'd be like, 'See you in twelve hours, guys!' and go and film on my own in the other room, with an earpiece for taking direction. Ian obviously had to do a lot of scenes like this, as his character was always with the dwarves, and he hated it, because it could be a lonely process. The end result, though, was stunning. I didn't see these finished CGI scenes until the premiere, when I sat there, open-mouthed at the spectacle. I thought back to that green room with the ball on the pole and was just in awe of those people who had sat at their desks for so many months to create an entire world that hadn't been there. When CGI is done well nobody notices it, but the time, effort, expertise and money that goes into it is just immense.

⋯

There was never a set wrap time on that shoot. If Peter wanted to keep filming, he just paid everybody overtime and got a hundred pizzas delivered to set from the local takeaway; we'd break for dinner, then keep working. The dwarves had to go through hours and hours of preparation to get in costume – fake noses, fat suits, giant hands – and sometimes Peter would bring them in and they'd spend the whole day sweltering in these prosthetics, only for them not to be used. His work ethic and energy levels were extraordinary.

Peter is a fascinating character. He's an obsessive collector of movie and military memorabilia and gave us a tour around his warehouse of treasures while we were filming the movie. Among his First World War artefacts were full-sized replica planes made out of wood and paper (Richard Armitage, who played Thorin Oakenshield, was the only one of us brave enough to go up in one) and original water-cooled German army machine guns. After calling the local police to warn them about the gunfire (though I imagine the residents of Wellington are well used to his explosions by now), Peter set up the guns and demonstrated them for us. He even took us out for a drive on one of his giant tanks: we assumed we'd go for a spin around the warehouse, but instead he drove out of the front gate and down a residential street with all of us actors sitting on the top, the tank's gun arm pointing forward as if about to take aim at the neighbourhood's cats. We also went for a drive in the *pièce de résistance* of his collection, the original vintage car from the movie *Chitty Chitty Bang Bang*. Not only did it make the famous 'chitty chitty bang bang' sound from the film, but as we turned onto the main road, Peter pressed a button and the theme tune blasted out of a hidden speaker as we drove along, waving at the astonished pedestrians. He was a big kid, living his best life, and we were lucky enough to enjoy it with him during these months.

...

During a break in filming, I went to Wales to visit my parents and asked if they'd like to come back to New Zealand with me. Apart from those few tricky years when I was a teenager, my parents and I have always been very close and I wanted them to be able to enjoy these incredible experiences I was having. Initially they were worried about leaving their dog, Georgie, but eventually agreed to come out for a week. I did explain that they'd need three days just to recover from the jet lag, but I supposed it was better than nothing.

Needless to say, once they got to New Zealand and saw my beautiful little house on the beach and met the wonderful people I was working with they decided to stay on for another week. They had the best trip: dinners with the cast, a visit to Wellington Zoo and a private tour of the magical Wētā Workshop from its founder, Sir Richard Taylor.

My dad has always been fascinated by the process of moviemaking. The first time he visited me on a set he couldn't understand why there were hundreds of people just standing around.

'But what are their jobs?' he kept asking. 'What are they all doing here?'

'Wait until they shout "cut" and then watch them move,' I said.

Sure enough, when the camera stops rolling a film set suddenly comes alive. As I explained to my dad, every single one of those people there was intrinsic to the process, whether they were checking make-up, changing a lens or touching up the fake snow.

One day during my parents' visit, we were filming a big sequence in Lake-town that would feature a lot of extras, so I asked Peter if my dad could be involved. I knew Peter would be open to the idea, because his own kids and dogs appear in the movie, while my daughters were played by Jimmy Nesbitt's children.

I took my dad to the tent where the extras got ready and left him to it. When it was time to do my scene with the crowd later that day, I scanned the 150-odd extras and spotted him instantly. The residents of Lake-town were usually dressed in sludgy tones of brown and grey, but somehow my dad had found the only bright red cloak in the basket of costumes. Together with the Gandalf-sized wig and beard he was wearing, he might as well have had a large arrow with DAVE pointing towards his head.

In the scene, Bard gives a speech to try to rouse the Lake-towners and encourage them to join him in fighting the dragon. Before the camera started to roll, Peter came over the God mic (which can be heard over speakers all around the set) and told the extras: 'Guys, I really need you all to look like you believe in Bard. He's one of the people! You're inspired by what he's saying! Lots of enthusiasm – okay?'

After we'd done the first take, Peter came over to me. 'Luke, just come and have a look at this.'

We went back to his tent and he played back the last take on his screens.

'Watch your father,' said Peter.

The camera slowly panned across the crowd, who were all reacting just as Peter had asked – nodding in agreement, looking inspired – then my dad appeared on screen in that red cloak. His eyes were wide and manic-looking; he was jerking his head about like one of those nodding dogs on the back shelf of a car. It was hysterical.

Next to me Peter was giggling away. 'Do you think you could tell him to take it down a notch?' he said.

I went and found my father in the crowd.

'How am I doing?' he said, his eyes bright with excitement. He was clearly loving the whole experience.

'Dad, what you're doing is great,' I said, 'but could you please just dial it down by about a hundred and fifty per cent?'

Dad also appears in scenes in *Dracula Untold* and *The Great Train Robbery*, but Mam's never been the least bit interested in getting her five minutes of fame. The closest she's come to being in one of my movies was on *Tamara Drewe*, when they came to visit me in Dorset during the shoot. Mam got bored while watching us film a scene in a field and decided to take Georgie for a walk. Moments later, we were in the middle of a take when all of a sudden Stephen Frears yelled: 'Stop!'

We all stopped; he sounded extremely pissed off.

'Who's that bloody woman in the background with the dog?' he shouted, gesturing towards a little figure at the bottom of the field. 'Get her out of my fucking shot!'

Oh Christ, I thought. *That's my mam.*

I know how proud my parents were of what was happening to me, but they were also a little perplexed. It was a world they knew so little about. As far as they were concerned, you went to work at nine, came home at five, had your tea and then went to bed, but now all of a sudden I was living out of a suitcase for months at a time. It was especially hard for them to relate to my job in the early days, because although I was working constantly, none of the films had yet come out. I don't think it had even crossed their mind that these films were going to be in the cinema and on TV. Once they had watched the movies it all became more real to them, because they could see the work I'd been doing and understand why I'd been away for so long. My whole family was impressed and very excited, because nothing like this had ever happened to anyone we knew. I would take them to all the premieres. 'You just enjoy every minute of this,' my auntie Helen would say. To this day, whenever I have a new film out, Dad will go to the pictures to watch it multiple times. He'll sit in the middle of the row and ask the people around him what they thought of it.

'See that actor?' He'll tell them, 'That's my son.'

It warms my heart to see how proud he is of me.

48

I had to make a second trip to New Zealand the following year to shoot some additional scenes, because Peter decided he wanted to make *The Hobbit* into three films rather than the two originally planned, and while I was there I was offered a role that would finally take me away from the long hair, swords and dragons.

I'd never seen any of the *Fast & Furious* movies – I knew they were about cars and that was about it – but when my agent told me they wanted me to appear in the sixth instalment of the mega-franchise I didn't need any persuading. I would be playing a British villain, they were shooting in London and Europe and the role of Owen Shaw would be me, front and centre of this giant, commercial blockbuster. The fact that I could cut my hair short was just a bonus.

I would have to get in serious shape for the role, not only because my character was a former SAS soldier, so I needed to be lean and sharp like a blade, but because I would be on screen next to the likes of Dwayne Johnson and Vin Diesel. A month before the shoot, I started working with Simon Waterson, the trainer who got Daniel Craig in shape for Bond. On our first day he told me we would begin with twenty minutes on the treadmill. My heart sank; treadmills are my idea of hell – any kind of cardio, in fact.

'I'm telling you now, Simon, this isn't going to work,' I said. 'If you make me go on the treadmill, I'm going to end up not turning up to the sessions. Isn't there any other way we can do this?'

Simon isn't known as the best in the industry for nothing. 'Of course there is,' he said.

He put together a regime of a high-protein diet and daily workouts combining strength exercises and dynamic moves to overload certain muscles. It wasn't traditional cardio, but I'd be out of breath within minutes. I stuck to it religiously and within a month I was in the most insane shape of my life. Ironically, I never took my top off once in the whole bloody movie, but I got to train with Simon, who I loved, and was getting paid to do it.

Though it can be nerve-wracking joining such a well-established group of actors, the cast was very welcoming. Vin, who is the producer as well as the star, is a musical theatre obsessive and would come up and sing *West Side Story* songs to me. Paul Walker was an absolute gentleman, while Dwayne was utterly charming. During filming in London, my cousin Dean, his wife Rachel and their kids came to visit me on set. Their daughter Caitlin, who was six at the time, was desperate to meet Dwayne, so I went and knocked on his trailer. Moments later, this giant of a man in a tight vest and sunglasses loomed in the doorway, his muscles bronzed and glistening.

'Hey Dwayne, would you mind saying hello to my family? They're visiting from Wales.'

'Sure,' he said, shaking everyone's hands. 'How you all doin'?'

Caitlin was staring up at him open-mouthed.

'Are you the tooth fairy?' she blurted out.

Dwayne grinned. 'Yes, I'm the tooth fairy,' he said.

I had no idea he'd played the role in a kid's movie.

Dwayne really is fucking enormous and you can't help but feel self-conscious around him so I had to keep reminding myself that they had cast me for how I looked. He always travels with an entourage, including his personal stunt double, a mountain-sized Hawaiian guy who's virtually his twin. After we finished filming in London, we spent seven weeks shooting in Tenerife and when we arrived at the airport I found myself standing at baggage reclaim with all of Dwayne's team, the other stars having already left for the hotel. The luggage began to arrive on the carousel and as we waited these very expensive-looking bags appeared, one of which looked as though it had got wet. There was a slick of something shiny behind it on the conveyor belt.

'Shit, it's happened again,' muttered one of Dwayne's guys.

'What is that stuff?' I asked.

'It's Dwayne's oil case. We pack it as carefully as we can, but one of the bottles must have broken. It happens nearly every time.'

It turned out that Dwayne travels with a suitcase full of bottles of a specific body oil he uses in films. He's always covered in it, to make the most of his muscles; his make-up artist rushes in and slathers him in it between takes. And by the time his team had managed to collect the bags, most of baggage reclaim at Tenerife airport was also smeared with Dwayne's oil.

Over the course of *Fast 6* I probably spent as much time working with the stars' stunt doubles as I did the actors themselves. From what I observed, Vin and Dwayne rarely did their own fight sequences: they would swing a punch for the close-up, but when the camera was back on me their doubles would step in and I'd fight them instead. You can understand why they'd rather not risk hurting themselves when they have their double on hand, because although every precaution is taken, these sequences certainly aren't without danger. Paul Walker and I had a fight on board an Antonov cargo jet, in which he was put on cables, and then flies at me and throws a punch. But during filming he landed awkwardly and the poor guy tore his ACL. It was such a shame, because Paul and I had spent weeks rehearsing that stunt together, but from then on he was injured and was unable to finish the fight sequence.

. . .

For me, the best part of the *Fast 6* experience was the press tour, because I got to take my cousin Dean along with me. On these big tours you are usually given a companion flight, plus one for your publicist, and because I was single at the time I took Dean. I've had some unbelievable moments working in movies and they are all the more joyous when I can share them with the people I love. The press tour went from London to the Philippines, South Korea and then Los Angeles. We flew by private jet, stayed in the best hotels and were treated like superstars everywhere we went. It was a treat for me, even more so for Dean, whose day job was working in a Pot Noodle factory.

It was on this tour that I first found out about the Luketeers. We'd been on an enormously long flight and I walked into arrivals at Seoul airport with Dean and my publicist Cara to be met by a crowd of 300 screaming girls. I glanced over my shoulder, assuming one of the other regular cast members must be following us, but there was nobody there.

'Luke, it's your face on the posters,' said Dean. 'They're here for you!'

None of us were ready for this, not even Cara; we had no idea that I had any presence in Asia at all. I knew I had fans by this point – when I got out of the car at *The Hobbit* premiere the noise from the crowd was thunderous – but this was something else. I couldn't believe all these Korean girls were screaming my name.

'We call ourselves the Luketeers,' they told me. It was a name inspired by *The Three Musketeers*. It would go on to be adopted by my fanbase and nowadays there are Luketeers all over the world.

I'm always shocked by how generous my fans are. When I returned to the West End in the play *Backstairs Billy* earlier this year, there were always gifts waiting at the stage door. Two of my most diehard Japanese fans, Zony and Sakko, came to the first thirty shows. Every. Single. Show. They could have gone to see every production in the West End for that money, but instead they sat in the same seats and were waiting for me at the stage door every night.

'It's so lovely of you to support me,' I said to them one night, 'but you do realise the show doesn't change? That it's exactly the same every time?'

'We know!' they said, smiling. 'We don't care!'

I've done a few of those charity auctions where you can bid to have a conversation with me, and invariably it's Zony I end up speaking to, or another fan of mine, Adele, who lives in New Zealand. Adele is in her seventies and has followed me for a long time, so I've got to know her quite well over the years. She's retired, yet often flies to see me wherever I am in the world. I do tell her she shouldn't spend so much money, but she says: 'Luke, you've given me a reason to travel the world and discover new things while supporting someone I admire.' I guess you can't argue with that.

While I can't relate to this intense level of fandom and do feel slightly indebted, I've only ever had good experiences with the Luketeers. Perhaps I've been lucky, but they are genuinely nice people and I'll always make an effort to spend time with them.

Once we arrived back in Los Angeles, Dean went home and my parents flew out to join me for the Latin American press junket in the glitzy resort of Cabo San Lucas in Mexico. The three of us flew there (by private jet, naturally) with my co-star, Michelle Rodriguez. Believe it or not, Michelle was brought up as a Jehovah's Witness and has a heart of gold, but she's got one hell of a mouth on her these days. You could be chatting to royalty and Michelle would be there happily effing and blinding – and she is unashamedly *loud*. It is quite brilliant to witness.

Before the flight I said to her, 'Babe, my parents are coming to Cabo with us, could you please just watch your swearing?'

'Sure,' she said. 'Of course.'

So we got on the plane, I introduced her to my parents – 'it's so nice to meet you, Mr and Mrs Evans!' – then she sat at one end of the plane, and me and my parents settled ourselves at a table at the other end.

As we prepared for take-off, Mam looked around at the cabin. 'Well, isn't this lovely, I—'

'Motherfucking *cunt*!'

Even with the background noise of the engines, the voice from the front of the plane was crystal clear.

I stood up. 'Michelle?'

'Yeah?'

'The swearing?'

'Fuck! Sorry!'

'No problem,' I said, sitting back down.

Yet moments later a steady stream of four-letter words started up. My publicist tried to warn me from saying anything, because Michelle gives off this *I will snap your neck* kind of attitude. She's created this fireball persona, but we'd had conversations during the shoot and when you got her on her own she was sweet and sensitive, plus we had stuff in common: we came from similar backgrounds.

So I walked up to the front of plane. 'Michelle. Please. The swearing? The flight is only two hours.'

'Fuck,' she said, looking genuinely contrite. She stood up and called out to my mother. 'Shit, Mrs Evans, I'm so sorry!'

'Please don't worry about it,' said Mam, smiling.

Michelle is such a character and I love her for being her authentic self. Mam still asks after her to this day.

• • •

There's a terribly sad postscript to my *Fast & Furious* experience. A few months after we finished filming, I was in Los Angeles for the premiere of the second Hobbit movie, *The Hobbit: The Desolation of Smaug*. A giant stage in the shape of a book had been built in the car park of the Beverly Hilton Hotel, which is where the cast of the movie assembled behind a curtain. Seconds before the grand reveal to the world's press, my publicist ran onto the stage. 'It's just been announced that Paul Walker has died in a car crash,' she whispered to me, then ran off just as the curtain went up. I plastered on a smile for the audience, but

I was almost frozen with shock and disbelief. I'd liked Paul very much; I couldn't fathom that this sweet, beautiful guy was no longer here. As the press knew that I'd just filmed *Fast 6*, the first question I got was: 'Have you heard about Paul Walker?' Thank God my publicist had warned me, as I was able to at least give some thought to my tribute to him, but it was horrible knowing I was in the same city where he'd died and here I was promoting a movie. It seemed so frivolous against the background of such a terrible tragedy.

49

After I finished *Fast & Furious*, I was invited to the headquarters of Universal Studios in Los Angeles for a meeting with the chairperson, Donna Langley. She told me that they loved me in *Fast* and wanted to offer me another movie: the title role in their remake of *Dracula*. It was the first time I was going to be leading a movie.

I remember walking out of Universal's offices in Burbank and getting into my rented car as if on autopilot. *So let me get this straight: I'll be playing one of the most famous characters in the world in a one-hundred-million-dollar movie that will be resting entirely on my shoulders?* In the world of movies it didn't get much bigger than this. I didn't have any hint of imposter syndrome, though, no sense that I wasn't worthy of this. I knew I couldn't keep wondering 'why me?' because for whatever reason it clearly *was* me. My dedication, professionalism and commitment had paid off, because they had been watching me and believed I could carry this movie – and I believed it too. I knew I could do this. I was ready.

I would be playing Vlad Tepes, the historical character on whom Dracula was based and a total badass. To top it all, I'd already got the fangs – not that my natural canines were anywhere near big enough for the part. My movie fangs were monstrous things, covered in veins, that fitted over two of my teeth, and were so sharp that I split my lip on them numerous times. They were made by Mark Coulier, the legendary special effects make-up artist who this year won an Oscar for *Poor Things* and who would also make my teeth for *Beauty and the Beast*. I had to have a full fake upper set that brought all my top teeth down to the same level, because they thought it would be distracting to see these two daggers jutting out of Gaston's mouth when he sang. They were so much longer than my normal teeth that I felt like Cilla Black when I had them in.

Dracula Untold is probably people's favourite film of mine and I'm always being asked when there's going to be a sequel. I'm proud that it's had that impact as it was a real test of my skill as a leading man, not just because of the emotion needed to fulfil my character's journey but because I was playing the title role. I knew how lucky I was to be in that position after only four or five years in the industry, but I really felt the pressure. As lead actor, both you and the director are captains of the ship and responsible for the atmosphere on set, and I was very conscious of wanting to make everyone feel part of the team. After all, you can't make a movie on your own: it requires an army of people, all specialists in their field and all of whom have fought hard to be there. No one can ever complain on a film set, because everybody's doing something they've always dreamed of doing – from the runner to the set designer. When that clapperboard slams shut for the first time, we know we're all on a train that won't stop until we reach the final sequence, by which point we'll be broken and exhausted, tears will have been shed and arguments, wet feet and sleepless nights endured – but we'll have got there together. My job as number one on the call sheet is to make people smile in those tough moments at 3am, when we're out in the middle of some forest and it's pissing down with rain. I want everybody to have a good time, because we're all so lucky to be on that set.

The shoot was exhausting, the most physical job I've ever done. We filmed the movie in Belfast and took over a warehouse in the dockland area for rehearsals, where we learned these enormous, complex fight sequences that were basically me against thirty or forty stuntmen. One of them was a 150-point fight, meaning I made contact 150 times in a row. In the movie it runs as a four-minute sequence: I plunge into the army of Turkish soldiers, swiping my sword and impaling with a flagpole (I am Vlad the Impaler, after all). For context, in *Fast & Furious* we'd have maybe a six- or seven-point fight before a cut, then they'd bring in the stunt doubles.

Movie fight scenes are genuinely dangerous. Consistency and accuracy are key, because you won't be doing the sequence just once; you'll be doing twenty or thirty takes on camera and using real weapons. We spent weeks rehearsing the battle scenes for *The Hobbit*, with wooden swords and in our normal clothes, and it was terrifying enough when you could see who you were fighting. But when you've got sixty stuntmen running at you in orc masks, with fake teeth and bloodshot contact lenses, wielding these giant axes, you absolutely feel the same fear you would in a real battle. At the moment 'action' is called, everyone wants to give their very best and adrenaline is sky-high, which means weapons can be swung too hard and too far, and when that happens people can get injured. On *Immortals* one of the stuntmen lost all his top teeth in a fight because someone swung their sword the wrong way; he was in the wrong place and it smashed into his mouth. The poor guy had to have a full set of implants once we'd finished.

I very nearly lost an eye on *Dracula Untold* because in the heat of the moment an actor forgot he wasn't fighting me for real. You only have to use 20 to 30 per cent of your force on film: you don't need to give it full power and push your weapon through like you would in a genuine fight, because you can trust the illusion works on screen. This actor was meant to swing his sword towards my face and then I would block it, but in that critical moment he forgot to fake it and swung so hard that when his sword made contact with mine it bent and the tip flicked the skin just under my eye. It was a bad cut and we had to stop filming for the rest of the day, but if it had been a few millimetres higher I would have been off the movie for good.

There've been occasions when I've had to tell the stunt supervisor that I won't do the scene with a particular actor, because he's fighting for real. I'm not prepared to be some dude's punchbag just because he isn't trusting the rehearsals or hasn't rehearsed enough. In that situation they'll usually pull the actor and put a stuntman in their place. When I was filming one movie, an actor had to whack his cane over my back and he did it so hard on camera that it snapped. I went home with three whopping black bruises across my back that day.

As I had to be in peak physical shape to tackle all the fight scenes in *Dracula Untold*, I made the decision to give up smoking. I'd always hated the smell of it and was well aware how bad it was for me, so one afternoon after filming I had a hypnotherapy session in Belfast. Within half an hour of going to bed that night I had unbelievably violent vomiting and diarrhoea that went on for four hours, which felt as though my body was trying to purge itself of something. I assumed it was food poisoning, but no one else got sick. The next morning I was exhausted, but completely over it – both the illness (or whatever it was) and the urge to smoke.

I never went back to cigarettes, but a year later I started vaping, which is less anti-social, though it's still caused me some headaches over the years. In the early days, vapes were huge battery-powered things that looked like hand grenades and produced a heavy water vapour. One time, during a long night flight, I stupidly thought I'd take a sneaky puff of this vape. I figured nobody would notice because the cabin was dark and the only illumination was coming from the low lighting on the floor. I was lying on my flat bed and blew the vapour under my blanket, expecting it just to disappear, but instead it drifted down and hung over the floor, looking worryingly like a thick cloud of smoke. *Shit, this isn't good,* I thought, wondering what I should do. I didn't want to draw attention to it, because smoking vapes was illegal on planes. Then, to my horror, a steward came walking up the cabin towards me. I immediately ducked under my blanket, pretending to be asleep. I heard his footsteps stop at my row, there was a pause, and then the sound of running towards the cockpit. Moments later a crowd of people, including the pilot and the purser, gathered by my seat.

'I'm telling you, I saw smoke!'

'Where did you see it coming from?'

'Just around here …'

They brought out some sort of smoke sensor, but of course as it was vapour nothing was picked up. I learned my lesson, though, and will never do that again!

• • •

Shortly after I finished filming *Dracula Untold*, I was invited to a Prince's Trust gala dinner at the Savoy Hotel in London. When I was asked to become an ambassador I chose to focus on bullying, an issue that's obviously close to my heart, and over the years I've shared my story with young people from all over the UK whose lives had been destroyed by bullying but were rebuilding them with the help of the Prince's Trust. It's a fantastic institution and I'm very proud to be part of it.

This dinner at the Savoy was the first time I got to meet King Charles, then Prince of Wales. I watched him work his way around the room, speaking to everyone, until he reached me.

'This is the actor Luke Evans,' an aide told him. 'He's just become an ambassador.'

Charles had a good, strong handshake.

'What are you working on at the moment?' he asked.

'I've just finished a movie called *Dracula Untold*. I play Vlad Tepes, the historical figure who was known as Vlad the Impaler.'

Charles's eyes lit up. 'I'll tell you an interesting story. I'm actually related to Vlad Tepes.'

To my astonishment, he then proceeded to talk me through his entire lineage all the way back to the 1400s. He told me he now owns a number of properties in Romania, where Vlad was ruler.

'That's the most incredible story,' I said.

'Yes, and not a lot of people know it,' he said, smiling, and off he went.

I noticed he had stayed a little longer with me than he had with other guests, probably because we had this fascinating thing to talk about. Charles makes you feel as if he's genuinely interested in what you have to say, which is remarkable when you consider he has to do this several times a day. You imagine he'd become robotic, just going through the motions every time, but he really seems to engage.

The King's sons are just as easy company. I've been invited to a lot of polo events over the years where William and Harry have been playing and on one memorable occasion I brought along a very good friend, my hair and make-up artist from *The Hobbit*, Ricci-Lee Berry, as my guest. Naturally, the two of us got extremely drunk (the champagne was plentiful and free) and at some point late in the afternoon I ended up saying hello to the princes, who I'd met before. The three of us were chatting when all of a sudden one of their security detail walked up to them and said 'incoming' very quietly. The princes immediately looked over my shoulder, so I turned round and saw my friend Ricci-Lee staggering towards us, champagne slopping from her glass, as she drunkenly weaved her way over.

'Helloooo!' she said, waving so hard she nearly fell over. I had to bite my lip to stop myself laughing.

'Great to see you, Luke,' said William quickly, and with that the princes were off.

50

In the early years of my movie career, rumours about my sexuality kept bubbling away, but because I was getting all these macho roles they never went anywhere. The brighter a star shines, however, the more people want to hear about you, and five years into my movie career – around the release of *Dracula Untold* – that's exactly what happened. All of a sudden, people started digging into the old press I'd done years before and speculation about my private life exploded online. I knew it was coming, but what I hadn't been prepared for was the vitriol and anger from other gay people. I was accused of closeting myself, just because of that one fake article about me and Holly. There were comments like: 'I hope he dies of AIDS' – really hideous, hurtful stuff. People wrote that I should be ashamed of myself, which particularly infuriated me: they had no idea what I'd been through, how I'd had to leave home at sixteen purely because I wasn't prepared to deny my sexuality. Yet as terrifying as it was thinking that no more movie offers would come in and my career could be over, I also knew I had to stand by who I was.

It was while I was doing press for *Dracula Untold* that I was asked outright about my sexuality for the first time by an American magazine. Before the interview my publicist had actually advised me that the subject might come up, because it was with a well-respected gay journalist, but even if she hadn't tipped me off I wouldn't have been fazed. I'd been prepared for this for years and I knew my answer would come from my heart. Sure enough, the journalist's first question was: 'How do you feel about being the world's first openly gay action hero?'

This actually took me by surprise – the action hero bit, not the part about being gay – but after a moment's thought I realised he was right. Back then it felt like I was the only one out there killing dragons, driving fast cars and blowing things up. There were other gay actors playing masculine roles, of course, but none of them were out – and sadly many aren't to this day. Because nobody connected the dots early in my career I was never pigeonholed in that way: people just saw this stereotypically masculine guy and accepted me at face value.

I told the journalist that I was glad people could look at me and see someone who was happy living his life and enjoying his career. It was a relief to be able to finally address the issue in public. The truth was out; *I* was out. I just hoped that audiences and the industry would accept me for who I was, and that I'd be able to continue with a career that I had loved.

On the back of that interview, there was an article in *TIME* magazine saying it would be easy to criticise me for not being more forthcoming about my sexuality, but the journalist acknowledged that I was working in an industry where 'queerness is a major strike against a star' and described my refusal to deny my sexuality as a step forward. The gist of it was: Luke may be doing this a little slower and less loudly than we would have wanted, but what he's doing is good.

That article was a turning point for me. I'd been constantly beaten up online about the fact that I wasn't out there shouting from the rooftops about my sexuality, but that hadn't been the sort of person I was before I was famous, so why would I change my personality now? The writer clearly grasped the fact that I was out there on my own, trying to be myself despite the challenges I faced, and I should be credited for that. Once the *TIME* article came out, I knew there was no going back. I had to own this now and if it affected my casting, so be it. And it made me realise that I didn't need to be waving a flag at the front of a Gay Pride parade to send a message: just being out here and living my life authentically – that was enough of a message in itself.

My experience of being an openly gay actor playing traditionally straight roles has been a double-edged sword. On the one hand it's been great to have international recognition, so I can use my platform for good. People will see that gay actors don't need to be pigeonholed, that we can play hard-as-nails characters and heterosexual romantic leads as convincingly as anyone else. The part that needs to change is the fact that an actor's sexuality is still such a topic of conversation. After all, do people refer to Brad Pitt as a 'straight actor'? It's reductive and lazy to make someone's sexuality their entire identity. There was a stage when I was referred to as 'gay actor Luke Evans' all the time, but once there was nothing more to say – no sensational story to go with this uninteresting fact – it eventually faded. Yet the fact that people see it as something that needs to be talked about means there's still an issue. If it wasn't a problem, it wouldn't ever be mentioned.

There's a famous straight actor in my peer group who I used to see at parties and whenever we met he'd always make a point of telling me how amazed he was that I was getting these macho roles. 'It's so incredible what's going on with you!' he'd gush. 'You! Doing *this!* Just … wow.' It happened so often that it was hard not to get a little paranoid. Did he think I wasn't worthy of playing these roles? Or was it because I was a gay man who was being cast in roles that perhaps he thought *he* should be getting? In the end, I tackled him on it.

'Look, I know why you're saying this,' I said, the next time we spoke.

'What? No! It's just because I'm so impressed!'

'I got the job because I was the right person for the role.'

'Oh yes, of course, but the fact that you're gay—'

'That's not even part of the equation. You've got to stop this. I can play alpha males, because that's how I appear. It's who I am. Being gay has got nothing to do with it.'

He's not mentioned it to me again since.

Nowadays I play both straight and gay roles, which is just as it should be. Right now I'm playing a father fighting monsters with my daughter; before that I was a hard-nosed ex-con, and before that a gay man going through divorce. As far as I can tell, I don't think my career or casting has been affected, yet I'm still in a very small group of Hollywood actors who are openly gay. The industry clearly has some way to go before an actor's sexuality is entirely irrelevant. Would I still be closeted if I hadn't done that early press during *Taboo*? No, I don't think I would be. But would I have had the same career if I'd been upfront about my sexuality from the start? Would I have got Owen Shaw in *Fast & Furious* and *Dracula*? The sad truth of it is probably not.

51

I still get freaked out when people know my name. I know I'm famous, but it blows my mind when I'm recognised as Luke Evans, rather than Gaston or Owen Shaw. I find it extraordinary that people have taken the trouble to look beyond the character and find out who I actually am. I was in the Maldives earlier this year and one of the guys who drove a buggy at the resort told me he was my biggest fan. That's the magic of this industry, that it carries you into people's lives, so that even on a tiny island in the middle of the Indian Ocean this young man knew who I was.

Fame is a weird one. For all its benefits, I'm not really sure I'd recommend it. The problem is that it's not something you can control, so while it's nice to be recognised at times, you can't turn it off on days you're feeling like shit. I remember having a horrible argument on the phone in Montreal with an ex-boyfriend and someone came running up to me, unaware – or ignoring – that I was crying, and asked for a photo, so I had to wipe away the tears and pose for a selfie. Maybe I could have refused, but I see it as part of the job and feel I have a duty to the people who put their hand in their pocket to buy into whatever I'm part of.

Even though I've now had a taste of fame myself, I'm certainly not immune to the power of it. Several years ago I was invited to the Museum of Modern Art's annual Film Benefit in New York, which that year was a tribute to Tom Hanks. The room was filled with Hollywood's elite, like a who's who of movie superstardom. You'd be reaching for a canapé and there would be Meryl Streep going for the same vol-au-vent. At one point during dinner I got up to use the bathroom and realised that the man sitting behind me was Steven Spielberg. I should explain that, although we'd never met, we did have a sort of history. A couple of years before this, at the premiere of the second *Hobbit* movie, Peter Jackson had told me about a text he had received from a friend of his, congratulating him on the movie and telling him what a phenomenal job he'd done. The friend mentioned me specifically and inferred that I had a bright future ahead.

And the name of the friend? *Steven Spielberg*.

Anyway, we finished dinner, Tom Hanks gave his speech and when we all stood up to applaud, Steven turned around, our eyes met and he said: 'Luke Evans!'

I just went: 'Steven Spielberg!' Totally starstruck, obviously.

'Lovely to meet you,' he said. 'I'm a big fan of your work. Maybe we'll work together one day.'

It's not happened yet, but the fact that this man, whose movies have been such an important part of my life, not only knew my name, but had seen and appreciated my work. It was the most incredible moment. It's not an exaggeration to say that the fantasy world of my childhood was entirely inspired by the movies of Steven Spielberg and George Lucas. *E.T.*, *Raiders of the Lost Ark*, *Indiana Jones and the Temple of Doom*: my family adored those films. They were some of the few movies my parents and I could watch together because there were no sex scenes, swear words, drugs or supernatural elements (the Jehovah's Witnesses are fine with aliens) so we could enjoy them without Dad muting scenes, fast-forwarding or stopping them altogether.

At the time I was living in New York, because I was going out with the model Jon Kortajarena. It was the first time I'd been out with someone famous. Generally, I'm drawn to people who live a normal life, because that's the life I've tried to keep. Real life is cooking your own dinner, paying your bills and working hard, not celebrity-packed premieres and parties. Jon, though, was a very unique individual.

When we first met, at the Cannes Film Festival amfAR (Foundation for AIDS Research) Gala in 2014, I couldn't believe how beautiful he was. He had a fabulous life of fashion shows, shoots and brand ambassadorships, travelling the world wearing gorgeous clothes. Jon's personality was as striking as his looks: he was confident, fun and very sweet. We were both at the party as guests of Bulgari, so we posed together on the red carpet and for some reason I put my arm around Jon's waist rather than his shoulders, which led to a flurry of stories linking us as a couple. We weren't at that point, although we were within a few weeks!

After those photos of us together in Cannes went round the world, the press attention on our fledgling relationship was instant and unrelenting. People had just started talking about me being gay, then suddenly I'm dating the most famous male model in the world. It was a big story at the time, especially in the Spanish press, because they love celebrity gossip. They all knew where Jon lived, so I'd be taking his dog Ator for a walk around the park in Madrid or Bilbao and suddenly a photographer would jump out from behind a tree and stick a camera in my face. They would follow us in cars as well, so we'd have to take secret exits from Jon's house. We were settled as a couple and tried our hardest to keep a low profile – if we were attending an event together, such as *The Hobbit* premiere, I would do the red carpet without him and then we'd meet up inside – so to have our private lives plastered all over the press made us nervous. It undoubtedly had a detrimental effect on our relationship, because we were constantly on guard and looking over our shoulders. We didn't handle it well at all and most of the time we ended up turning our frustration and fears on each other.

We were a volatile couple and had the most dramatic arguments. On several occasions I stormed out of his place in New York in the middle of winter and walked the streets with my suitcase, before getting cold and sheepishly coming back again! I remember once he took me to see a flamenco show. The dancer looked so angry, stamping her foot and flipping her hair, then the man started to sing and it was like wailing – such a painful, beautiful sound. As I didn't speak Spanish at the time, I asked Jon to explain what was going on. He told me that the woman was angry because this man had treated her badly, yet she still adored him. That was the moment I realised that Jon and I were in a flamenco relationship: full of love and passion, but also fury and torment and just so much bloody drama.

It was addictive. Jon was addictive, the drama was addictive, but in the end it was all too much. Even without the press interest it was never going to work. We were both focused on our careers, so we were travelling separately a lot, and we were both very well-known. He was a famous model, adored by everyone. Even closeted gay actors would flirt with him, which annoyed me on two levels: one, you're hiding the fact that you're gay, and two, you're trying it on with my partner! At the same time, there was a lot of attention on me; my star was rising very rapidly during our relationship and I think Jon was probably worried it would all go to my head.

It was very sad the way it ended – too painful to go into details – but in retrospect I certainly could have done a better job in how I handled the break-up. You think you're doing the right thing, but you end up hurting people – and I did hurt Jon. It took us a long time for us to be able to be in the same room as each other. We finally reconciled, five years after we split, at a mutual friend's fortieth birthday party. It was so lovely to see him; we gave each other a hug and the wonderful thing is we're now good friends and can laugh about the past.

52

My agent, Ruth, had told me that Disney were keen to meet me for their live action remake of *Beauty and the Beast*. It seems ridiculous now, but I wasn't interested at first; I didn't want to play another bad guy. Ruth persisted – 'Luke, they really want to see you for Gaston' – but I kept putting off the audition.

While this was going on, I went to see my friends Olly and Lorna, who by this time were parents of two. We talked about work and I mentioned that I'd been approached about playing Gaston in *Beauty and the Beast*, but that I wasn't sure about the role.

Olly gawked at me. 'Are you mad? Gaston's the best character in it.'

'Really? I thought he was just another baddie.' I had seen the animation years ago when it first came out, but couldn't remember much about it.

'Honestly, Luke, if you saw how the kids react to him I think you'd change your mind.'

So we played the movie and I sat on the sofa watching it with my two godchildren and, sure enough, the second Gaston appeared on screen these two little humans were perched on the edge of the sofa, booing and shouting, and then when his song came on they jumped up and were dancing around the room. That was the moment I decided to go for the part. If a cartoon character could have that effect, imagine the potential for the real thing.

So I went to the audition and sang for the director, Bill Condon, but as I was walking out, Idris Elba was walking in. My heart sank. The part wasn't going to be mine, clearly; not with Idris in the mix. Yet somehow – by some Hollywood magic – it was. I was Gaston. *Holy fuck*.

Most of the work you put in on movies happens before you even set foot on a film set: learning the lines, creating layers to the character, working with costume and make-up to bring it to life. When I got the script I could see there was so much fun to be had with Gaston that my only caveat was that I wanted to make him somewhat likeable before he turned and became the evil antagonist. There was a lovable idiot side to him and the script was so brilliant I could instantly see the moments where I could make the most of this, such as the scene in which he's saying, 'You're the most beautiful thing I've ever seen …' and then the camera pulls out and you realise he's talking to his reflection in the mirror.

In terms of his look, Gaston went through several iterations before he became what you see in the film. The first costume we tried involved a gold pigeon-chested armour plate, which was authentic for the 1600s, when the story was set. It was a beautiful piece with ornate buckles and must have cost thousands to make, but when they put me in it on horseback I looked ridiculous, the chest plate jutting out from under my cloak. Next, they tried me in a dark brown coat, but it was too far removed from the appearance of the animated character to work. It was important we get the costume right, because there were elements of the cartoon character that were quintessentially Gaston that we knew we wouldn't be able to recreate. In the animation he's unnaturally gigantic, but I was never going to be able to train my way to Disney-sized muscles, so we had to find the other ways to connect my version to the cartoon. Which we did with the bouffant wig, the perfect white teeth, the line on my chin (to recreate Gaston's bum-chin) and my red and brown coat, which mirrored the colours of the original costume. The second I put everything on, together with the boots and ring we'd created, it totally worked.

For me, one of the best parts of the film was getting to sing the beautiful music, written by Howard Ashman and Alan Menken, the multiple-Oscar-winning team who also worked on *Aladdin* and *The Little*

Mermaid. Someone who worked in the music department told me a wonderful story of how in the original recordings of Howard composing the movie's title song, you can actually hear him picking out the notes on a keyboard, trying out different combinations and then suddenly landing on that now famous sequence of notes in the song 'Beauty and the Beast'. On the tape there's a long pause, then you hear Howard say: 'I think I've found it'. I get goosebumps just thinking about it.

. . .

The table read tends to be one of the most boring bits of making a movie. You're all nervous and feeling self-conscious because you're about to read the script together for the first time, while the producers and bigwigs in LA listen to it live. The table read for *Beauty and the Beast*, though, was extraordinary; an all-singing, all-dancing extravaganza. It created a spirit of wonder, magic and closeness among us that continued for the whole of the shoot.

The read-through took place in a room at Shepperton Studios with the tables set out in a huge square, in the middle of which were the prototypes for the models of Mrs Potts, Cogsworth, Lumière and Chip the cup. I'd already had a few weeks working on the choreography, so when it came to the Gaston song in the tavern they called in the ensemble – many of whom I'd worked with during my theatre days – and we performed the entire number in front of the creative team for the first time. I was in my element; it was everything I loved most about my job in one performance. I've still got a note that Emma Thompson, who was sitting a couple of seats along, passed to me that day, which says: *For fuck's sake, can you stop being so fucking good, it's a fucking table read!!*

Gaston has been one of the most enjoyable roles of my career. I had so much fun with Josh Gad, who played my sidekick, LeFou. During our scenes together the crew would always be pissing themselves. It took Emma Watson and I quite a while to be able to get through our scenes together without her laughing at me – or me laughing at myself. I remember walking on set with Josh, and Bill Condon saying: 'Ah, happiness has arrived!'

My parents came to see me on that set and brought along my grandmother, who by this time was sadly suffering from dementia. On the day of their visit we were filming the movie's big opening sequence in Villeneuve, Belle's village. It was a glorious sunny day and I made sure there were chairs set up so they could watch me work in comfort. I went over to say hello, dressed in my full Gaston regalia and make-up.

'Hiya, Nan!' I said. 'What do you think of all this, then?'

We had a little chat and it was lovely to see her so engaged and interested, then off I went back to set. It was only later Mam told me that as soon as I'd walked away Nan had turned to her and said, 'Who the bloody hell was that?'

...

Whenever Disney releases a movie they make sure the whole world knows about it. The launches are enormous. For *Beauty and the Beast* we did the press in Paris, flew to a huge event at Shanghai Disneyland (where they kept the park open until midnight so the cast could go on the rides) and the final stop was Los Angeles and the Hollywood Boulevard premiere, where I met John Legend and Celine Dion, who all sing on the soundtrack. Then the movie came out and, of course, everyone loved it. The reviews were wonderful. I'm very proud of the effect my character has had; I still have kids running up to me, shrieking: 'It's Gaston!' I'm just so glad Olly made me watch the movie that day, otherwise I might have missed out on such a magical experience. (Cheers Ol!)

Soon after the film came out, all of the cast received an email from Celine Dion asking if she could use some of the footage in her Las Vegas show, because she wanted to include her song from the film, 'How Does a Moment Last Forever'. She came to us all personally to ask if we'd mind. I replied that it was absolutely fine with me, on one condition – that I could come and see her in Vegas. So a few months later I took all my friends on holiday to Acapulco in Mexico and from there arranged a private jet (which I'd been loaned as a thank you from the *Fast & Furious* team) to fly to Vegas. We went backstage to see Celine before the show, and when she came into the room she flung her arms towards me and yelled, in her French Canadian twang: 'Gaston!' It's another one of those moments I've thought: *This is nuts!*

When I originally got the part of Gaston I was told that I could hire a personal assistant for the duration of the shoot. I already had an executive assistant, Matilda, who Gemma Arterton had recommended to me early in my career when I was away working for months at a time and would come home to red bills and chaos. Matilda is my friend and confidante and I couldn't live without her; I call her 'the wife'. She still does a brilliant job of sorting my life out, but she has a family so she wouldn't be able to join me on set. I needed to find a second assistant who would be able to travel with me.

I had recently met up with my friend Jamie (the same Jamie who loaned me the money to buy my parents' house) who had been visiting the UK from the French countryside where he'd been living for the past few years, renovating a barn and working in a bar. That day I'd been left with the impression that he was bored of France and missing his London life, so when I started thinking about possible assistants Jamie sprang to mind. I knew we got on really well, plus he was super organised and obsessed with movies. When we shared the flat on Charing Cross Road he used to make me stay up all night to watch the Oscars with him. We'd get a bottle of champagne and some popcorn, then we'd sit there and watch the entire ceremony.

When I offered him the job he jumped at the chance. Neither of us had any idea if it would work out, but within a week it was as if Jamie had been doing it his entire life.

We initially assumed it would be just that one job, but it worked so well that I asked Jamie to join me on my next movie; that was ten years ago and we've been together ever since. Before Jamie came on board I would often be alone on location for months at a time. I would hang out with the cast and crew, but it took effort to build a three-month relationship that generally wouldn't last beyond that job; Jamie and I knew each other so well that we could go out to dinner and chat about our days and it was easy and relaxing. Also, I'd been missing out on so many important moments in my friends' and family's lives – birthdays, wedding, funerals – that I had been beginning to question whether it was really worth it, being away from home so much, but having Jamie with me was like a link to reality and the rest of my life.

Jamie gets on with everyone and brings me out of my shell, which gives me the confidence to go out more while I'm on location. It's changed the dynamic of our friendship for sure, but we're thick as thieves and love each other like brothers (and argue like brothers, too). He's supremely calm and patient, both with me and everyone else, and acts a bit like my filter. I can rant and rave to him about a director who keeps giving me the script at 9pm to shoot at 6am next morning – 'It's unacceptable! This is unbelievable!' – and he will then go and speak to the director on my behalf, but with far less swearing and a lot more charm.

'Luke would love it if you could bring the script a little earlier so he just has a couple more hours to work on it. Would that be okay? Thank you *so* much, he will really appreciate it.'

Whatever the problem, he will always sort it out. He's my rock and my pal and I'm so glad he's with me on this journey.

53

'So, the movie's called *Murder Mystery*. Jennifer Aniston *and* Adam Sandler are the leads and—'

'I'll do it,' I told my agent.

There was a pause at the other end of the phone. 'Don't you want to know what it's about?'

'Nope. I'll do it.'

The chance to work with Jennifer Aniston and Adam Sandler? Come on! It would be worth it even if the movie turned out to be shit (which it didn't). And when I discovered that I would be playing a millionaire and wearing beautiful clothes, that we'd be filming in Italy over the summer and that the movie was a comedy, which I hadn't done before … it was even better than I'd hoped.

That shoot was so much fun. We were in Portofino for three weeks, then Lake Como for a month, staying in the most exquisite hotels. One night I went out to dinner with Jennifer, Adam and David Walliams, who also appears in the film. The restaurant was on the water with a view of all the yachts. At one of the other tables was Adrien Brody, who came over to say hello as we'd worked together before, then I was chatting to Jennifer when something over my shoulder caught her attention. 'Oh my God,' she said, 'is that Cher?' She started waving. 'Cher! Cher!'

My eyes went wide. *Did she just say* Cher?

Moments later this iconic figure in sunglasses and a cowboy hat appeared at our table. The sheer Cher-ness of her was just dazzling. Jennifer had known her for years because she had gone to school with Cher's son, Chaz Bono, so she introduced us. As I shook her hand, it struck me that we had two Oscar winners and two of the biggest movie stars in the world in this one tiny restaurant.

Later that night, David went over to talk to the woman Cher was dining with, mentioning that he was a close friend of Elton John and David Furnish.

'Did you hear that, Cher?' said her companion. 'David knows Elton really well.'

Cher put down her cutlery, looked up and said, 'Thank you very much.'

When he came back to the table and told us the story we were all in hysterics. I have no idea what she thought David had said – or even if she had bothered to listen to him – but she clearly couldn't have given a shit if he'd known the Queen of Sheba. I love it when a celebrity turns out to be just as you'd expected, and for me that moment was pure, 100 per cent Cher.

At the end of the shoot, Jennifer told me to give her a call when I was next in Los Angeles. People often say that sort of thing, but I got the impression Jennifer actually meant it: she comes across as a really genuine person. So when I next found myself in the city, I thought: *Fuck it, I'm going to give Jennifer Aniston a call.* Well, I'm so glad that I did. She told me I must go and have a facial with the woman who did her skin (naturally it was the best facial of my life) and then she invited me to dinner that night at her house, where I met Jason Bateman and his wife and a whole bunch of lovely people. We had drinks in the garden and then went in to have dinner – Asian food, as I remember. Jennifer sat on my right, but the seat to the left of me was empty, until the doorbell rang and in walked ... Lisa Kudrow. *Play it cool, Luke. Play it cool.* I grew up with *Friends*, so to be sitting at dinner between Rachel and Phoebe was beyond ridiculous. At first I didn't feel I should be there, but they were both so lovely – genuinely curious and interested to hear about me – that I soon relaxed. It was surreal though, because I was so familiar with the sound of their voices that I was half-expecting Ross or Joey to turn up.

54

I was finishing filming *The Pembrokeshire Murders* in Cardiff in early 2020 when this thing called coronavirus started being mentioned in the press, although at this point nobody knew much about it and there were no restrictions on set. The morning after we wrapped, I was on a flight out to Miami at 7am to see my then-boyfriend, Rafa, who worked as an art curator and hotel events director and lived in an apartment on the beach. Little did I realise at the time that it would be the final tourist flight that was allowed to land there before the world started to lock down.

We filed off the plane and were walking down the gangway towards the main building when a crowd of police and airport staff came rushing towards us. They were all carrying PPE, but they obviously hadn't been trained on how to put it on: some had their masks on upside down; others were wearing the face shields like sun visors. And they were yelling at us like we were criminals: 'Backs up against the wall! Everybody stand still and DON'T MOVE!'

All of the passengers from the flight, a few hundred of us, had to line up against the wall like *The Usual Suspects*, wondering what the hell was going on. The staff formed a hastily assembled checkpoint, but again they clearly had no clue what they were doing. The woman with the thermometer gun would put it in one person's ear, then they'd hold it against the next person's forehead, while someone with a clipboard was asking us random questions that seemed to change with every passenger. It was chaos. Even taking into account that we were in America, where everything is a major drama, this was the moment I was like: *Okay, something is happening.*

Outside the airport, however, everything seemed normal. I got to Rafa's apartment and the next morning we went down to the beach. Even though it was just outside Rafa's building, that was the last time we would set foot on the sand, because the following day they closed the whole of Miami Beach. Perhaps we would have got a couple more weeks out of it, but spring break had just started, which is when thousands of US college students descend on resorts like Miami to drink and party, and they were worried about the virus spreading. As it was, there was a big spike in cases in the city that month thanks to the spring break invasion.

Once Miami Beach had been shut down, the rest of the city quickly followed. Rafa got temporarily laid off from his job, because they closed the hotel, and within a week of my arrival the pair of us found ourselves stuck in his apartment, in the stifling spring heat, with only a balcony as outside space. With Covid restrictions getting increasingly prohibitive by the day, I made a snap decision and found a house on Airbnb in Vero Beach, an hour and a half north of the city, and rented it for a month. The day Rafa and I left they were already setting up patrols on the bridges to stop people leaving and entering the city. As we joined this long trail of cars fleeing Miami it felt as though we were in a disaster movie.

The beach our rental house was on was closed to the public, but thankfully the people living there could use it. There were far worse places to spend lockdown and we so appreciated our daily walks along the beach. Amazon was our saviour during that time. There's an enormous distribution centre in Florida – virtually the size of a city – so you can order something at 9am and it'll be with you by midday, whether that's frozen clams, a glue gun or a skull.*

We had thought the restrictions would be lifted within weeks, but then Airbnb shut down. We couldn't stay in our rental and we struggled

---

* As there wasn't much else to do I got into crafting while we were staying there, collecting shells from the beach to make into necklaces and a shell-covered skull.

to get back into Miami, which by now was like Fort Knox, but by chance we'd met a real estate agent and she found us another house nearby.

A few months previously I had been offered a role in a TV miniseries with Nicole Kidman, called *Nine Perfect Strangers*, that was scheduled to shoot in Los Angeles later that year. After Covid hit I'd assumed that would be the end of it, but while we were in Vero Beach my agents called to say that the production company had struck a deal with the Australian government to allow the cast to fly to Australia and shoot it there. The show was happening, and I would need to be there in two weeks' time.

By the time Rafa and I arrived in Sydney that June, the world was in Covid chaos. We had to wear full PPE on the flight and were taken straight from the plane to a car and driven to the hotel, where we were tested and then taken to our room for Australia's mandatory two-week quarantine. From Sydney the cast were then put on three private jets to Byron Bay in New South Wales, which had barely been affected by Covid because the borders had been closed between the states. As a result, only the crew had to wear PPE on set. It was extremely chilled compared to what was going on in the rest of the world.

For the duration of the shoot, I stayed at a beautiful wooden house in Myocum, a heavily forested area a little way inland from the sea. The house was built on stilts, so had the most incredible views, and it was next to a field of very friendly cows who'd come to say hello when I would go down there with my morning coffee. In the afternoon, I'd wake after my siesta to find a swamp wallaby sunbathing in the garden. After the sun went down, though, this laid-back paradise was transformed into something out of a horror movie. After my first night in the house I thought I'd have to move, because I didn't get a moment of sleep. The noise coming from outside was unbelievable. As the roof was made of corrugated metal, whenever any creatures crossed over it – and there were a *lot* of creatures around there – it sounded as if a small child was running back and forth above my head. I would shudder at the sound of something large and heavy slowly dragging itself across the roof; other times I'd have to put a pillow over my head to block out the noise of God knows what having a party on the decking outside my bedroom. Once or twice I went out to take a look, but most nights I just hid under the covers until the sun had come up.

It's my mother's fault, but I absolutely fucking hate spiders. Thankfully you didn't usually see any around the house unless it rained, but when it did, the huntsman spiders came out. These things were the size of my face. They would climb the screen on the windows and if you approached them, instead of running away like a nice polite British spider, they would rear back on their haunches, ready to launch themselves at you and attack. One day my housekeeper, Shanti, was cleaning the terrace outside my bedroom when she heard me shrieking from inside the room.

'What's wrong?' she said.

'Look at that!' I pointed to the monster clinging to the screen between us.

'Oh, it's just a huntsman,' said Shanti, casually grabbing it by the leg and aiming it off the terrace, but instead it flipped in mid-air, landed by her feet and then scuttled straight into my bedroom and under the bed.

I immediately moved bedrooms and never slept a night in that room again.

One morning the landlady came round to see how I'd settled in. I told her how much I loved the area and was enjoying her beautiful house.

'You're very lucky,' she told me, 'because you've got a big old python living in the roof above your bedroom.'

My face fell: I'm not that keen on snakes, either. 'A python?'

'Oh yes, she's been there for years. And when you have a python in your roof, you don't get any rodents. If you're *really* lucky you might wake up one morning, come out your bedroom and find she's shed her skin on the terrace. It glistens like petrol on water, like a beautiful decoration.'

'Uh-huh,' I said, trying to look enthusiastic. 'Right. Lovely.'

Thankfully, Rafa was brilliant at dealing with the local wildlife. He was very outdoorsy and while we were dating he encouraged me to step outside my comfort zone and embrace new experiences, such as getting up before dawn to ride our bikes along the promenade in Miami and watch the sun rise, or camping in a canyon in Hawaii with him (and millions of bugs). Sadly, our relationship ran its course during our time in Byron Bay, but I'll always be grateful for the adventures I shared with him.

After Rafa went home, I had to get used to the idea of sharing my space with all these creatures and from then on I grew to appreciate my unusual neighbours. I discovered a family of bats living inside a tribal mask hanging on the outside wall, and when I sat on the terrace sofa in the morning I'd often move the cushions to find these bright green tree frogs, sparkling in the early morning sun. I'd only ever seen these sorts of creatures in David Attenborough documentaries and all of a sudden I was living in the midst of them.

. . .

Each of us on *Nine Perfect Strangers* knew just how lucky we were. Not only were we among the few hundred actors in the world to be working, but we were on location in one of the most beautiful places on earth. Yet my time in Australia was bittersweet, because it coincided with the last few painful months of my nan's life. We knew she was nearing the end, but due to the travel restrictions I couldn't leave the country to see her. The evening before she died Mam called me on Facetime from Nan's bedside to tell me she'd been asleep for the past two days; I should probably say my goodbyes, she said gently. It was a beautifully warm evening in Australia and I was sitting outside on my deck in that stunning landscape, yet at that moment I would have given anything to be back in chilly Wales. I asked Mam to hold the phone close to Nan's ear and began to sing the Joe Cocker song 'You Are So

Beautiful'. I didn't know if she'd even hear me, but as I sang to her I saw her eyes flicker open. I'm crying even now, just thinking about it. It was as if in those final hours of her life the magic of music had brought her back to us for the briefest of moments. Nan drifted off again soon after and she died the following morning peacefully in her sleep.

Nine Perfect Strangers was a really interesting, challenging project – my first opportunity to play a gay man on screen – and I enjoyed bringing a lot of myself to the character of Lars.

The cast was a delight, including Melissa McCarthy, aka the funniest woman in the world. We all got to spend a lot of time together, because there were quite a few ensemble scenes in that show, such as when we're all sitting together at breakfast, and these would take a day or two to shoot because of all the coverage. For those who don't know, 'coverage' basically refers to when the camera is focused on you. When it's your coverage, the other people in the scene will be behind the camera. If part of another actor's body is in shot with you that's called a dirty frame, while a deep shot is when you see both people together, but the camera is only focused on one of you. When you film a scene with multiple actors, you shoot each of your coverage in turn; a thoughtful director will keep swapping round the order of filming, but I've worked with some very established, powerful actors who insist on always having their coverage first. Or others might be superstitious and want to go second or last. Personally, I prefer being first, because I like the spontaneity that comes with that, but having worked in the theatre I'm very good at replicating a scene multiple times, so I don't mind waiting my turn.

For the first month of the shoot, Nicole rarely came out of character. She was playing a mysterious Russian and at first would keep apart from the rest of us, disappearing after each take, and never dropped the accent. It was a little unsettling, but I understood her reasons: her character had to be enigmatic to the rest of the cast, so it made sense to keep her distance. As the weeks went by, however, she became more herself.

I'd be standing next to her on set and she'd suddenly turn to me and say: 'You having a nice time, babe?' in her Aussie accent. I'd be like, 'Nicole! Hi!' Then moments later it would be back to the mysterious Russian and Nicole would vanish again.

Although I'm not a Method actor, I do understand how a character can consume you like that. When I was in *High-Rise*, I played a very complicated, angry man who I based on Oliver Reed and George Best in their worst moments: he was always under the influence of alcohol and steadily lost himself as the film went on. He was so unlike me as a person that I stayed in his mindset for the duration of the film and found it tough to brush him off when it ended. It wasn't that I was difficult to be around, but I was certainly much more intense. Watching the movie when it came out, there were scenes I had no recollection of shooting because I had completely surrendered to the character. Worse, I woke up one morning after a night of drinking with the cast and discovered two bite marks on my torso, but I had no memory of what had happened. I was later told that I'd had a drunken friendly tussle with a fellow actor in the restaurant, which was not like me at all. There had been nobody else in the restaurant, just the cast, and we'd had a lot to drink, but still – it was unnerving. It was as if the character was bleeding into my after-hours existence.

I spent a whole day filming a scene in bed with Nicole and between takes we talked about our lives.

'Can I give you one piece of advice?' she asked me at one point.

'Sure,' I said, wondering what it might be. Don't sell yourself out? Stay humble? Save your money?

'Have a child,' she said. 'It's the most amazing thing I've done.'

Her face shone when she was talking about her daughters. I asked how she and her husband, Keith Urban, balanced their careers with parenthood.

'Being a parent can be tough, but the rewards are extraordinary,' she told me. 'It's something you will never regret.'

I thought it was such a lovely thing to say, and it's true: the most important thing in life is nothing to do with the business or money. I do want to have children, and hope I'm able to do so in the next five years, whether that's through adoption or surrogacy. I've talked about it with my partner, Fran, a Spanish architect who I've been with for the past three years and with whom I can certainly see myself becoming a parent. I always thought I'd be a young dad, but I've realised now that I needed to find my feet and have my own journey before I could slow down and make changes in my life in order to focus on children. As long as I look after myself, I can hopefully be an able-bodied, energetic seventy-year-old with a twenty-year-old kid. Fran and I are currently talking about getting a dog together, which sort of feels like the first step in bringing a new life into our relationship!

Fran is my best friend. We've built a fashion business, we travel together and, best of all, he's as close to his family as I am. That's probably why we didn't hesitate about getting our parents together, even though they don't speak the same language. It melted our hearts to see our mothers walking along the beach, picking up shells, one talking in Spanish and the other in English, with no idea what the other was saying. And then my dad discovered Google Translate and that was it: there was no need for us to be around any more!

I have so much respect for Fran. He is kind and loving, and never has a bad word to say about anybody, which is an extraordinary quality. I'd like to say I'm the same, but it's hard at times! He is the cool air and the calm water in our relationship, while I'm the fire and lightning; it works because we balance each other, and we have a very fun, fulfilled life together.

...

After we'd finished *Nine Perfect Strangers*, Nicole and Keith invited me and the rest of the cast who were still in Australia to their house in

Sydney for dinner. After a lovely evening on their terrace, Nicole asked if I would like to sing.

'Go and tell Keith which song and he'll accompany you on the piano,' said Nicole.

I hesitated. I didn't really feel I could go up to a multiple-Grammy-award-winning singer-songwriter and ask him to play some random song for me.

'Go on, he won't mind,' said Nicole. 'Keith! Luke's going to sing.'

'Alright, mate,' said Keith. 'What's it gonna be?'

'Um, do you know any Adele …?'

'Course I do!'

So Keith played 'Make You Feel My Love' on their grand piano and we all sang along. Nicole was lying on the floor listening; later that night she sang too. It was a very special evening and it would go on to plant a seed that would come into beautiful bloom a year or so later.

55

After *Beauty and the Beast* I began to be more widely recognised as a singer as well as an actor and was asked to perform at the Queen's 92nd birthday concert at the Royal Albert Hall. I sang 'Oh, What a Beautiful Mornin'' from *Oklahoma!* – apparently one of Her Maj's favourite musicals – with the Royal Philharmonic Orchestra and then joined Kylie, Sting, Tom Jones, Jamie Cullum and Shaggy (quite a combination!) for the finale of 'What a Wonderful World'.

Following the concert, I was approached by Ste Softley, a record producer I had met through friends, who asked if I'd like to record a solo album. I got a sudden flashback to that night, fifteen years before, when I'd been asked the exact same question – although this time I was confident it might actually happen. I told Ste that I would love to do it; he pitched the idea to various record companies and we ended up signing a deal with BMG.

We recorded my first album, *At Last*, at AIR Studios with Kylie's producer, Steve Anderson, who I already knew from his work on *Rent Remixed*. The record company told me I could sing whatever I wanted on the album: talk about a kid in a candy store! I chose all the songs I had ever wanted to perform, including, of course, 'The First Time Ever I Saw Your Face'. I couldn't do an album without Roberta, as that song meant so much to me when I was young. I suppose it was quite a risky move, bringing out an album when I was still far better known as an actor, but I loved singing and I knew I was good at it. After all, it was what had got me on the path to where I am now, even though I hadn't had the chance to do much of it since leaving musical theatre. So I was confident the album would sound good; whether or not people would buy it or not was another matter, but to be in a recording studio, hearing the orchestra play for the first time – it was joyous. I was completely in my element. The album landed in the charts at number 11, nudged out of the top ten at the last minute by Ed Sheeran, but seeing my debut album in such prestigious company was consolation enough. I sang on all the TV shows to promote the album and when I appeared on *Strictly Come Dancing* it shot from 35 all the way up to number 6 overnight – the power of salsa and sequins!

At Last sold almost 70,000 physical albums, an enormous achievement in this digital age, and the record company asked if I wanted to record a follow-up. I jumped at the chance; this time, however, I said I wanted to duet with guest stars and write some of my own music. While I was in Cardiff for *The Pembrokeshire Murders* I reached out to songwriter Amy Wadge, who's worked with the biggest stars, and she came to meet me in my trailer. I told her that I had a few ideas, but had never written songs before and had no idea how to go about it, yet out of those unpromising beginnings a wonderful working relationship grew. Amy is very special, an amazing person and an incredible talent. We wrote together during lockdown over Zoom: me in Vero Beach, Amy at her home in Pontypridd. She told me what equipment to order so we could record demos – a mic, the right software, a small mixing desk – and Amazon, as ever, delivered the lot (though I wish they could have also delivered someone to set it all up, because it was bloody impossible). Still, I got it working and we went on to record four demos together on opposite sides of the ocean, two of which eventually ended up on the album.

When I was considering who I would like to sing with on the album one of the first people I thought of was Nicole. She had told me how much she liked my voice when we first met: 'Keith and I thought your album was amazing,' she had said, which just about blew my mind, as you can imagine. So I sent her a text asking if she might be interested in a duet, imagining it would be a no or that it would get lost amidst all the other requests she must get, but to my delight she got back to me and she said yes, she would love to. She sang her part of our song, 'Say Something', in Nashville – Keith sent me a video of her at work in the recording booth – while I sang mine in London. When I heard our voices mixed together on the finished track I got goosebumps.

I also asked Charlotte to sing with me on the album, because I thought it would be a beautiful full-circle moment. We had so much history together; I had been there when she became this huge star and now we had both achieved success, and I wanted to celebrate that. She wasn't keen on the song I suggested, 'Come What May' from *Moulin Rouge*, because it had an operatic feel to it and she had moved on from using that huge soprano voice of hers that she was famous for in the early days. It took some effort, but I finally got her round to the idea, convincing her we could do something really cool with the song. We recorded it in London and it was magical. I think even Charlotte was happy. She might not use it so much these days, but that voice is still the most incredible instrument.

After the second album, *A Song For You*, came out, a Welsh production company got in touch to say that the BBC were interested in producing a one-off entertainment show with me. They had an established formula for this kind of show, but we told them we wanted to do something even bigger and more spectacular. To this end, I put my fee back into the production; I wouldn't get paid, but we would be able to get better lighting, bigger guest stars and make my show the best it could possibly be.

While we were prepping for the show, I posted something on Instagram about my song with Nicole Kidman and among the comments was one saying: 'Babe, when are we doing our duet?'

It was from Nicole Scherzinger.

Nicole and I had met for the first time a few months earlier at the Queen's Platinum Jubilee Pageant. I'd been invited to drive a vintage Land Rover in the parade and Fran was coming with me as passenger.

Early that morning, we were put in a room to wait for the parade to start with literally every single person from the last fifty years of entertainment. There were the supermodels – Naomi and Kate – and the likes of Sir Cliff Richard and Gloria Hunniford over in one corner, and sports personalities, including Dame Kelly Holmes and Sally Gunnell, in another. It was like we'd just walked into a copy of the Christmas *Radio Times*. And at the far side of the room, sitting a little apart from everyone else, was a beautiful woman in a very elegant hat.

'Oh my God, it's Nicole Scherzinger!' gasped Fran. 'Will you introduce me?'

'I don't know her,' I said.

'Well, just go up and say hello.'

'Fran, I know celebrities, and sometimes they don't like that.'

But after a moment I thought, *Fuck it – why not?* We were in a room full of famous people; it wasn't like we'd be hassling her on the street. So I walked over and introduced myself. Nicole didn't really know who I was, but she was the sweetest person and we ended up chatting for about an hour and swapping numbers.

So when I saw Nicole's comment on my Instagram, I sent her a text: 'Hey babe, if you're serious about the duet I'm doing a one-off show for the BBC this Christmas and you could be one of the guests.'

She wrote back: 'If you can fly me over, I'll do it.'

And that's exactly what happened: I gave up my wage and flew her over for the show!

I have Fran to thank for this, because without his encouragement I would never have spoken to Nicole that day. I get quite nervous at those sort of things anyway and would never want to force myself on people, which is probably why I don't have a lot of celebrity mates, but we're now solid friends with Nicole and her partner Thom.

Luke Evans: Showtime aired nationally on 22 December and in Wales on Christmas Day, straight after the King's Speech on BBC One. People loved the show, and the icing on the cake was winning a Welsh BAFTA for it. I was especially proud because we filmed it in Wales with a Welsh production team. Not everyone knows about our little country, so whenever I get the chance I like to wave our flag.

It's a funny thing, being from Wales. Whenever someone is on the radio or TV I have this compulsion (as do most Welsh people, I think) to immediately point out their Welshness.

'You know this song? By Bonnie Tyler? She's Welsh.'

'That footballer? No, he's actually Welsh.'

It comes from a sense of pride in the other successful people who've come from my country. I even did it on a plane the other day when the flight attendant came round with the bread rolls. 'See this little pack of butter? It's Welsh.'

It's been fantastic to see Wales getting itself more on the map these days – and I'm proud to have played a small part in that. I've worked with the tourist board, travelling around the country to film commercials for Visit Wales, and early in my career I'd always make a point of telling interviewers they should describe me as a Welsh actor, rather than British. It might seem unimportant, but we're only a small country and I always want to shout about the fact that I came from this tiny village in the mining valleys of South Wales and have gone on to find international success.

My family still live in Wales, and whenever I go home to Aberbargoed and talk to people they always seem proud that I came from their village. It's a lovely thing, knowing that my own achievements have had such a positive effect on a wide range of people. Whether or not they've had a direct role in my life, everyone back home is lit in the glow of this mad experience I've been lucky enough to be part of.

56

My agents tell me I'm one of the hardest-working actors on their books. I remember, at a dinner a few years ago, talking to a fellow actor who I'd worked with on a movie several years before, and when I asked what he'd been up to, as I hadn't seen him for a while, he casually told me he'd taken a couple of years off. I was stunned. *Can you do that?* It was a totally alien concept to me. It's a working-class thing: even though I've been fortunate enough to earn the sort of money that my parents would never have dreamt of being able to make, I still worry I'm one step away from losing it all. I'm sure it's easier to take your foot off the pedal if you come from financial stability, but I know what it's like not to be able to pay the bills. I'm always thinking of ways to be happier, less stressed and more secure; how to be safe.

Safe. That's the word. At the heart of it, that's what drives me to keep working so hard, because when it comes down to it I'm a one-man band. There are numerous people that help and support me, but I'm the one carrying and playing all the instruments. I'm grateful for every penny that comes in and extremely careful about how I look after it. I'm possibly now at the point that if I did have to give it all up tomorrow then my future, and my parents' future, would be secure. I think I've got there, finally. And when I stop and consider the fact that I've achieved the one thing I've been striving for all these years – feeling safe – well, it takes my breath away.

So perhaps I will take a year off one day. It would be lovely to relax and enjoy what I've built for myself. I'm always on a schedule; I'd like the chance to feel what it's like to be bored! And yet … I love my job. *Love it.* I was sitting in a forest in Northern Ireland last night in the pouring rain, mud seeping into my supposedly waterproof boots, watching as they filled the forest around me with lights and fire and smoke, and it struck all over again what a magical industry I'm lucky enough to work in. As long as I'm enjoying myself and still feel I've got something to give, then I'll keep going as long as I can.

I think the reason I still find this job as interesting as ever is my choice of roles. My film career started on such a high, then the tent-pole movies just kept coming: *Fast & Furious 6, Dracula Untold, Beauty and the Beast.* After a few years, however, I realised that while it was wonderful to be in these huge studio productions and enjoy the recognition that goes with them, it was time for me to dig a little deeper. There's always a risk of being pigeonholed as an actor: you can become so closely associated with a certain type of role that people won't consider you for anything else. When you're an unknown you really have to work to build a profile and get as many people to see you as possible, but as I've got older and my experience and work has broadened, my choices are for very different reasons. It's the character first, then the story, the script, the director – not just the size of the movie. These days I mix up the big films with more diverse indies to hopefully forge a path towards a longer career.

For the past few years, Duncan had been telling me I should go back to the theatre. Ruth, my agent, agreed it was time. The only person who wasn't convinced about a return to the stage was me. It was partly a matter of logistics: I was so busy with movies, TV projects and travel that I wouldn't be in one place for long enough to fit in a three-month play. More importantly, I hadn't found the right script. If I went back to the theatre it would be a very different experience from when I was younger: rather than being an anonymous performer in a famous show, this time it would be about Luke Evans in a particular play. There would be a lot of attention on me specifically, so it was crucial to find a script with a story I loved and a character I could get excited about – and that's not easy to find. So I waited. And I waited. And then along came *Backstairs Billy*.

Set in 1979, the play is a fictional story inspired by the real-life relationship of the Queen Mother and her loyal servant, William 'Billy' Tallon. When I read Marcelo Dos Santos' brilliant script it ticked every box. It was a new play, so my performance couldn't be compared to anyone else's; it was a comedy, which I've always loved but don't get the chance to do very often; and, most importantly, I knew straightaway what I could do with the role of Billy. I'd never played such a nuanced, vulnerable character: there was no machismo, no fighting – it would free me from everything I'd done up to this point in my career. To top it all, the play would be directed by Michael Grandage, who'd been the artistic director of the Donmar when I appeared in *Small Change* and *Piaf*. If I was going to return to the stage I wanted to work with an experienced director who I could trust entirely – and for me, that person was Michael.

When I walked into that rehearsal space on the first day I was ready. Fifteen years might have passed, but it was as if I'd just stepped out of the theatre the day before. I quickly remembered that lovely feeling of support and kindness in a company when you're building a production together. The cast ranged in age from 20 to the wonderful 77-year-old Dame Penelope Wilton, who played the Queen Mother. I'm not sure if they were expecting some Hollywood actor who wouldn't mix and kept to themselves, but I turned up in my sneakers and hoodie and happily became part of the gang. Michael Grandage later said we were one of the closest companies he's ever worked with.

We opened at the Duke of York's Theatre, which was where I had appeared in *Rent Remixed* all those years ago. As I stood in the dark on that first night alongside the actors playing the other servants, waiting for the curtain to go up, I was well aware of the possibility that my performance would be ripped to shreds by the press – and if that happened I would still have to come back the next night and carry on. I think there was probably a fleeting sense of: *Why on earth am I putting myself through this …?* Then the lights went down, I turned to the others and said, 'Have a good one,' opened the doors at the back of the set and all those thoughts and worries instantly vanished. I was onstage for the first thirty-seven minutes of the play and when I eventually came off everyone backstage was asking how it was going, whether the audience were enjoying it, but I had absolutely no idea! I'd been totally in the moment as Billy.

When the curtain came down that night, all of us formed a big huddle on stage, hugging and congratulating each other. We truly were like a family by this point. I texted Penelope the other day and she signed off with: *I miss holding hands with you at the curtain call.* What a beautiful soul she is – I'm honoured to call her my friend.

Although the three-month run was physically exhausting I loved every second. And yes, it has made me think I'd like to do more theatre. There are two iconic roles in musicals that I would love to play: Valjean in *Les Misérables* and Phantom. Who knows? Perhaps that's something for the future.

. . .

When I was first approached to write a memoir, my first thought was *Aren't I too young?* With luck I'm still only halfway through my life! But this book is hopefully as much a story that can inspire young people, who might see some of their own experience in what I've been through, as it is about me. We are not defined by others' behaviour, however cruel and overwhelming it may seem at the time. We can move beyond it. I want people to understand that there is always hope, no matter how shit you feel about yourself. Even when things are at their darkest, brighter times could be waiting just around the corner.

If this resonates with you, then I hope giving this insight into my life will perhaps inspire you and help you realise that wherever you start out doesn't dictate where you can potentially end up. You may not want to be in the movies, but I know you can write the happy ending to your own story.

Generally, however, I prefer not to dwell on the past. I have moments of reflection, but I would never want to live my life looking in the rear-view mirror. We walk forwards – our vision goes ahead of us. So what do I see in the future? Hopefully many more years doing the job I love, enjoying the fruits of my success with my family and friends. I also see a ticking clock, like the one on that card I sent to Anne McNulty at the Donmar all those years ago, a constant reminder to squeeze every bit of joy out of life for as long as we have left, because while none of us have any idea what happens next, the most wonderful thing of all is that we're still here, with the chance to do something amazing and be proud of ourselves every single day. Sometimes I wonder, if I could've had the chance to tell my younger self these words, whether it would've helped him. Who knows? But unbelievably, he did it all anyway, without my help.

Acknowledgements

This is a thank you to the people who have an impact on my life and have helped me fulfil my dreams.

Fran
David and Yvonne
Dean and Rachel
Holly
Olly and Lorna
Tim
Enid and Gary
Helen, Elaine, Carol and Shirley
John
Kevin
Terry

Alison Lane
Amy Wadge
Andrew Dunlap
Anne McNulty
Ashley Greene
Ashley Morris
Barry Buren
Ben Dey
Benji Bar-David
Boy George
Cara Tripicchio
Caroline Hazeldine
Catherine Woods

Charlotte Hardman
Christopher Brown
Craig Logan
Cynthia Blaise
David & Philip
Duncan Millership
Emyr Afan
Esmeralda Brajovic
George Freeman
Gray Eveleigh
James Morgan
Jamie Nelson
Jamie Sivewright
Jess Anderson
Jo Myler
Jo Power
Joe Machota
John Grantham
Jonathan Davies and Afanti
Josh Lieberman
Juliet Fairbairn
Juliet Pochin
Kate Davie
Kylie Minogue
Laura Belnavis
Laura Ohnona
Laura Woods
Lena Roklin
Lennard Hoornik
Lewis Shaw
Louise Ryan

Lucy Bevan
Lupe Fairman
Matilda Morrogh-Ryan
Michelle Warner
Millie Hoskins
MK Crook
Pål Hansen
Patsy O'Neill
Peter Gill
Philip Foster
Pippa Beng
Randi Hiller
Richard Agnew
Rick Lipton
Roma Martyniuk
Ruby Zinner
Ruth Young and her team
Sally O'Neill
Sarah Armitage
Shaun Stafford
Shelise Robertson
Simon Waterson
Ste Softly
Stephanie Kazanjian
Steve Anderson
Tim Blakely
Todd Interland
Tom Stubbs
Tracy Brennan
Vikki Josephs
William Baker